PRESERVATION

Issues and Planning

EDITED BY

Paul N. Banks
Roberta Pilette

AMERICAN LIBRARY ASSOCIATION

Chicago and London

2000

While extensive effort has gone into ensuring the reliability of information appearing in this book, the publisher makes no warranty, express or implied, as to the accuracy or reliability of the information, and does not assume and hereby disclaims any liability to any person for any loss or damage caused by errors or omissions in this publication.

Cover design by Design Solutions

Text design by Dianne M. Rooney

Composition by Todd Sanders in Janson Text and Korinna using QuarkXpress 4.0 on a Macintosh platform

Printed on 50-pound white offset, a pH-neutral stock, and bound in 10-point coated cover stock by McNaughton & Gunn

The paper used in this publication meets the minimum requirements of American National Standard for Information Sciences—Permanence of Paper for Printed Library Materials, ANSI Z39.48-1992. ∞

Library of Congress Cataloging-in-Publication Data

Preservation : issues and planning / edited by Paul N. Banks and Roberta Pilette.
    p. cm.
   ISBN 0-8389-0776-8
    1. Library materials—Conservation and restoration—Planning.
  2. Archival materials—Conservation and restoration—Planning.
  3. Library materials—Conservation and restoration—United States—
Planning. 4. Archival materials—Conservation and restoration—
United States—Planning. I. Banks, Paul N. II. Pilette, Roberta.

Z701.P739 2000
025.8'4—dc21   99-057119

Printed in the United States of America.

04   03   02   01   00   5   4   3   2   1

To the memory of

Carolyn Harris

CONTENTS

CONTRIBUTORS

PAUL N. BANKS
Consultant. Formerly, senior lecturer, Preservation and Conservation Studies, Graduate School of Library and Information Science, the University of Texas at Austin; conservator and head, Conservation Department, the Newberry Library.

SALLY A. BUCHANAN
Associate professor, School of Information Science, the University of Pittsburgh. Formerly, chief, Preservation Department, Stanford University Libraries.

MARGARET CHILD
Retired consultant. Formerly, assistant director, Smithsonian Institution Libraries; head, Research Resource Programs, Division of Research Programs, National Endowment for the Humanities.

JOHN F. DEAN
Director, Preservation and Conservation, Cornell University Libraries. Formerly, head of Preservation, Johns Hopkins University Libraries; head of Bindery, the Newberry Library.

PAULA DE STEFANO
Barbara Goldsmith Curator for Preservation, New York University Libraries.

PETER S. GRAHAM
University Librarian, Syracuse University.

CAROLYN HARRIS
Until her death, director, Preservation and Conservation Studies, Graduate School of Library and Information Science, the University of Texas at Austin. Formerly, assistant director for Preservation, Columbia University Libraries.

BARBARA LILLEY
Conservation/Preservation program officer, New York State Program for the Conservation and Preservation of Library Research Materials, Division of Library Development, New York State Library.

JAN MERRILL-OLDHAM
Malloy-Rabinowitz Preservation Librarian, Harvard University Library. Formerly, head of Preservation, University of Connecticut Libraries.

CAROLYN CLARK MORROW
Formerly, Malloy-Rabinowitz Preservation Librarian, Harvard University Library; assistant director, Preservation Directorate, the Library of Congress.

ROBERTA PILETTE
Associate chief, Preservation Treatment, Preservation Division, the New York Public Library. Formerly, senior lecturer, Preservation and Conservation Studies, Graduate School of Library and Information Science, the University of Texas at Austin.

JUTTA REED-SCOTT
Formerly, senior program officer for Preservation and Collections Services, Association of Research Libraries.

NANCY CARLSON SCHROCK
Chief collections conservator, Harvard College Library.

DON C. SKEMER
Curator of Manuscripts, Department of Rare Books and Special Collections, Princeton University Library.

ELEANORE STEWART
Formerly, head, Replacement and Reformatting, Preservation Department, Stanford University Libraries; head, Conservation Treatment, SUL.

RICHARD STRASSBERG
Kheel Director, Kheel Center for Labor-Management Documentation and Archives, Martin P. Catherwood Library, Cornell University.

EILEEN F. USOVICZ
Consultant. Formerly, operations manager, MAPS (now Preservation Resources).

CHRISTINE WARD
Chief, Archival Services, New York State Archives.

DUANE A. WATSON
Aaron and Clara Greenhut Rabinowitz Chief Librarian for Preservation, the New York Public Library, retired. Formerly, head of Preservation, the New-York Historical Society Library.

SARA R. WILLIAMS
Collections management coordinator, University of Tennessee, Knoxville, Libraries. Formerly, head, Preservation Department, University of Colorado–Boulder.

LAURA J. WORD
Senior program officer/administrator, Division of Preservation and Access, National Endowment for the Humanities.

PREFACE

Carolyn Harris entered the field of library preservation during what might be considered its early youth. As the preservation administrator of a major research library, as a preservation educator, and, at the time of her death in 1994, as director of the only full preservation and conservation education program in the United States, she contributed in countless and significant ways to the maturing of the field. It is a measure of her stature in library preservation that many of its ablest and most respected practitioners contributed chapters to *Preservation: Issues and Planning*, which Harris began planning in 1989. It is also remarkable that all the original authors were willing to update their chapters for publication, in some cases nearly ten years after they originally wrote them.

Early in the history of the book, Don Skemer joined Carolyn Harris as co-editor. After her death, other responsibilities forced Skemer to relinquish his role in the work, but he has been consistently supportive of the efforts to bring the book to fruition. In 1996, the current editors took over the project, feeling that the book was too valuable to allow simply to disappear.

As institutional preservation programs multiplied and the field coalesced into a recognizable series of policies and procedures, preservation management replaced artifactual conservation as the leading edge of a growing movement. In the 1990s, a shift occurred toward concern with electronic and digital media, both as potential means of preservation and as forms of information that present formidable preservation challenges. Despite this current emphasis of the preservation field, traditional collections—both primarily artifactual and primarily informational—will continue not only to exist, but to dominate. Thus, effective library and archives preservation must now concern itself with three broad and overlapping areas: care of materials of artifactual value, preservation management of paper-based collections of primarily informational value, and the still largely uncharted management of information in new media. *Preservation: Issues and Planning* presents a balanced view of these three essential areas.

Preservation has often been called a technical problem requiring managerial solutions, and that is precisely the thesis of *Preservation: Issues and Planning*. The book will not tell you "how to do it right" but rather presents the issues that need to be considered within an institutional context. The professional requirement that every librarian and archivist understand preservation from a managerial perspective is regarded as far more important than knowledge of specific actions and techniques. Preservation must become an integral activity in every library and archives, managed by specialists but understood and supported by all.

Preservation: Issues and Planning was written by working library administrators, archivists, conservators, and educators who found the time in their busy schedules to present up-to-date surveys of key issues. Although the book is a coherent whole and may be read cover to cover with minimal duplication, each chapter stands alone and may be read separately with occasional references to other chapters. For the librarian, archivist, or student, or indeed for institutional managers wishing to understand the role of preservation in their organizations, it is hoped that this book will fill a need as a succinct one-volume overview of the principal preservation issues inherent in the responsible stewardship of collections and the information they contain.

Many people beyond the authors have contributed immeasurably to this work; indeed, some of the authors have contributed assistance beyond the writing of their chapters. There are surely those we cannot now identify who assisted with the earlier state of this work, and we regret that we cannot publicly acknowledge their contributions. Among those whose more recent assistance is gratefully acknowledged are Paula De Stefano, Janet Gertz, Barbara Lilley, Karen Muller, Barbara Paulson, Don C. Skemer, and Ann Swartzell.

We believe that *Preservation: Issues and Planning* will serve as a fitting tribute to Carolyn Harris, who was both our friend and our colleague.

PAUL N. BANKS
ROBERTA PILETTE

1

■■ ■ ■■

Defining the Library Preservation Program: Policies and Organization

■ ■ ■

CAROLYN CLARK MORROW

Every library seeks to keep the materials that comprise its collection in usable condition after they are selected and acquired, and for as long as they are needed as defined by the library's mission. In addition, all libraries supply myriad services to provide users with access to information and library resources in a timely manner, regardless of where they may be located. This they do to the best of their ability given institutional policy and current finances. Research libraries assume an additional responsibility. They seek to create and maintain for use collections of great depth and breadth—collections that build, generation upon generation, on the research, publication, and documentary record of human endeavor. Although irrelevant materials are sometimes removed from the collection, for the most part the record is cumulative, both intellectually and physically. Therein lies the preservation challenge.

The so-called brittle-book crisis caused by the acidic nature of industrial-age paper overtook research libraries before its impact on the traditional use of and access to research resources was well understood. The awakening of research libraries to this awesome reality also caused them to consider the permanence of all the diverse materials and formats that comprise collections—vellum, paper, leather, cloth, polyester film, videotape, photographs, compact disks, etc.—as well as the many variations in chemical and physical structure and preservation potential within these primary material types. In addition, the brittle-book crisis encouraged research libraries to consider the impact that physical format, access to originals, and the physical integrity of the collection as a whole have on the user, and the consequences, and perhaps even the opportunities, inherent in the imperative of crumbling collections. By acknowledging the impact that the brittle-book crisis would have on access to research resources, librarians were forced to build an infrastructure to share the burden of preservation. This national and increasingly international preservation program is positioning libraries to take advantage of the new electronic technologies for preservation and access, thereby gradually creating an information environment that promises greater access through electronic distribution of digital images than would ever be possible with the traditional book and microfilm formats, but that entails its own serious preservation issues.

Comprehensive, balanced, and responsive institutional preservation programs enable academic and research libraries to do more than merely preside over the decay of their aging collections, or even address today's brittle-book crisis. A programmatic approach to preservation allows libraries to address the prospective preservation challenge that is constantly changing in response to new patterns of use and the acquisition of new information formats. Furthermore, just as information networks and library consortia seek to extend the walls of the traditional library, preservation programs are, of necessity, linked together through cooperative, collaborative action. The capricious, creative, and increasingly interconnected and interdisciplinary nature of research makes it impossible for one institution to "have it all," let alone preserve it all.

At their most basic, preservation programs seek to keep core materials in usable condition for the benefit of on-site users working in today's library environment at the same time as they seek to address the long-term retention of and access to information for the users of the future. In fact, preservation programs are designed to bring today's cumulative, linear, analog collections forward to meet the future where technology continues to transform the way libraries acquire, describe, and provide access to information resources, as well as change the way library users exploit those resources.

The Institutional Context

Libraries are not all the same and their response to the preservation challenge also varies, institution by institution, and even within a particular collection. Some libraries serve special research interests or are built around a particular genre, subject, or discipline. They may collect and preserve comprehensively in certain areas and may accept the responsibility for conserving unique originals in perpetuity. Some libraries serve the general teaching and research needs of their host institutions and rely on other libraries, databases, and consortial arrangements for access to specialized materials. They may emphasize the preservation of core subject collections in open stacks.

Despite their differences, both specialized and general academic and research libraries may make a contribution to the nationwide program to preserve endangered materials and share copies. Both may host a world-renowned institute that sponsors postdoctoral students doing research in depth, and both may hold unique materials that attract scholars for the express purpose of examining original artifacts. Thus, regardless of their primary emphasis, academic and research libraries need comprehensive preservation programs capable of delivering the full range of preservation options. However, the proportions of the program and the extent to which a particular option is used will vary institution by institution. There is no magic formula for a library preservation program; rather, it is the result of a continuous process of definition, planning, and priority-setting keyed to the needs of a particular library and its users, and affected by the nationwide cooperative program and advances in preservation and access technologies.

Finally, regardless of their individual mission and priorities, all academic and research libraries have a responsibility to the community of research libraries and their users to identify and preserve unique materials and particular collection strengths that may exist as the result of the peculiarities of institutional history, collecting philosophy, region and location, entrepreneurship, and serendipity. Some portion of the collections held today will undoubtedly not reflect an institution's current priorities or collecting patterns. However, to the international community of research libraries and their users, possession of materials and the broadcasting of ownership through national databases imply acceptance of the responsibility to secure and preserve.

Despite their differences, research libraries also have many things in common. All must acquire or provide access to an ever-expanding universe of information. All seek to exploit evolving technology to manage their collections and provide access to collections beyond their own. All face the reality of limited resources and all are overwhelmed by the magnitude and complexity of the preservation challenge. Indeed, to a library already struggling with zero-growth budgets, the sky-rocketing cost of serial subscriptions, and personnel freezes, the magnitude and cost of the preservation problem when viewed in its totality appears insurmountable and invites paralysis. These realities, when combined with the reality of the limited resources that can be devoted to preservation, demand that libraries develop a highly focused preservation effort. Priorities for the preservation program are developed in conjunction with overall priorities for the institution, and libraries join with their peers to share the burden and the fruits of preservation work beyond their own institutions.

Developing an institutional sense of preservation priorities and a firm direction for the program is critical to the success of the preservation effort and enables libraries to make the most effective use of local resources that can be devoted to preservation and make their own unique contribution to cooperative preservation efforts.

The Development of Institutional Policy for Preservation

Suggested policies for the preservation of library collections, for access to preserved materials, and for the physical treatment and reformatting of library materials are found throughout this book. However, it is useful to review the benefits of developing an overall institutional preservation policy that can support the development of a comprehensive preservation program and enable implementation of the specific components of a preservation program.

A number of explicit and implicit purposes are served through the development of institutional preservation policy. The process of developing policy, or the periodic review of an established policy, allows a library to establish and shape an institution-specific context for preservation activities. This process is crucial to acceptance and promulgation of the program throughout the institution. For example, without the existence of a preservation policy that represents institutional consensus, the preservation program will be seen as competing with collection development and access programs, instead of being an integral part of both.

An explicit policy statement also allows the library to establish lines of authority and assign responsibility for certain activities—such as selection for preservation or collection security—to functional groups within the library. Assignment of specific responsibility is the only way to ensure that the job will get done. Although the bulk of the preservation task will typically fall to a preservation department, many activities—such as emergency preparedness, selection for preservation, cataloging of preservation copies, and stack maintenance—will cross departmental lines. A preservation policy will explicitly list the preservation goals and priorities that have been discussed and agreed upon and will broadcast those decisions with the cachet of administrative sanction. The existence of a formal preservation policy statement will make it easier for a library to codify preservation practices and implement preservation activities evenly throughout the various semi-autonomous custodial units that make up most larger libraries. The development of preservation policy is also an opportunity for a library to reexamine those activities that it may take for granted—such as library binding or reshelving—in light of overall preservation goals and priorities.

In addition to the explicit goals listed above, an institution-specific preservation policy has many implicit goals. Most importantly, it creates an atmosphere that will support institutional change. In many academic and research libraries, the enthusiasm to build comprehensive collections caused libraries to seriously overcommit. As they continue to add to (and brag about) their collections, libraries are nevertheless loath to acknowledge and broadcast the enormous and very real cost of maintaining those same huge collections. In the course of developing a preservation program, libraries may acknowledge the reality that collecting alone cannot ensure continued access.

Finally, the development of an institutional preservation policy reflects the reality that libraries are systems built on standard practices. Standardization is necessary to maintain order and ensure quality and cost-effectiveness; however, unexamined practices lead to entrenchment. All those who work in libraries can list many practices that are slavishly followed but whose origin and rationale are no longer remembered. Because the development of comprehensive preservation programs in academic and research libraries is relatively new, many practices that negatively affect the longevity of materials are entrenched in decades of use. For example, "book drops" were adopted as a convenience to users and to promote the timely return of library books. From the point of view of preservation, the use of book drops is absolutely senseless, yet many libraries continue the practice because they assume that change is impossible or too difficult. The circulation department could not adjust and users would be outraged. In fact, circulation departments all over the world have made the mammoth transition from manual to online systems. Likewise, users have learned to use online catalogs and adjust to off-site storage. Obviously, both users and library staff members are capable of being educated about the damage caused by book drops and adjusting to their removal. The task of determining preservation policy brings such issues as these to the fore where they can be discussed openly and the complexities and trade-offs acknowledged.

Change requires human agents, and the process of developing policy necessarily involves key decision makers and influential staff. Academic and research libraries distribute leadership and responsibility throughout the organization; thus, powerful people and agents of change will be found at all levels. Increasingly, strategic planning efforts and the introduction of self-managing work teams are encouraging library staff to initiate change at all levels in the organization. Thus, the process of developing preservation policy is an opportunity to involve as well as educate the library staff and gain their support for the implementation of a library-wide preservation program. This process is crucial because the implementation of a preservation program involves staff in every department of the library. For example, if a library contributes to the national preservation program by creating master negative microforms, the cataloging department will need to report the existence of a master negative, while the interlibrary loan department will have to loan service copies, even though past policy may have prohibited the loan of microforms.

Despite the distribution of power and functional responsibility, libraries are also hierarchical organizations. Thus, the development of library policy of any kind must first be sanctioned by the library administration. The existence of a preservation policy signals that the library administration considers preservation an important, central function rather than a noncontroversial topic that the library pays lip service to, but virtually ignores.

A typical library preservation policy includes the following elements: (1) a statement of need that describes and qualifies the preservation challenge; (2) definitions of preservation concepts and terms; (3) descriptions of general preservation principles and practices; (4) discussion of institutional preservation priorities; (5) strategies for selection for preservation; (6) an outline of the preservation program, including its organization, staffing, facilities, funding, and services to the collection; and (7) a discussion of consortial and cooperative relationships and opportunities with other libraries. Each of these elements will be discussed in more detail in the following sections.

A Statement of Need

The outlines of a preservation program for a particular library will derive, first of all, from the size and nature of the general and special collections that comprise the library and the libraries of any allied institutions or branches. What is the physical and intellectual makeup of the collections? Are there large collections of uniquely held manuscripts and archives or photographic materials, and what importance does the institution place on them? Are there long runs of serials that few other libraries hold? Is there a large graduate student body in the humanities or the sciences or both? How does the library serve its visiting scholars?

In addition to qualifying the preservation challenge, research libraries also find it useful to conduct statistically valid condition surveys in order to quantify needs. Surveys enable libraries to closely tailor their preservation efforts to actual problems and provide the basis for more precise preservation planning, including cost projections. Candidates for condition surveys would include materials in circulation, the reference collection, materials left beside photocopy machines, subject collections that may be targets for grant projects, and special collections.

Concepts and Terms

Librarians have their own professional language that arises from functional specialties, but is adopted by everyone so that the library can exist as a single, working organism whose parts communicate effectively with one another. Just as most librarians understand the key concepts and terminology of bibliographic access, they should understand the concepts of collections conservation, prospective preservation, and rehousing, to name a few. On the more nitty-gritty level, fore-edge shelving should be universally recognized as detrimental to books, while the term *alkaline* should be understood in the context of the paper deterioration problem. The concept of mastering as it relates to newer formats, such as videotape and electronic media, should be understood and contrasted with the characteristics of traditional formats. When preservation terms are defined and used throughout the library, the preservation mission can become just one more part of the library's overall mission.

Preservation Principles and Practices

What principles guide the preservation program? What preservation actions does the library take and why? An institution-specific preservation policy should outline the basic principles and practices ascribed to by the library. Are videotapes added to the permanent collection copied before they are put on reserve? Are audiotapes stored as played, rather than rewound? What portion of the budget is used for library binding and how does it relate to the size of the serials budget? Are all paperbacks bound upon receipt? Are materials from developing countries deacidified upon receipt, held as is, or selectively deacidified? Does the library always produce a duplicate master negative microfilm or does it wait until a request for a copy is made? Are brittle materials discarded following microfilming or sent to off-site storage? Does the library produce a backup microfilm copy of digitized materials? If the purpose of preservation policy is to develop consensus about what the library's preservation program will be, then a discussion of the general principles that guide the library is a useful exercise. Elements of the library's preservation policy will also be found in the policy statements and procedures manuals of other functional groups, such as the training manual for the stack assistants, the serials cataloging manual, and the collection development policy.

Institutional Preservation Priorities

In times of budget crisis, library directors often ask department heads to "warm up" by describing how they would reduce services in the face of large cuts. Although severe budget cuts can decimate programs, create gaps in the collection, and result in backlogs that mortgage a library's future, the process of "cutting" can also be a useful exercise in setting priorities and in examining new ways to get the job done. In addition, the exercise of setting priorities demands that an institution focus on those activities that will have the most impact on the overall preservation of the collection, such as environmental control. It also identifies priorities, such as retrospective conversion, to which the preservation program can lend its support because the benefits to preservation processing are significant. Finally, the identification of portions of the collection that are the highest priority for preservation will allow the institution to proceed with the development of special projects, grant proposals, and fund-raising. When policy- and priority-setting are conducted as an open process, the entire organization can move forward with actual implementation without undue argument and delay.

Selection Strategies

A critical precursor to a successful preservation program is the understanding on the part of the institution as a whole that the selection and collection management process does not end with acquiring an item and providing access points. The importance of the work and its relationship to the collection as a whole requires periodic reassessment, even if it only occurs every fifty years. This process of reselection also benefits users by protecting the research utility of the collection, and it is the only way that libraries will be able to realistically address the enormousness of the preservation challenge. Assigning responsibility for collection management—including collection reassessment and preservation decision making—is the first task of a library's preservation program. Problems can occur if preservation of existing resources is seen to compete with the acquisition of new information resources; therefore, the resolution of this tension is critical to the success of the preservation program and is another good reason to develop an institutional preservation policy.

Program Outline

A description of the functions encompassed by the library's preservation program belongs in a policy statement along with the assignment of responsibility for each function. Clarifying responsibility allows the program to move forward and makes explicit the breadth of the program. Preservation can be found in many different locations in the organization precisely because it touches every part of library operations; thus, it can logically be associated with many different functional units. However, precise location on the organization chart is less important than assigning a locus of responsibility and authority, without which nothing can proceed. Equally important is a description of how the program will be accomplished, the staff and facilities that are needed for the various activities, and what services—in-house and contracted out—will be provided.

Cooperative Relationships

Libraries do not meet the preservation challenge by acting alone. In developing cooperative models for preservation, libraries have adopted the successful models of retrospective conversion, shared cataloging, and union catalogs. Regional and national bibliographic networks and consortia provide the infrastructure and opportunities for cooperative action. The nationwide "brittle-book" program administered by the National Endowment for the Humanities is built on the premise of sharing the products of preservation work with other libraries. In addition to the contribution of individual libraries to the collective good, libraries with collection strengths in common can join together on projects to preserve materials cooperatively. After all, from the point of view of the scholar or researcher, it is not helpful to identify and preserve resources pertaining to a particular discipline or subject that have been collected in only one library without regard to the existence of important materials held elsewhere that also deserve preservation. Likewise, institution-specific projects may not make the best use of funding provided by federal agencies and national foundations that are more interested in access by the community of scholars, regardless of their home institution. A description and characterization of cooperative and consortial relationships belongs in an institutional policy statement because the extent of involvement in extra-institutional projects, including the requirements for cost-sharing, must be considered alongside local priorities for preservation. A balance must be struck that makes sense for the particular institution and also contributes in a meaningful way to regional, national, and international initiatives.

Developing the Preservation Program: Articulation, Infrastructure, and Implementation

Most institutions view their library collections as capital goods, acquired and organized at considerable expense, and worthy of a long-term commitment to maintain and preserve. Therefore, most academic and research libraries have some kind of preservation program in place. However, the extent of their development varies widely depending on the length of time the library has been engaged in actively developing a program and the level of commitment that the library administration and its host institution have made to the activity. The larger, older libraries have tended to develop more comprehensive programs in response to the brittle-book crisis, but many smaller and specialized libraries also have effective programs that reflect a substantial commitment to the preservation of their collections.

The preservation program in an academic or a research library is a complex of policies, activities, and services that enable a library to preserve and protect physical objects and retain or reformat intellectual content. Many libraries go beyond this goal of item-by-item preservation to attempt to preserve the integrity of the on-site collection as a whole, or portions of it, so that it may effectively serve as a laboratory for individual research and directed graduate study.

Preservation activity is an integral part of the larger task of collection management and should be woven through the strategies libraries use to build collections, provide access to them, and facilitate their use. A preservation strategy, as illustrated in figure 1, should encompass the entire collection, but in varying degrees of intensity depending on the nature of a particular segment of the collection (its intellectual and physical composition and its condition), the relative importance of the materials, the kind and level of access provided (open stack or off-site storage), and the frequency and type of use a group of materials or an individual item is expected to receive. Regardless of decisions made about individual items, however, all library materials will benefit from umbrella preservation programs designed to protect them from extremes of temperature and humidity, prepare for emergencies, provide a proper storage environment, actively discourage theft and

Figure 1
Preservation Strategy

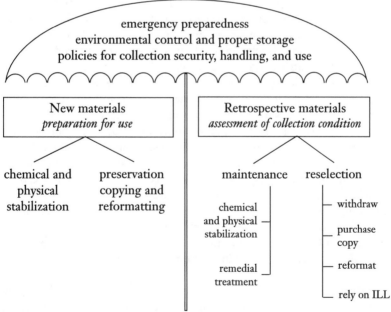

mutilation, and encourage proper handling and use. Without these umbrella programs in place, it makes little sense to invest resources in the preservation of individual items.

The cost of preservation should be considered along with the cost of acquiring materials and making them available for use. Funds designated for building the collection in a specific discipline or subject area should include funding to provide for necessary preservation treatment. Materials should be acquired, when possible, in formats that are conducive to preservation, or receive preservation treatment or reformatting at the time of acquisition. If possible, negotiations to acquire a special collection should include the funding necessary to provide both intellectual access and needed preservation action.

Development of the overall preservation program involves three major subactivities that are carried out simultaneously: articulation of the program components and strategy; development of the infrastructure that supports preservation action; and implementation of preservation activities throughout the collections.

Articulation

Articulation of the preservation program includes the development of an institution-specific preservation policy as described earlier. Articulation of the preservation program takes place during the time the policy is being developed, while it is being promulgated throughout the organization, and during the periodic review process that every institutional policy undergoes, especially at the time of a change in leadership. Articulation is part of the advocacy for the preservation program that occurs naturally when staff members attend training sessions or special seminars on preservation topics or when library users are exposed to a preservation awareness campaign. The need to develop goals for fund-raising is another important opportunity to articulate the goals of the library's preservation program and can be crucial to sustaining the momentum of preservation program development during tough financial times. However, the most important measure of success in the process of articulating the library's preservation program is the full incorporation of preservation goals and objectives into library planning that is initiated from the director's office.

Strategic Goals   An important part of the process of articulating the preservation program is determining those activities that are strategic. A strategy followed can powerfully advance the library's goals for preservation because it is action and results driven—that is, if action X is taken, Y will result. However, as a program matures and changes, strategies will change, too. The following are examples of strategic goals for preservation.[1]

Improving the storage environment for library collections will retard deterioration and reduce the need for expensive preservation treatment and replacement of library materials. Excessive heat and humidity, air pollution, and exposure to light, especially ultraviolet, accelerate the deterioration of library materials and cause irreversible damage. The capital outlay to add, replace, or renovate air-conditioning systems can be prohibitively expensive, but is the single most important preservation action that can be taken. Significant improvement in environmental conditions is often possible through improved maintenance procedures, affordable changes to existing systems, or more vigilant monitoring and adjustment.

Storing lesser-used library materials off-site in an optimum preservation environment will stabilize their condition and enable the library to concentrate preservation resources on the more heavily used portions of the collection. On-demand preservation services will ensure access when deteriorated materials are stored off-site.

To solve the problem of ever-expanding collections, many large libraries have built or are planning to build off-site storage facilities. When a facility is intended for storage and retrieval only—items are used in the main library or delivered to the individual's office or departmental library—it can be designed to optimize the preservation environment and is a powerful preservation action in itself. The condition of fragile or deteriorated materials can be stabilized and treatment or reformatting accomplished on demand, when an item is recalled for use. Improved access services, such as online holdings records and document delivery, will mitigate the negative effects of off-site storage to the user. One of the most critical preservation selection tasks is to determine what materials will remain on-site and thus be candidates for more intensive and expensive preservation activity, and what materials can be stored off-site and benefit from a low-unit-cost optimum preservation environment.

Coordinating the library's preservation microfilming or imaging efforts with that of other research libraries will avoid duplication of effort and result in more research materials being preserved worldwide. Although estimates vary among individual libraries, approximately 10 percent of the paper-based collections in most research libraries are already so deteriorated that they cannot be handled without danger of loss, and another 25 percent are extremely fragile. No library acting alone can afford to solve the brittle-book problem through replacement or refor-matting; the cost is simply too great. Fortunately, the existence of a nationwide brittle-book program allows individual libraries to make their unique contribution while taking advantage of the work of other libraries.

Taking advantage of technology to deacidify nineteenth- and twentieth-century materials on unstable, acidic paper, when combined with collections conservation and stack maintenance activities, will retard the deterioration that renders library materials unusable and enable the library to maintain the physical integrity of its collection. The majority of the paper-based collections in academic and research libraries are not yet brittle, but they exist on acidic paper that is inex-orably weakening and will eventually result in materials being unusable in their original format. It is questionable for libraries to spend money to repair and rebind books that are part of the permanent collections without also addressing the acidity of the text block. At the time of this writing, several research libraries are engaged in launching mass (whole book) deacidification programs based on over twenty years of research and development in the private sector and at the Library of Congress.

Providing expert conservation treatment for rare materials and special collections will preserve their historic, artifactual, and aesthetic value and permit their safe exhibition and use. The collections of most acad-emic and research libraries contain materials prized for their artifac-tual, historic, and intrinsic value, including individual rare and unique items as well as great collections. These materials require an optimum preservation environment and, when necessary, expert conservation treatment. A number of research and specialized libraries have in-house conservation laboratories staffed by professional conservators. Other libraries contract for services with regional conservation labora-tories or private conservators.

Using emerging digital imaging technologies, intelligent character recognition, distribution of electronic information over networks, and print-on-demand services will provide improved access to preserved research resources and leverage the investment made in preservation microfilming. Research libraries began using microphotography in earnest in the mid-1930s to make rare and unique materials more widely available. As paper deterioration became a more urgent prob-lem, microfilming became the standard method of preserving intellec-tual content. In the future, digital and electronic technologies and print-on-demand services will enhance access to all research resources, including deteriorated materials that were microfilmed as part of local or national preservation efforts. Libraries are alert to the possibilities of new imaging technologies even as they develop new access and research services that employ online databases, electronic publishing, and electronic distribution of information. Demonstration projects in imaging technology are providing insight into new applications that leverage the collective investment that libraries have already made in preserving their collections.

Infrastructure

Although the articulation of preservation policy is an important step in the development of a preservation program, development of the infrastructure to support a wide array of preservation program activities and components positions a library to make actual progress in meeting the preservation challenge. If the program is to function effectively, all the necessary program components must be in place. For example, if a low-cost replacement for a brittle, unusable book is located, but the library does not have replacement funds or a processing mechanism in place, the knowledge that the replacement exists is useless, preservation action will be incomplete, and backlogs will develop. Many research libraries developed just such backlogs when they participated in federally funded preservation microfilming projects, but did not make provisions for the additional preservation needs that accumulate as the result of conducting a large-scale project.

In addition, libraries require a comprehensive array of preservation options so that the appropriate options can be applied and the preservation process can proceed efficiently. For years, libraries were frustrated in their need to efficiently and effectively address the acidic paper problem because mass (whole book) deacidification technology had not yet developed to the point of practical application. On the other hand, most large libraries during the same period successfully completed the infrastructure needed for conservation and repair of general collections materials. Obviously, it is questionable for a library to invest in a careful repair of the binding when the book is acidic and destined to deteriorate from the inside out. Having mass (whole book) deacidification available as a viable option will allow libraries to complete the preservation picture and maintain hard-copy originals at a low unit cost through selective deacidification and rebinding. This is a particularly sensible option for scholarly and core research resources that have received consistent use over several decades.

The development of infrastructure goes beyond the ability to complete individual preservation tasks to encompass an institution's ability to position itself for preserving whole collections. For example, if a library holds a preeminent collection of documentary photographs that is at risk of loss from chemical deterioration, but staffing levels do not permit the development of a grant proposal, the library cannot fulfill its preservation responsibilities and should consider giving the collection to an institution that can take effective action rather than preside over decay.

Completing the technical infrastructure for preservation is important, but only if the library is also successful in developing the ongoing operational budgets or raising additional funding to apply the various options at the level that the institution decides is appropriate. As discussed earlier, the appropriate level is determined through the process of articulating preservation policy, strategies, and priorities. More importantly, it is only through a library-wide planning process that the administration can determine and articulate priorities for the library as a whole and gain the support of its parent institution. Such planning is a crucial precursor to the process of reallocation of resources. In an era of reduced or zero-growth budgets for institutions of higher education, reallocation is critical to maintaining the viability of an organization. The reallocation process can and should occur at all levels and will, of necessity, cross departmental lines. For example, as a result of strategic planning, the library administration may decide to reallocate funds from the original cataloging program (cataloging department) to automation of cataloging functions (systems department) to take advantage of shared cataloging programs. Likewise, funds devoted to purchasing positive film copies of deteriorated books (preservation department) might be better used to record in the library's online catalog the existence of a national master microform produced by a sister institution (cataloging department) and encourage interlibrary loan. Because reallocation often crosses departmental lines, consensus among library staff is crucial and the library administration must be involved in making reallocation decisions.

Balance among the components of the program is also important. Too often, libraries have developed one option, such as special collections conservation or library binding, quite completely while they have ignored other, perhaps more important elements of the preservation program, such as major improvements to the library's environmental control system. Intensive development of one option to the exclusion of others interferes with flexibility because it locks resources into staffing and benefits and thus reduces an institution's ability to change directions or priorities or take advantage of lower costs through contracting for services. This mistake is common among programs that have developed from the bottom up and do not have the support or interest of the library administration. Most importantly, however, a balanced infrastructure for a preservation program means not only a full array of preservation options, but also the application of those options in an appropriate proportion as determined by an assessment of collection needs and consensus about the priorities of the program.

Implementation

Although each library situation will be unique, the following list describes appropriate steps or phases of preservation program development. The list is shown in rough priority order, but in practice many development aspects would take place simultaneously. More importantly, however, elements of the preservation program may be developed when the opportunity to do so arises—for example, through a strategic planning initiative, a grant project, new leadership in the library or a key department, organizational or personnel changes, a capital fund-raising campaign, or participation in a regional or national program.

Establish institutional policy for preservation activities.

Identify and stop damaging practices.

Improve environmental control and storage conditions.

Educate library staff to recognize items in need of treatment or protection.

Raise awareness of library users so that they will cease thoughtless practices.

Identify and isolate those items in immediate danger.

Survey the collections to qualify and quantify needs and problems and estimate costs.

Examine current preservation practices and assess their quality and effectiveness.

Develop a preservation selection policy and institute procedures for withdrawal, replacement, reformatting, and remedial treatment.

Identify priority collections/classes/formats for treatment and develop special projects.

Develop and streamline preservation work flows and routines.

Despite the progress that many research libraries have shown in acknowledging the preservation challenge and moving to meet it, some libraries have been unsuccessful in launching or implementing programs whose size and breadth of activity is commensurate with the size and complexity of the problem. Even among some research libraries that have engaged in formal planning studies, involving significant numbers of staff over a period of time and resulting in a strongly worded report and far-reaching recommendations, success in implementing a comprehensive preservation program has often eluded the organization.

Why are some libraries successful in developing and implementing comprehensive preservation programs and some are not? Although it is perhaps simplistic to say so, the single most important indicator of success is leadership from the library administration. If the administration supports the development of the preservation program, then even without the resources needed to launch a multifaceted, well-endowed program, the library can still implement the most important elements and make significant progress in preserving its collections.

In addition to support from top-level library management, several other elements are crucial to successful program development, such as inclusion of preservation planning in overall library planning, a firm implementation plan that phases in improvements in preservation practices and describes priorities and a timeline for the introduction of new preservation activities, and assignment of responsibility for discrete portions of the program to competent people.

Although support from the top and a structure for implementation are important, the individual elements of the program must also make sense and be cost-effective. Significant progress can be made if the individual tasks associated with developing a program are broken down and aligned logically with each other. This helps set the stage for change and builds momentum for the program. The checklist shown in figure 2 is an example of the kind of tool that can be used to measure steady progress in preservation program development.

As in most things, timing is crucial. A library that is planning a new building or bringing a circulation system online or engaging in a massive retrospective conversion project will not be able to devote energy to developing and implementing a preservation program during the same time frame. However, though the development of the preservation program is not uppermost at such times, the library's preservation manager has a key role to play in pointing out the preservation aspects of these library-wide efforts. A new library building is an opportunity to improve the preservation of the entire collection through improved

Figure 2
Preservation Program Implementation Checklist

Collection Maintenance

☐ Regular monitoring of temperature and humidity throughout the library?

☐ Temperature and humidity consistently maintained within the recommended limits?

☐ Temperature and humidity stabilized even if not within the desired ranges?

☐ Light sources, including windows, filtered to exclude UV light?

☐ Timers installed so lights in stacks go out when not in use?

☐ Air filters regularly replaced and air ducts cleaned?

☐ Shelving, cabinets, book trucks, book supports upgraded?

☐ Book drops abolished?

☐ Book drops made less damaging?

☐ Photocopy machines upgraded to edge copiers?

☐ Ban on eating and drinking in library buildings except in restricted areas?

☐ Rodent and insect control program?

☐ Routine cleaning of the collections?

☐ Materials housed in archivally sound enclosures?

☐ Library binding upgraded to improve preservation of bound materials?

☐ Program to repair/replace deteriorated bindings?

☐ Environment controlled in exhibit cases?

☐ Appropriate preservation procedures in place for archival materials, visual materials, and audio materials?

Disaster Planning

☐ Disaster plan complete?

☐ Disaster supplies in place throughout the library?

☐ Staff trained in disaster procedures?

(continued)

Figure 2   *(continued)*

☐ Disaster plan periodically reviewed and updated?

☐ Problems with physical plant (such as leaks or defective wiring) corrected promptly?

☐ Cooperative arrangements for prompt responses to emergencies set up with the local police, fire safety, and facilities management offices?

☐ Insurance policies reviewed to ensure full coverage against theft, water damage, fire, and natural catastrophes?

Organizational Changes/Funding

☐ Preservation plan completed?

☐ Responsibility assigned to a professional librarian for the direction of preservation functions?

☐ Library policies, procedures, and practices reviewed and revised to include preservation considerations?

☐ Policies and procedures written for preservation functions?

☐ Staff informed about the implications of changes and given training where appropriate?

☐ Staff reassigned within the library to assume preservation responsibilities?

☐ New staff hired to assume preservation responsibilities?

☐ Funds reallocated within the library budget to preservation uses?

☐ New funds for preservation added to the library budget?

☐ Grants obtained for preservation projects?

☐ Gifts or donations received for preservation purposes?

☐ Use of library friends group to seek resources to meet preservation needs?

☐ Other mechanisms used to raise money for preservation?

☐ Campaign to inform the university administration and library users about the importance of preservation?

☐ Posters, handouts, bookmarks, exhibitions, meetings, one-on-one discussions, news releases, other?

☐ Initiation of a program to inform users about how to handle books and other library materials safely?

Replacement and Reformatting Programs

☐ Initiation of a program to replace or reformat brittle books?

☐ Written policies incorporating ANSI standards to guide this program?

☐ Use of quality control tests/procedures (i.e., checking microforms for quality and completeness) to ensure that standards are met?

☐ Master negatives stored according to ANSI standards?

☐ Use of archival photocopying as an alternate means of reformatting brittle books?

☐ Use of digital imaging as a means of reformatting deteriorated materials?

☐ Appropriate bibliographic control of preservation materials?

Adapted from a survey conducted by Margaret Child for the Association of Research Libraries on the effectiveness of the ARL Preservation Planning Program

---

environmental controls. The introduction of an online circulation system is a good time to explore the relationship between circulation of materials and their condition and to plan improvements to remedial treatment programs that target materials receiving heavy use. A retrospective conversion project will have important resource implications for the preservation program, as it will increase the use of older materials and result in a surge of interlibrary loan requests.

Despite significant progress in the past decade in developing effective preservation programs in libraries, the difficulty in establishing a program that largely exists to address the needs of retrospective materials should not be underestimated. Tremendous pressure exists for libraries to acquire new materials and new information resources in expensive electronic formats in order to meet the demands of library users for current resources. The intensity of the preservation effort will and should vary depending on the primary mission of the institution and its values.

Organizing the Preservation Program

A 1991 publication of the Association of Research Libraries, *Preservation Program Models: A Study Project and Report*, laid out the basic components of a research library preservation program from the library administrator's point of view.[2] The ARL report also suggested organizational and staffing models for four different-size libraries. The two accompanying organization charts (figures 3 and 4) are possible examples.

The ARL report was conceived as a concise guide for library administrators engaged in developing programs. What is the rationale for each activity and how does it contribute to the effective functioning of the library? What are the administrative issues and policy considerations, and what are the human and material resources needed to conduct each activity? Finally, what are the steps, or phases of development, that the library administrator should anticipate initiating or supporting? The report also gives benchmarks for core preservation activities keyed to four levels of program development. This milestone document, although brief, reflects twenty-five years of preservation program development in research libraries. It represents consensus in the library field about the current outlines of a preservation program. The discussion of the organization of preservation programs contained in *Preservation Program Models* is still relevant and should be consulted in conjunction with this chapter.

The chapters that follow describe in detail the components of a preservation program and suggest additional sources of information. Contributors review the development and evolution of the preservation field within librarianship and discuss the experience and value of cooperative programs. However, a cooperative national program is only as strong as its individual parts. Although the existence of standards, federal funding, and service bureaus is critical, the real key to the success of cooperative programs and initiatives is the existence of strong institutional programs. Individual libraries with strong preservation programs for their own collections are in a position to take coordinated action.

After approximately twenty-five years of development, most large research libraries and many smaller academic and special libraries have preservation programs in place to keep core materials accessible in usable, readable condition and to protect the artifactual value of special collections. According to statistics compiled annually by the Association of Research Libraries, research libraries typically spend between 5 and 10 percent of their overall budget on actions to prevent damage and deterioration, to physically prepare materials for use, and to repair or copy materials. These figures do not include the cost of maintaining the building and its systems to create an environment conducive to preservation.

Figure 3
Organization and Staffing Model for a Preservation Program for a
Small Academic Library

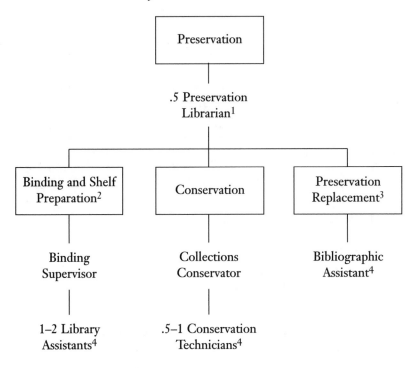

Personnel: 8.5–13.5 FTE (2 professionals)
Budget: $.2–.5 million
% of Total Library Expenditures: 5–10%
% of Total Materials Expenditures: 15–30%

---

1. In most libraries, this position will also manage another unit, such as circulation, stack maintenance, or collection development.
2. Includes traditional binding and shelf preparation activities and personnel needed for preparation for mass (whole book) deacidification.
3. In many libraries this activity would take place within the acquisitions or collections development department.
4. Paraprofessional positions could be filled with a combination of support staff and student assistants to equal FTE.

Figure 4

Organization and Staffing Model for a Preservation Program for a Large Academic Library

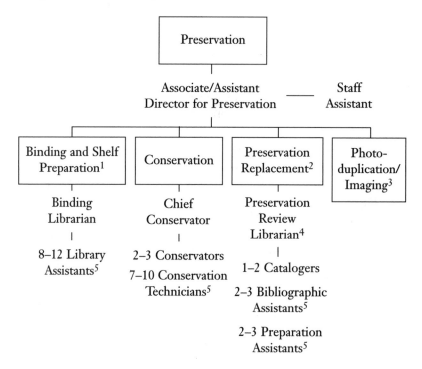

Personnel: 27–38 FTE (7–9 professionals)
Budget: $.8–3 million
% of Total Library Expenditures: 5–10%
% of Total Materials Expenditures: 15–30%

1. Includes traditional binding and shelf preparation activities and personnel needed for preparation for mass (whole book) deacidification.
2. Excludes staffing for externally funded microfilming/imaging projects. Without a photoduplication unit, reformatting services would be contracted out.
3. A photoduplication unit is often associated with preservation and would typically handle microfilming/imaging in addition to some public services functions.
4. In some libraries this position may serve as the assistant head. Cataloging may be done in the cataloging department.
5. Paraprofessional positions could be filled with a combination of support staff and student assistants to equal FTE.

Most preservation activities are recognizable and commonplace in libraries. They become part of a comprehensive preservation program when a library defines its preservation goals and acts to integrate preservation into all of its functions and services. This is mainly a matter of seeking consensus and establishing library policies. Without consensus among library staff and periodic reexamination of routine activities, some elements of the program may be overemphasized while others languish. In addition, although significant costs can be associated with individual preservation actions, many important goals of a preservation program can be accomplished by reorienting current activities, raising the preservation awareness of staff, and providing training and retraining as needed to institutionalize standard preservation practices.

Many libraries assign responsibility for the core functions of a preservation program to a preservation department headed by a professional librarian. Depending on the organization of the library and the interests of key personnel, preservation departments can be found attached to technical services, collections development, or public services, or reporting to the director of the library. Because preservation activities cross departmental and functional lines in a library, there can be logic behind each of these configurations. The exact location of the preservation department within the organization of a library is of much less importance than appropriate support of the program by the library administrator to whom the preservation department reports.

Research libraries, like all large organizations, periodically undergo a process of long-range planning and reconceptualization of their mission, goals, and objectives. The preservation of the library collection will be found within the mission statements of most libraries in recognition of the fact that libraries preserve their collections not for preservation's sake, but to enable access and facilitate use and research. Because preservation fits within the larger goal of library services, the mission of a library preservation department could be expressed as follows:

> The Preservation Department plans, coordinates, and implements activities to maintain collections in usable condition to support the teaching and research needs of the institution, and, as appropriate, contribute to national preservation efforts. Preservation activities protect the institution's investment in its library collections and ensure that materials will remain available for as long as they are needed. To accomplish its mission, the Preservation Department enforces proper storage and handling practices; develops preservation

review and replacement strategies; contracts with outside vendors for services; applies conservation techniques to return damaged materials to a usable condition; provides for the timely transfer of deteriorated materials to a stable preservation format; and investigates and adopts, as appropriate, new preservation technologies.

Conclusion

Academic and research libraries are necessarily focused on the challenge of preserving their deteriorating retrospective collections, and they are engaged in the implementation of extra- and intra-institutional responses that position them for success. But they are also haunted by the prospect of the future challenge as today's magnetic and digital resources become tomorrow's "brittle books." The infrastructure and institutional programs that research libraries build and operate to address the brittle-book problem are in the process of being modified and extended to all information formats in a meaningful way and at an operational level that is commensurate with the problem. The library response to the preservation challenge will necessarily change the way scholars exploit information resources and holds the promise of creating new opportunities for research using library collections.

Notes

1. Adopted from Harvard University Library, *Ten Year Plan for Preservation and Continued Access to the Collections* (September 1992). This plan was developed as part of a university-wide planning effort initiated by President Neil L. Rudenstine and designed to position Harvard University for a major capital campaign commencing in 1994.

2. Jan Merrill-Oldham, Carolyn Clark Morrow, and Mark Roosa, *Preservation Program Models: A Study Project and Report* (Washington, D.C.: Association of Research Libraries, Committee on Preservation of Research Library Materials, 1991).

Suggested Readings

Association of Research Libraries. *ARL Preservation Statistics.* Washington, D.C.: ARL, published annually since 1988.

Association of Research Libraries. Office of Management Studies. Systems and Procedures Exchange Center. *Preservation Organization and Staffing.* ARL SPEC Kit 160. Washington, D.C.: ARL, 1990.

Cloonan, Michèle. *Organizing Preservation Activities.* Washington, D.C.: Association of Research Libraries, 1993.

Feather, John, and Paul Eden. *National Preservation Policy: Policies and Practices in Archives and Record Offices.* Boston Spa, England: British Library Research and Innovation Centre, 1997.

Williams, Sara, and Diane Lunde. "Preservation and Collection Development in Academic Libraries of the United States." *Advances in Librarianship* 21 (1997): 73–89.

2

Preservation Programs in High-use Library Collections

SARA R. WILLIAMS

Although preservation has grown into a prominent topic for research and discussion within librarianship over the past twenty years, there appears to be a lack of agreement on the nature of preservation itself. Preservation is inextricably linked in the minds of many librarians with large-scale, grant-funded microfilming projects and laboratory conservation of rare and valuable books. These activities are associated with the great research libraries in which preservation administration first became a regular function. The association was probably inevitable, growing as it did out of the large research library's role as permanent repository for the materials that will support the scholarship of the future.

By contrast, the small to middle-sized academic or public library conceives its mission as the provision of immediate access and services for the needs of a specific clientele. Is a preservation program needed in a library that neither actively collects rare books nor has a significant concentration of brittle books in its stacks, and in which the chief measure of success is a high circulation rate?

The middle-sized high-use library faces deterioration of its collections as a result of its very success in meeting its users' needs. Books that circulate frequently become dilapidated long before their paper succumbs to the "slow fire" of paper embrittlement. Many libraries can no longer bear the costs of frequent replacement purchases, extra copies of high-demand titles, or multiple subscriptions to heavily used journals. The rising costs of purchasing and maintaining collections in any medium make it essential that every library have some kind of collections maintenance strategy if its collections are to remain accessible to users.

Collection maintenance includes all preservation activities that preserve library materials in their original format for as long as they are needed in the collection. How long that will be depends on the nature of the material and on the nature and purpose of the library. Even small libraries usually have core collections of books and other materials that must be permanently kept in their original form. Most of the volumes in the collection of any circulating library, however, will be valued for the information they contain, rather than for any intrinsic value of the materials themselves—their content is interesting, but their physical structure is not. Preservation of these materials focuses on maintaining their original structure until they are either no longer needed, or until they deteriorate to the point that their intellectual content must be translated into some more durable form.

Collections maintenance is an appropriate and practical preservation strategy for the small to medium-sized library that collects information in a variety of media and in which the ratio of circulating to noncirculating material is high. A collections maintenance program will develop strategies adapted to a specific library's needs and resources.

The High-use Library

This discussion will focus on planning a preservation strategy for the small to medium-sized academic library that has a high level of circulation and use. Many of the points to be considered here can also be applied to public libraries with similar characteristics.

The library's mission is defined as the support of the teaching and research activities of the parent institution. The size of the collection will be no larger than 2 to 3 million items housed in open stacks. Collection policy is designed to meet the specific information needs of a specific clientele, with basic rather than comprehensive collections on most subjects. Certain subject areas will be collected at greater depth, depending on local research needs and interests. Levels of use for the collection as a whole will be heavier than would be true in the large research institution, with reference collections and materials related to current course work bearing the brunt of the activity. There is a great deal of interlibrary loan traffic, usually both lending and borrowing.

Causes of Deterioration in High-use Library Collections

If paper embrittlement is a "slow fire," then circulation fans the flame. A brittle book that is otherwise intact may last for years if stored in a stable environment and not often used. It will fail quickly, however, if it is subjected to frequent circulation, photocopying, or interlibrary lending.

Books that are not brittle, even those produced on alkaline paper, may deteriorate because of poor construction and heavy use. Libraries are often compelled to add the cost of binding or rebinding to the purchase price of the volume in order to get a durable copy.

Print on paper is no longer the only form in which information is marketed and stored. In addition to films, slides, and audio disks, which have long been staple items in library collections, information may now be packaged as videotape, compact disks, laser disks, and various products on magnetic tape. With the advent of the online database, information is available by means of a machine, but is not physically present on the library's premises. These new media for storing information are themselves physically fragile, and the machines required to read them present problems of maintenance and obsolescence.

The typical small to medium-sized library can rarely offer optimal environmental conditions for all the materials and media it collects. Overcrowded shelving and excessive variations in temperature and humidity are common and present serious implications for the useful life of the collection.

The sum of these local factors will create a set of preservation problems unique to each library. A successful collections maintenance strategy will reflect both the actual pattern of use in the collection and the intellectual goals of the institution.

Mission and Goals

The small to middle-sized library may find it useful in the beginning to think of preservation as an aspect of collection development planning. A new preservation program, if it is to be a successful and sustainable part of library operations, must be closely related to the library's over-all goals and objectives. Library staff must perceive preservation as a benefit to the daily operations of the library, rather than as a fashion-able add-on. Development of a successful program is much more likely if those doing the planning take time to consider some of the following questions:

> What is the library's mission? Does it have a written mission state-ment defining its character and relationship to the goals of the college or university? Who does the library serve? What changes are expected in the library's mission during the next five to ten years?

> Does the library have a collection development plan or policy? If so, is it up-to-date? Is the collection mostly composed of paper-based materials, or are collections of other media important? Is the collection weeded regularly and by whom? What criteria are used to make weeding decisions? What needs to be retained in the collection and for how long? What changes are anticipated in the focus of collection development over the next five to ten years?

> What kind of relationship does the library have with the parent institution, governing board, and so on? How do these people perceive the library? Is it seen as a valuable resource or as a bot-tomless pit? Is this relationship expected to change in the next five to ten years? If so, how?

> What kind of physical plant does the library have? Who is respon-sible for cleaning, maintenance, and security? Is the building air-conditioned? Is there a remote storage facility? If so, does anyone inspect it regularly for water leaks and other dangers? Is the collection insured?

A detailed picture of institutional goals, needs, priorities, and restraints, and of anticipated changes in the near future, is essential if the collections maintenance program is to support the needs of the individual library.

Physical Condition of the Collection

The next step in designing a preservation strategy is to develop an accurate picture of the physical state of the collection. Staff in a small or medium-sized library often have a good empirical sense of what parts of the collection are in jeopardy. A condition survey of the collection, however, is needed to provide explicit and reliable data on the nature and size of the library's preservation problem and of the amount and kinds of resources needed to deal with it.

Because the library will allocate resources based on the results of the condition survey, both the survey instrument and the sample to be tested should be planned carefully, and the questions the survey is to answer must be carefully defined. Should the survey be limited to those areas of the collection perceived to be at greatest risk, or should the entire collection be examined? If the library collects media in other than paper-based formats, will these be included in a general survey or examined separately? What kinds of damage or deterioration should the survey be designed to detect and measure?

Both training and experience are required to design a trustworthy survey instrument. A college or other small academic library may be able to find the necessary statistical expertise on campus. If not, a professional consultant will be well worth his or her fee.

Designing a Preservation Strategy for Local Needs

In an active circulating collection, the causes of deterioration can be grouped into three categories:

- Building environment (the conditions under which the collection is housed)

- Dilapidation (damage caused by the way the collection is used or abused)

- Inherent vice (deterioration caused by weaknesses inherent in the chemical composition and physical structure of the materials)

Deterioration caused by inherent vice, of which paper embrittlement is the classic example, is the most difficult and expensive preservation problem to solve. A small or medium-sized library preservation program can make a good, cost-effective beginning by correcting problems in the way the collections are housed and handled.

Environmental quality is the single most significant factor in long-term library preservation. Improved building environment is also probably the most frustrating aspect of a preservation program to bring about. An ideal environment is impossible to maintain in an open-stack collection in constant use by the public. As a further complication, responsibility for the physical plant is often administratively separate from the library. A physical plant manager faced with spiraling energy costs may be hard to persuade of the need for year-round climate control for the library.

If optimum climate control for the entire library building is impossible, it may be more feasible to install strict temperature and humidity controls in a room or rooms separate from the circulating collection, one set aside for volumes with real artifactual value or for unstable media of long-term research interest, such as photographs or magnetic media. The balance of the collection, which is valuable for the information it contains, can be adequately maintained in an environment that is suitable for human health and comfort.

Disaster prevention and general housekeeping are essential to a stable environment for library collections. Any disaster, whether caused by fire, water, earthquake, or other agency, does some permanent damage to the collection; recovery efforts never give perfect results and are always expensive. Prevention is better, and usually cheaper, than recovery after damage is done. An organized effort to check for open windows, water leaks, fire hazards, and other potential sources of trouble as a regular part of the library's opening and closing procedures will do much to prevent a costly disaster. Regularly scheduled vacuuming in the stacks will remove dust and dirt that would otherwise damage books and other media. Wastebaskets should be emptied frequently, and patrons politely discouraged from bringing food and drink into the stacks, thus discouraging insects and other undesirable fauna.

Dilapidation can be reduced and the useful life of library materials extended by means of good handling, shelving, and storage practices. Any book, even one printed on acidic paper, will last longer if stress on its physical structure is kept to a minimum. The newer, electronic forms of information storage media, such as audiotape and videotape, are also extremely vulnerable to damage from improper handling.

Good basic handling procedures cost nothing except the effort needed to train the library staff. The following simple procedures should be included in every new staff member's orientation:

> Books should be shelved upright and supported by bookends, but not packed so tightly into shelves that patrons have trouble removing them. Oversized volumes are best shelved separately so that they can stand upright or lie down flat.

Audiocassettes, compact disks, floppy disks, and so on should all be stored in their protective cases away from heat, light, dampness, and magnetic fields. Playing equipment should be cleaned regularly according to the manufacturer's instructions.

Jamming a thick wad of forms into a book can seriously weaken its binding before it leaves the library's technical processing area. A slim volume can accumulate a thick bundle of invoices, processing forms, computer printouts, notes, and a security strip before it reaches the library shelves.

Metal paper clips, pressure-sensitive tape, or rubber bands should never be used to attach messages to books during processing; they can tear pages and abrade covers. Any necessary notes can be written on a slip of paper large enough not to get lost inside the volume.

If a book drop must be maintained (and it may be politically impossible to get rid of it), it should be emptied before it is full. The staff member in charge of emptying the book drop should have a large, stable book truck available for the job. If the book drop is located outside the library building, a sheet of plastic or some other protective cover may be used to protect books in wet weather.

Modern publishers' bindings are not manufactured to stand up to the stress of frequent, heavy use. Even books issued in hard covers are often bound with "perfect" bindings, burst bindings, and hot-melt adhesives; the results are only marginally more durable than paperback books. As a result, librarians are often forced to add the cost of binding to the purchase price and processing costs to obtain a durable copy of a heavily used title. Library binding is the most basic preservation measure taken for the longevity of paper-based library materials; it also often consumes a large portion of the library's operating budget. A good-quality binding by a reputable library binder can add years to the life of a book; a poor-quality binding wastes funds and often breaks up the book faster. A careful review of the library's binding policy or contract should be part of the preservation planning process.

Book repair in a collections maintenance program refers to limited treatment of books whose case structure has failed, but which are printed on nonbrittle paper and have no artifactual value. Unfortunately, much of what is done in the name of "book mending" is destructive. The self-adhesive "book repair materials" commonly marketed for use in general library collections reduce openability, damage paper, and may make later rebinding impossible. Repairs in a collections maintenance program preserve the book's margins and openability and do not interfere with any future rebinding. Nondestructive book repair does not necessarily cost more per volume than damaging repair techniques. Confusion may exist between the meticulous, time-consuming, and expensive conservation operations used on materials with artifactual value and the simple, cost-effective repairs suitable for volumes with informational value only. Nondestructive repair requires a certain investment in staff training and expertise, but the results last longer than those done with unsound techniques and materials.

The crumbling of brittle books printed on acidic paper is the preservation problem with which smaller libraries feel least able to cope. All the solutions devised to date are expensive in terms of money, time, and labor. Fortunately, all the books in a library will not deteriorate at the same rate, nor is it likely that all the books in the collection will need to be retained once they deteriorate past the point of use. If a good collections maintenance program is in place, the point at which books become too brittle to remain in use can be postponed for a considerable time. When the day of reckoning finally comes, there are several solutions that are practicable for the smaller institution.

> *Withdrawal:* If a brittle or hopelessly deteriorated book no longer serves any useful purpose in the collection, and is neither rare nor valuable in itself, the simplest solution is just to get rid of it. Weeding the collection of outdated or out-of-scope materials allows the preservation program to concentrate its resources on items in genuine need of attention.

> *Replacement:* If a brittle title is valued only for its intellectual content, a commercial reprint or later edition of the same work is an acceptable substitute. A well-planned replacement program is less costly than filming or photocopying deteriorated titles. A further advantage is that most libraries already have staff and procedures in place for this activity.

> *Enclosure:* If a brittle book is going to be used infrequently, its life may be extended by placing it in some type of protective enclosure.

> *Photocopy replacement:* This is a good solution for obtaining a local copy of a brittle book if the title is not available as a commercial reprint. Cost per unit is high, but may be worthwhile if it is essential to have a copy in book form. Several commercial firms and some library binderies are now offering this service.

Some libraries produce their own photocopy replacements as a regular part of their preservation activity. Production costs should be carefully considered before setting up a program of this kind. A photocopy replacement operation is very labor intensive, requiring careful collation of both the brittle original and the copy, binding of the completed copy, and modification of the catalog record for the title being replaced, in addition to the actual copying. It is essential to purchase or lease a high-quality copier that will produce a sharp, durable image, and to use a good grade of alkaline paper for the replacement copies. Unless the library anticipates making very large numbers of photocopy replacements, it will probably be more cost-effective to contract with a commercial vendor for this service. In all cases, the library should be aware of its parent institution's copyright policy.

Microfilm: The cost of microfilm production can be prohibitive, and some microfilm service bureaus refuse to accept small projects. Costs of maintaining a microfilm collection mount rapidly. Roll film readers require careful maintenance and cleaning if they are not to damage the film. The cost of proper off-site storage for preservation master negatives is an additional burden. Experience has also shown that many patrons (and librarians) intensely dislike the medium.

Small and mid-sized libraries would be well advised not to commit any portion of their preservation budget to microfilming unless the material to be filmed is unique and of great scholarly importance. If there are titles in the general collection for which microfilm would be a suitable substitute, it will be far more cost-effective to buy copies of existing film either from a commercial vendor or from a research library that has been actively engaged in preservation microfilming.

Case Studies in Collections Maintenance Strategies

The subjects of the following case studies are composites based on libraries with which I have had personal experience. They illustrate how practical collections preservation programs can be designed to meet the needs of libraries with very different facilities and clientele.

Library A: Large Urban University

Library A serves an urban university with approximately 20,000 students. The university was founded in the nineteenth century as a teachers' college, but had grown to university status by World War II. The university now offers undergraduate courses in a full range of subject concentrations, as well as several prestigious graduate programs. Areas of special research strength include the physical and biological sciences, psychology, and political science.

The library is located in a large central facility built in 1965. Several branch libraries were eliminated at the time the central library was opened. The collection grew rapidly during the 1960s and 1970s, and now totals 1.5 million cataloged volumes, plus 9,000 active serial titles, and extensive microform holdings. In addition to the general collection, the department of special collections includes several important collections of books and manuscripts that have attracted scholars from across the country and from abroad. The collection is heavily used, with over 250,000 circulation transactions in the past academic year, together with 31,000 interlibrary loan transactions. Shelving has filled rapidly and is packed almost to capacity in some areas.

The building is air-conditioned, but modifications to the system over the years have resulted in poor humidity control. Budgetary difficulties have forced periodic shutdowns of the air-conditioning system during the summer months. Since the architectural style in vogue at the time of the library's construction called for large glass window walls, heat gain during the summer is severe. The department of special collections has a fireproof vault with a separate cooling system, but most of the special collections are housed under conditions no better than those of the general collections.

Preservation activity in the past has been limited to commercial binding and repairs with various types of self-adhesive book-mending tape. Because of periodic budget shortages, most paperback volumes have not been rebound and there is a sizable backlog of unbound periodicals. A condition survey showed that almost 30 percent of the collection was in serious need of either rebinding or repair.

The same survey revealed that approximately 18 percent of the library's collection was in brittle condition, and that nearly 70 percent of the serials collection was printed on acidic paper, which could be expected to become brittle in the future. Further investigation, however, indicated that a large portion of the brittle books in the general collections rarely circulated. Furthermore, nearly half the titles searched had either been previously filmed by other research libraries or were available as commercial reprints.

A disaster plan has been drawn up for the library, a piece of planning prompted by a near catastrophe involving a frozen water pipe during the Christmas holidays.

Plans are being made to construct an addition to the library within the next ten years. Although the details are still being discussed with the university administration, the proposed new construction will include both stacks and office space and new facilities for special collections.

Strategy for Library A   The chief preservation problems for library A are the environment created by the structure of the building and the deterioration caused by the high level of use that the collection receives. Some relief will be obtained for the first problem with construction of the new library addition. A preservation program for this situation would properly focus on providing as much protection as possible for the important special collections and on identifying heavily used items in need of treatment. Best results would be achieved by a comprehensive program providing a wide variety of options, including a strategy for dealing with books that were not brittle, but worn and deteriorated from heavy use.

The strategy that would be most effective for library A emphasizes identification of deteriorated materials after circulation, rather than at the shelves in the stacks. In this way, volumes in current use receive priority for treatment. A collections conservation unit can be set up to provide quick, nondestructive repair for books from the circulating collection, with special attention given to reference and reserve materials. Such a unit would relieve pressure on the binding budget by reducing the number of deteriorated monographs to be rebound and allowing more funds to be committed to serials binding.

Brittle-book replacement should likewise focus on circulating titles. After a preliminary search to determine reprint status and previous microfilming history, subject bibliographers can be given an opportunity to withdraw duplicate or nonessential titles, and to replace those still commercially available either with hard copy or microfilm. Photocopy replacement would be the option of choice for brittle titles that have not been filmed elsewhere, have not been commercially reprinted, and are still needed for local use. Library A might find the demand for copy replacement great enough to justify setting up its own photocopying operation.

The special collections are among the collections chosen for relocation to the planned addition. It would be appropriate, therefore, to concentrate on protection for these collections, rather than more aggressive treatment, and to design an optimal environment into the new location. Phase boxes and other protective enclosures could be constructed for fragile or deteriorated volumes.

Library B: Suburban Liberal Arts College

Library B is attached to a small, four-year liberal arts college in a prosperous suburban community. The college was founded late in the nineteenth century under church sponsorship. Although the college is now officially secular, a strong traditional association with the church persists; many members of the college's governing board are church members, as is a substantial portion of the student body. The college prides itself on its rigorous liberal arts curriculum, with particular concentrations in languages, literature, and art.

The library was built in the first decade of the twentieth century in the "university gothic" style and has appeared on the cover of the college's catalog for years. The top floor is occupied by a large central reading room, with stained-glass windows and several large murals decorating the walls. Research by a member of the faculty recently revealed that these murals are quite valuable.

The library maintains basic collections on all subjects taught at the college. As a result of faculty research interests, art history and French and Italian literature have been collected at greater depth. Total collection size is about 500,000 volumes, with 1,000 active periodical subscriptions.

The library also owns a small but distinguished collection of seventeenth- and eighteenth-century books acquired as a bequest from an alumna. This collection is housed in a small locked room adjacent to the chief librarian's office. The library also has custody of a series of diaries and letters written about the time of the Civil War by the college's founder. These are stored in a locked filing cabinet in the chief librarian's office, no other secure space being available.

The library has no air-conditioning system and is heated by steam in the winter. Stack space on the lower levels is filled to capacity. Staff work areas are cramped and inadequate. Study space is at a premium; an empty chair is almost impossible to find during examination periods, and students are forced to make do with stairs or the floor. The college administration is well aware of this situation, but recent declines in the value of the endowment have forced postponement of any new construction for the immediate future.

Preservation activity at library B has so far been limited. Attention has been given to security measures and to maintenance of the physical plant. A determined effort is made to keep the library clean and free from fire or water hazards. All paperbacks are bound before being sent to the shelves, and periodicals are bound on a regular schedule, although the cost is beginning to strain the operating budget. No book repair has been attempted because of lack of the necessary skills and work space. Dilapidated volumes are sent out for commercial rebinding. Subject bibliographers weed the collection as time permits. Although no formal condition survey of the collection has been done, staff members have a strong perception that brittle paper is not a significant problem.

Strategy for Library B   A successful collections maintenance program for library B will require planning to make the most use of very limited resources in staff, funds, and space. Because most of the collections are easily replaceable, binding of paperbound books can be postponed, at least until they begin to show signs of wear. Exceptions might be made for any titles with long-term research value. Another possibility is to not bind periodicals at all and replace back runs with microfilm to reduce pressure on already limited stack space.

If improvements in the library's environment are not immediately possible, the room containing the rare books collection should be altered to permit a better environment for the most valuable parts of the collection. This collection, together with the letters and diaries of the college founder, are worthwhile candidates for individual conservation treatment or for microfilming.

Given the close relationship of these materials to the history of the college, it may be possible to solicit funds from alumni or other interested individuals to support such a project.

Conclusion: Local Efforts Count

Any library that is regularly used must concern itself with preservation of its collections if it is to continue to meet user needs. It is unfortunate that the attention given in the professional literature to the microfilming efforts at the great research libraries (necessary and beneficial though they have been) may have persuaded librarians at smaller institutions that preservation of high-circulation collections is either unnecessary or hopelessly expensive. However, professional appreciation of the value of preservation efforts in such institutions is growing, as one can see in recent library literature. A well-thought-out collections maintenance strategy, designed with the needs and resources of the individual institution in mind, clearly can prolong the useful life of circulating collections and allow the library to make better use of its resources.

Suggested Readings

Boomgaarden, Wesley L. "Preservation Planning for the Small Special Library." *Special Libraries* 76 (summer 1985): 204–211.

Brown, Charlotte B., and Janet E. Gertz. "Selection for Preservation: Applications for College Libraries." In *Building on the First Century*, edited by J. C. Fennell, 288–294. Chicago: Association of College and Research Libraries, ALA, 1989.

Buchanan, Sally. "Preservation Perspectives: Notes on the Care of Collections." *Wilson Library Bulletin* 68 (October 1993): 64.

Drewes, Jeanne M., and Julie A. Page, eds. *Promoting Preservation Awareness in Libraries: A Sourcebook for Academic, Public, School, and Special Collections.* Westport, Conn.: Greenwood, 1997.

Gertz, Janet E., Charlotte Burbank Brown, and Jane Beebe. "Preservation Analysis and the Brittle Book Problem in College Libraries: The Identification of Research-Level Collections and Their Implications." *College & Research Libraries* 54 (1993): 227–239.

Kyle, Hedi. *Library Materials Preservation Manual: Practical Methods for Preserving Books, Pamphlets, and Other Printed Materials.* Bronxville, N.Y.: N. T. Smith, 1983.

MacDonald, Eric. "Creating a Preservation Department from Existing Staff Resources: The UC Irvine Experience." *Conservation Administration News*, no. 55 (October 1993): 6–7.

Milevski, Robert J. "Book Repair Manual." *Illinois Libraries* 77 (spring 1995): 76–112.

Morrow, Carolyn Clark, and Carole Dyal. *Conservation Treatment Procedures: A Manual of Step-by-Step Procedures for the Maintenance and Repair of Library Materials.* 2d ed. Littleton, Colo.: Libraries Unlimited, 1986.

Nasland, Cheryl T. "Preservation Programs in Small Academic Libraries." In *Operations Handbook for the Small Academic Library*, edited by Gerard B. McCabe, 153–167. New York: Greenwood, 1989.

Ogden, Sherelyn, ed. *Preservation of Library and Archival Materials: A Manual.* Rev. and expanded ed. Andover, Mass.: Northeast Document Conservation Center, 1994.

Page, Julie A., and George John Soete. "Preservation Orientation for Library Staff." *College & Research Libraries News* 55 (June 1994): 358–360.

Reynolds, Anne L., Nancy C. Schrock, and Joanna Walsh. "Preservation: The Public Library Response." *Library Journal* 114 (February 15, 1989): 128–132.

Rowley, Gordon, and Ivan Hanthorn. "Designing a Conservation Treatment Facility: Charting a Course into a Less Familiar Region of Planning for Libraries." *Journal of Academic Librarianship* 22 (March 1996): 97–104.

3

Preservation Program Planning for Archives and Historical Records Repositories

CHRISTINE WARD

An archives is a place in which records of long-term, or enduring, value are systematically preserved and made available for use. Preservation ensures the continued availability and usability of the information contained in those records. In a traditional sense, preservation is the archives' raison d'être. But preservation of information is a means to achieve a desired end. A modern archives' primary goal is to provide access to its holdings. Attaining this goal depends on how effectively, comprehensively, and systematically preservation planning is employed throughout the institution. Without an organized preservation program, the archives' ability to sustain access will be limited and eventually become impossible.

Archives and Archival Records

Archives are primary and generally unique documentary resources that possess long-term value because they offer evidence about the function or activity of their creator(s) or because they contain information that supports historical, legal, social, public policy, scientific, personal, and other research. Archivists appraise and select for permanent preservation those records that have fundamental and continuing value for administrative, fiscal, legal, evidential, or informational (historical) purposes.

Records can be public or private. They are created by organizations, governments, businesses, or individuals, and are the direct result of a specific function, activity, or transaction. They are arranged and accessed at the series or collection level. Each item in a file, series, or group of records is related to the others in a consequential or contextual way. Records are unique individual items that have a collective significance. Therefore, they must be maintained, both physically and intellectually, according to their organizational and functional origins and in their original order.

Archives are said to be used less extensively, but more intensively, than library materials (for example, each series may be used infrequently, but the use is steady, focused, and often for lengthy periods). Some records with special qualities or historic significance become the objects of continual display or excessive review. Such concentrated handling destroys fragile materials.

Even though the materials and methodologies vary considerably from library to archives, their program goals, preservation concerns, and management issues are not unrelated. Libraries and archives exist to preserve and provide access to information. Although preservation programs designed for libraries may not be immediately transposable to the archival environment, with creative adaptation, archivists can successfully employ library models.

In recent years, the archival community has developed some new approaches to preservation programming, adapting and applying library preservation methods and procedures, but packaging these approaches in an archival context. To be successful, archival preservation programs must conform to the archival program. Moreover, archivists have to be persuaded to modify their way of thinking about the preservation responsibility and, as a result, make significant changes in the organization and operation of their programs.

Unique Problems of Archives

Archives exist in a variety of physical formats and media. The multiformity and quantity of materials that the archivist must manage; the fact that different formats are often scattered throughout the archives, sometimes mixed within a series; and the numerous ways in which archival materials are, or might potentially be, used are all factors that make it impossible to find a single strategy to preserve archival records.

The voluminous size of archival collections makes it difficult to identify all the preservation problems that exist in every box. Even if all problems were known, the frequency with which they occur throughout the collections makes it impossible to deal with each individual problem. In federal and state government, fewer than 5 percent of records produced in the course of business have long-term value. Given the vast number of records created, however, this translates to great quantities. Even small historical records repositories and manuscript collections are threatened with being overwhelmed by the sheer size of their collections relative to the size of staff and institutional capacity to care for them.

Archival records are unique. Because replacement of their information may be impossible, difficult to carry out, or exceedingly expensive, this becomes a key issue in preservation planning. With archives, there are no second chances; once archival information is destroyed, it cannot be recovered. Similarly, once the context within which archival information exists (that is, the documentation relating to a record's original purpose and uses, as in the case of electronic systems) is lost, the usability of those records for future research may be compromised.

Archival repositories exist in a variety of organizations and within diverse administrative structures. Most archives are not autonomous entities; most are subsumed within a larger organization, such as a research library, historical society, corporation, or government agency. The success of archival preservation programs depends upon the ability of archives administrators to make decisions and take action for the preservation of their holdings. To the extent that archival administrators cannot act autonomously, they must at least be positioned to influence the decision makers.

Responsibility for Preservation

Preservation is the responsibility of every member of the archives' staff, every user of archival records, and every administrator accountable for the archival program. The administrator sets an example and provides leadership by encouraging planning, ensuring adequate staffing and resources, and pledging ongoing support for preservation activities.

In a large institution, the actual programmatic responsibility for preservation may be delegated to a member of the staff who has an aptitude for administration and who should have some experience managing one or more of the core archival functions. It is important that this individual receive training in preservation management, that the job description be amended to include preservation administration as a formal duty, and that a reasonable amount of time be allotted for activities related to managing the preservation program. The individual should be at an organizational level high enough to influence policies and procedures throughout the archives and to work effectively with those who direct functional operations. In a well-developed and well-supported program, a full-time preservation administrator may be hired. This person should have an understanding of preservation management as well as a familiarity with archival functions and operations.

Because of the small size of many archives, there may be only one professional staff member responsible for the entire operation. This is such a common situation that it is imperative that graduate and in-service programs in archival administration include training in preservation program management. Every archivist should know the basic principles of archival preservation and how to integrate them into the overall program.

The individual responsible for preservation must be able to make informed decisions about the program based upon an understanding of the mission and collecting policies of the institution; the condition of the collections as a whole and, as far as possible, of records scheduled to come to the archives; the facilities and environment in which collections are stored; the needs of archives users; the resources required to support the program; and the options available for preserving all formats in the collections.

Managers of preservation programs must be aware of the sources of information and able to analyze and evaluate such information to make appropriate decisions for the collections. Conservators and conservation scientists can provide information on the physical and chemical properties of archival materials, treatment options, and storage environments. Technical experts from such fields as film and audiovisual production and information technology can advise on the preservation of special media records. A challenge facing the archival preservation community is to identify what specialized technical information is important to support archival preservation and to find a means to package and deliver it in a format that nontechnicians can understand and use. Another related challenge is to develop methods, guidelines, and procedures for preserving information in records created in electronic and machine-readable formats.

Staff members also have a responsibility for preservation. Orientation workshops and in-service training help to create a work environment in which every member of the staff handles and cares for the collections in a responsible manner. And researchers must assume some responsibility for proper use of archives. Rules governing use and handling of records should be prominently displayed and enforced. The attitude and actions of staff handling records in the presence of the public set an example. Public relations materials describing preservation issues and outlining the reasons for strict adherence to preservation rules not only offer researchers the courtesy of explanation, but may persuade some to become active supporters of the program.

Preservation in an Archival Context

Most archival records are valuable for the information they contain. Therefore, preservation of information in its most usable form and through the most cost-effective means should be a goal of the program. There are, of course, some records with intrinsic value because of historic, literary, or other association or significance (an Abraham Lincoln letter or an original James Joyce manuscript) or because the information they contain must, for legal or other reasons, be maintained in its original format (maps in which the scale is difficult to reformat accurately or the color is significant). The valuation of archival material is often relative and should be determined locally, based upon the appraisal or collecting policies of the institution and other institutions holding similar or related materials. Whatever an institution's interpretation of the concept of intrinsic value may be, archivists should be aware that "value" is a key criterion in identifying materials for preservation.

The identification of archival material through the appraisal process is the first cut at selecting information with long-term value for preservation. Because preservation is expensive, appraisal archivists must be rigorous in their analysis and evaluation of potential accessions. Every institution should have a collecting policy that clearly states the scope of collecting and the criteria employed to identify archival records. Appraisal analysis should include a review of preservation needs, costs of long-term maintenance and preservation, and the impact of the decision on the rest of the holdings. Preservation planning begins with appraisal. The more that is known about the physical needs of records before they enter the archives, the easier it is to plan for their maintenance once they arrive. Likewise, records that present overwhelming preservation problems upon appraisal review should be carefully considered using a cost/benefit model before deciding to accession them.

Archives should be guided by the principle of responsible custody. It is neither practical nor professionally ethical to acquire records for which the institution cannot ensure at least a basic level of preservation. Every archival repository must provide conditions that support long-term maintenance and usability of records in its custody. Responsible custody relates not to an ability to carry out preservation treatments, but to the institution's capacity to achieve and maintain such conditions. These include: an environment appropriate to the needs of the formats and media in the collections; protective housing for all collections; fire protection systems; security systems; a disaster prevention and recovery plan; and a program of staff and user training.

Beyond these basic provisions, those institutions that maintain records on unstable media (for example, color film, magnetic tape, floppy disks) must have the capacity to monitor and evaluate the condition of those records on a periodic basis and provide for transfer of information before irretrievable loss or obsolescence occurs.

The principal goal of archival preservation is to stabilize the collections as a whole. At the same time, if resources permit, decisions can be made about preservation actions to be taken for collections, or parts of collections, that require more concentrated attention. Because there are simply not enough resources to treat all records that are designated "archival," the majority of resources should be allocated to upgrade and stabilize the condition of all holdings. Then, analysis can continue to identify materials most in need of additional preservation action and to determine the types and levels of treatment to be applied. These decisions should be based not only on physical condition, but also on assessment of risks posed by current storage practices and by the amount and nature of current and potential use. This concept of preservation management is akin to the Utilitarian principles advanced by British philosopher Jeremy Bentham: "The greatest good for the greatest number."

Preservation Policy in Archives

An institution's preservation policy should contain statements of principle that define the institution's approach to meeting its preservation responsibility. Such statements provide a framework for setting priorities and making decisions. The policy should define preservation in an archival context and should endorse the primacy of preserving information over artifact except when intrinsic value is a factor. The preservation policy should delineate the function of preservation in relation to the other archival functions and indicate other policy areas that are affected by preservation policies (for example, policies on researcher services, staff training, public relations, or emergency response).

The preservation policy must also reflect the mission, goals, and priorities of the parent institution, particularly with respect to ways in which the records are serviced or used and the needs of the institution's clientele. This does not mean that the preservation policy should be silent on points at which the practices of the parent institution conflict with sound preservation principles. It does mean that compromise may be required to unify conflicting policies. Sometimes, however, the policies of the parent institution will have to change in order to meet preservation requirements and preserve the integrity of the collections.

Planning the Preservation Program

The preservation program is a set of activities that address, in a comprehensive manner, the preservation needs of the institution. Because institutions differ in mission, size, character of holdings, and clientele, the actual design of the preservation program will vary somewhat from place to place. The specific elements and activities of each individual program are determined after a thorough assessment of needs throughout the institution, and developed through a planning process that should include input from staff at all levels.

All archives and historical records repositories, even small ones, need a comprehensive and integrated preservation program. Because the issues cut across all archival functions, they cannot be compartmentalized. Individual staff members, who are exposed in their daily work only to the symptoms of larger preservation problems, may not understand fully the systemic nature of the problem or see the implications of their actions. The preservation program must generate a broad base of support, cutting across functions, providing for staff education, and involving staff at all levels in identifying problems as well as in developing solutions.

From a management perspective, a carefully planned program ensures that limited resources are expended consistently and economically. For example, stabilization or reformatting measures implemented now will alleviate the need for expensive conservation treatments later. Moreover, an institution that bases its preservation decisions on a clearly defined set of selection criteria and careful assessment of preservation needs is better able to justify treatment decisions and resource requests to support the preservation program.

Finally, establishing a preservation program will necessarily involve a substantial ongoing commitment of both staff and monetary resources. A long-range preservation plan offers continuity of direction over time. It makes it possible for staff to understand the program goals and to see how their activities help to achieve those goals. Comprehensive preservation programs are products of decisive action on the part of both administration and staff. The planning process requires introspection and honesty and should encourage consensus building on directions and goals.

The successful program will have three additional characteristics: It must be integrated into the overall archival program, it must be proactive, and it must be flexible. An integrated program is one that makes preservation a part of every archival function and adds preservation responsibility to every staff member's job description. A proactive program is one that does not simply react to solve a problem, but focuses on preventing them from occurring or on eliminating situations that would give rise to the problem in the first place. A flexible program is one that has the ability to adapt to changes. For instance, increasingly archives must respond to the needs of a growing quantity of records in machine-readable formats, while continuing to deal with problems posed by vast quantities of paper-based material. This transition to dealing with new media that have different needs from paper is forcing major changes in archival preservation programs.

Five steps are necessary to lay the foundation for a comprehensive preservation program: assign responsibilities, determine needs, develop plans, establish ongoing monitoring and evaluation procedures, and provide for staff training.

Assign Responsibility

At every level and in every department of the archives, responsibilities must be determined, agreed upon, and assigned. One individual or group of individuals (for example, the preservation department or collections management unit in a larger operation) must be accountable for developing, implementing, and monitoring preservation activities.

If the program is truly integrated, every functional unit of the archives will have preservation activities that must be routinely carried out. Procedures within many functional units may have to change to conform to accepted preservation practice. The head of each unit should be accountable for overseeing these activities on a daily basis and for coordinating with the preservation staff to ensure that they are properly carried out.

Determine Needs

A thorough assessment of the preservation needs of the institution must be carried out. Data should be collected on the condition of, and risks to, collections, the environment, and the physical facility in which the collections are housed.

The collection needs assessment should be carried out on two different levels in order to obtain a detailed picture of preservation needs. Initially, an overall survey of all holdings will provide enough information on general condition and needs to develop broad goals for the program. Sampling is an effective means of gathering this kind of information. So too are interviews with staff, particularly those involved with storage and use of materials. Data on the actual physical condition of the collections should be gathered, including information on formats and the percentage of unstable materials, including brittle paper.

As the planning progresses, more detailed information at the series or collection level will be needed. Analysis of these data will provide a basis for selecting materials for preservation action and for setting priorities. Sampling can be used for large series. Staff should gather information on archival significance or value and use as well as summary information on the actual physical condition and status of housing for each series. Once a retrospective needs assessment is completed, staff should continue to gather condition, significance, and use information for new accessions and maintain it in a comprehensive database for all holdings.

A survey of storage facilities and the equipment on or in which records are stored provides necessary information on existing and potential dangers to the records. Such a survey can be completed by a consultant or by institution staff who have had some training. A facilities survey should review the structural and mechanical components of the building, particularly the heating, ventilating, and air-conditioning systems; the storage systems; the security systems; the fire detection and suppression systems; the building's surroundings; and the climate and environment in which the building exists.

Finally, policies and procedures for storage, handling, and use should be reviewed and evaluated to determine their effects on the general physical condition of the records. In each of the needs assessment areas, it is important to compile information on preservation activities that have already been carried out. For instance, an institution may rebox and refolder new accessions in acid-free materials or may have procedures for denying access to materials in extremely fragile condition. An analysis of data from all of these sources should provide a complete picture of the actual preservation needs and any risks to the security or continued safe use of these records.

Develop the Plan

The product of this systematic process should be a written plan that states in clear and practical terms: (1) the goals of the preservation program, (2) the activities necessary to reach those goals, (3) designated responsibility for each activity, (4) resources required to carry out each activity, and (5) a schedule for beginning and completing each activity. Some examples of preservation goals are: to create and maintain an environment that retards deterioration, reduces risk, and provides for recovery in case of emergency; to revise procedures for records processing to improve housing and identify critical preservation needs; or to integrate preservation and security measures into procedures for moving or exhibiting records. A section of the plan should be devoted to a statement of the preservation needs and should relate the plan's goals to the needs that each addresses. Another section of the plan might explain why a preservation program is essential and what this will mean to the long-term accessibility of important archival records or information. The plan is the document that will be used to justify program development and to support resource requests.

Planning should involve as many members of the archives' staff as possible. In a large institution, it is neither practical nor likely that all staff will have the time to devote to the planning activity, but those not involved directly might be interviewed and might be asked to comment on drafts of the plan. Institutional assimilation of the program may depend, as stated before, on staff feeling some ownership of the plan under which they will be operating. The plan should include both short- and long-range goals, and it should clearly indicate those activities that must be carried out right away. This will make it possible to implement the program in phases or stages, dealing early on with immediate needs and priorities and beginning activities that require little or no funding and minimal preparation. It is important to indicate the relationship between short and long-range goals that are dependent upon each other. For example, a long-range goal may be to plan and build a new facility that meets appropriate preservation standards. A related short-range goal might be to complete a thorough study of environmental and space needs for the program.

Establish Procedures to Monitor and Evaluate

A plan is useful only if there is a way to measure progress. Staff should meet regularly to review and measure accomplishments against the plan's goals. This serves two purposes: First, it makes it possible to observe strategies that are not working and gives staff the opportunity to revise, adjust, discard, or simply change methods, activities, timetables, and cost estimates. The plan should be flexible, and staff should have the opportunity to suggest revision at any point. Second, regular review provides a means to measure success; to chart the progress of the program; and to document achievements, difficulties, scheduling needs, and costs.

Provide for Staff Training

Ongoing staff development makes it possible for every member of the staff to participate fully in the preservation program. Staff should receive training in preservation at whatever level is necessary to ensure each person's understanding of, and commitment to, the program. This includes such simple but important issues as continuing communication between the manager(s) of the program and staff members carrying out the actual activities to keep them abreast of developments, accomplishments, and directions. Although this seems simple, it can be critical to the success of the program. In a large institution, particularly, where the preservation program is diverse and integrated throughout many other functions, it is not always possible to maintain close contact with all staff carrying out preservation activities. A concerted effort must be made to ensure communication.

Preservation Program Design

The preservation program is designed to respond to the institution's specific needs and achieve its stated goals. The design both allows and limits the development of program activities.

Following is a list of possible preservation program elements. The number and nature of activities associated with each element will vary from institution to institution, depending upon the identified needs and the resources available.

1. Needs assessment
   a. ongoing for new accessions
   b. retrospective

   for collections already in institutional custody

   for facilities (carried out during planning process, but must be reviewed and updated periodically)

2. Stabilization/protection of holdings
   a. holdings maintenance program, including basic preservation activities
   b. environmental control
   c. security and emergency preparedness
   d. ongoing policy and procedures review

3. Staff and user training

4. Conservation treatment of material of intrinsic value

5. Reformatting

The first three elements constitute a core preservation program. A program that combines these elements focuses on stabilizing and providing a sustained level of basic preservation for the entire collection. For institutions that do not have the resources or the need to become involved with treatment or reformatting, these elements can comprise the full preservation program. For other institutions, these three elements might represent the first steps toward developing a broader and more comprehensive program. For financial reasons, institutions may begin with the most basic elements and then expand the program later.

Needs assessment has already been discussed in the context of planning a program. It is also an essential part of a functioning preservation program. Evaluation of the physical needs of all materials coming into the archives will provide information necessary to plan for future preservation activities and to set priorities for preservation treatments. This can be accomplished by reviewing materials as they are accessioned. It is preferable, however, to incorporate the assessment activity as early as possible into the life cycle of records. The appraisal of records should include an analysis of their preservation needs. For those archival programs that include a records management function, the preservation needs of permanent records can be assessed, and perhaps addressed, before their transfer to the archives. This becomes a particularly critical activity for records in nontraditional formats, such as electronic records or videotapes, because of media instability, dependency on hardware and software for retrieval of information, and dependency on associated documentation (metadata) for use or understanding of recorded data.

Ongoing needs assessment allows the program to remain current and to maintain flexibility, changing priorities as needs change. Although a basic retrospective needs assessment will have been carried out in the planning phase, it is important to review this periodically and reevaluate the identified needs. Needs will change as the program matures. For example, better control over environmental conditions may alleviate an early concern over the spread of mold; a project to provide boxed storage for all records may reduce the need for lighting control in the stack area, or the installation of a new roof may mitigate the necessity for certain protective procedures.

The assessment will undoubtedly reveal more needs than the institution is prepared to handle. The next step is to identify priorities among the full range of needs. For every need, the cost of implementing activities necessary to address that need must be balanced against the cost or risk of doing nothing. "Costs" are not always monetary. Problems that accrue as a result of inattention to a currently identified need can certainly be defined as a "cost."

The single most important element in a modern archives preservation program, and certainly the broadest in terms of the range of possible activities, is that of stabilizing and protecting collections. This aspect of the program focuses on creating and maintaining a benign environment to slow the ongoing deterioration of the whole collection. The goals are simple: store and handle records in a manner consistent with preservation standards and ensure their ongoing protection in storage and in use. Achieving these goals will depend upon many related activities occurring at once. The physical condition of the collections must be stabilized as far as possible. At the same time, procedures for the physical care, handling, and use of these records should be reviewed and revised to ensure that all actions related to these functions contribute to the long-term preservation of the records and remain compatible with preservation standards. Finally, the facilities in which the records are stored and used may need upgrading.

Multiple strategies may be employed to stabilize and protect the collections. These include: establishing a holdings maintenance program; maintaining an environment at levels appropriate for long-term preservation; providing for collection security and emergency preparedness; and initiating ongoing policy and procedural review.

Holdings maintenance is a systematic program, developed at the National Archives and Records Administration, that uses a range of basic preservation procedures to improve the housing and storage environment on an institution-wide basis. A holdings maintenance program defers or eliminates the need for individualized conservation treatment. In a small institution, holdings maintenance might be applied to the entire collection; in large repositories, the program may be carried out only for specific segments of the collection, basing priorities upon an evaluation of the needs of each discrete group of records. Holdings maintenance involves procedures that offer a high level of physical protection and chemical stability within the limits of institutional resources and needs. These procedures include rehousing in containers (equipment, boxes, and folders) that are chemically stable and do not contribute to the deterioration of the records; isolating records that could contribute to the degradation of other records; ensuring that records are properly aligned and supported in housings; providing appropriate housing (and appropriate environment if necessary) for special formats; removing or replacing damaging fasteners; and unfolding and flattening material.

A holdings maintenance program attends also to the environment in which records are stored and used. An environment in which temperature, humidity, and airborne pollutants are maintained within acceptable ranges is required for the long-term preservation of archival materials. Ideally, records storage and work areas should be separated, but this is rarely an option in most archives. Therefore, the archives should attempt to maintain as cool a temperature as is compatible with other activities being carried out in the storage areas.

Without an adequate security program, including an emergency preparedness component, an institution's preservation investment can be negated. The security requirements, and associated risk factors, of the archival repository should have been reviewed and evaluated as part of the overall needs assessment. Particular emphasis should be placed upon the structure, construction, location, and surroundings of the facility itself and the adequacy of its surveillance, fire detection, and fire suppression systems. Institutional procedures relating to research room security, movement of records between locations, exhibitions, copying, and emergency response should be reviewed to determine their efficacy and to identify areas that will require change. To be effective, security procedures must be integrated into the everyday routine of the archives. Ongoing staff training and communicating with users about the importance of, and the reasons for, strict security procedures are fundamental to a successful security program.

Emergency preparedness is an essential component of the security program. Every archival repository should know its risks and have in place a plan to deal with them. Based upon the needs assessment, the manager should be able to pinpoint specific conditions and situations that cannot easily or economically be changed and that may pose a potential threat to the collections. Preservation emergencies may be as mundane as a broken air-conditioning system in the middle of August, as potentially explosive as a bomb threat, or as devastating as a fire or flood. The plan may be the collection's salvation, allowing for immediate, efficient, coordinated, and, therefore, effective response to any unexpected emergency or disaster.

Institutional policies and procedures can run counter to sound preservation practices. During needs assessment, certain practices that are harmful or pose a risk to collections may have been identified. These might relate to handling of materials in the field and during transfer to the archives, storage and handling procedures, research room procedures, or exhibit policies. The preservation manager must be in a position to bring improper practices to the attention of the staff and to effect changes in institutional procedures to ensure the appropriate use and handling of archival records.

Staff training, communications, and public relations guarantee a well-informed staff and public who will pay attention to the preservation needs of the records and support preservation activities. As changes are made in institutional procedures, staff must be informed and retrained if necessary. They will accept new methods and procedures when they understand the reasoning behind the changes and are made to feel a part of the new program. Researchers are far more likely to acquiesce to stricter regulations if they, too, understand why such measures are necessary and see they are being applied uniformly. In fact, some users are so interested in the preservation activity and respect the necessity for these new strictures that they themselves become advocates for preservation. Researchers can often be counted on to bring deteriorated materials to the archivists' attention and to report breaches in preservation practice in the research room.

The degree to which conservation treatments are employed largely depends upon the size, maturity, needs, and resources of the preservation program. Conservation treatments are expensive. The volume of material that benefits per dollar expended for conservation is significantly smaller than the volume benefiting from each holdings maintenance dollar. Available resources will necessarily limit the number and type of treatments possible; it will be necessary to establish priorities. As the program matures and needs are fully assessed, the manager can confidently make treatment selections against established criteria that are uniformly applied.

The manager must also decide if an in-house treatment program makes sense and, if so, what level of treatment can be supported in-house. For example, should a conservation lab be established on-site, or should a contracted conservator provide training and supervision for technicians who work in-house? The most familiar solution is to establish contractual arrangements with a conservation service to have materials treated on an as-needed basis. This eliminates the overhead of work space, equipment, and staff and, for most institutions, meets the conservation treatment need in a cost-effective manner.

The last major element in the preservation program is reformatting archival information. In most instances, the preservation of information is the archivist's paramount concern. Therefore, copying paper-based records to a more permanent medium can reduce bulk while improving access. Reformatting may be carried out for two purposes: preservation of the original, which can then be retired from active use, or preservation of information in a record of no intrinsic value, which may be destroyed after the film is certified to meet technical and legal requirements. The film then becomes the record copy. Microfilming is the technology most commonly employed in archives. However, digital technologies, and a hybrid approach using a combination of micrographic and digital technologies, are currently being tested for preservation applications, as discussed in chapter 17, Digitization for Preservation and Access.

Several alternatives are available for meeting reformatting needs. A large institution may determine that an in-house micrographics or digital scanning operation is cost-effective because the institution has a level of ongoing need that justifies a substantial investment in equipment and staff. Most institutions will find it more economical to contract for commercial services. In either case, the archive is responsible for ensuring quality, maintaining standards, and monitoring the products of the copying activity.

Finally, electrostatic or digital copiers may have some application in archives for copying individual acidic, brittle, or otherwise unstable items. Massive copying programs, however, are generally not cost-effective and do nothing to reduce the need for space. Copying a large volume of archival records is labor intensive and should be undertaken only when other options are inappropriate or impossible. For the smaller institution without a space problem, and for which other reformatting options are not possible, copying may be a reasonable solution to preserve relatively small quantities of information.

Whatever elements are determined to be appropriate to the design of the preservation program for a specific institution, it is important that the overall program remain vital and effective. To ensure that the program continues to be proactive, flexible, and responsive to changing needs, planning cannot be abandoned once the program is functioning. Ongoing collection and facility needs assessment to revise or set new priorities for the program is essential. Also essential is ongoing review and evaluation of the effectiveness of each program activity in meeting the archives' identified needs. Built-in review allows program personnel to monitor and evaluate the program's ability to achieve the desired goals. Are the needs identified during the planning process being met? Do they still exist? Have they changed such that the strategies are no longer adequate or appropriate? It may be useful to establish annual benchmarks against which to measure progress toward the goals. This can be a useful approach when dealing with goals that will realistically take many years to reach. It is also a useful tool to help maintain staff morale in the face of overwhelming needs. Benchmarking allows the program to achieve visible successes on its way to reaching the larger long-term goals.

Resources and Priorities

As the program is designed, the costs in staff time and other resources for each program element and associated activity being considered must be identified. This information is then reviewed against the needs, the short- and long-term impact or benefit of carrying out that activity, and the risk of not doing it. This analysis of cost against need, impact, risk, and available resources makes it possible to identify and eliminate unrealistic solutions and reduce overly ambitious solutions to reasonable proportions.

The resources—staffing, equipment, and funds—required to develop and implement a comprehensive preservation program are directly related to the ambitiousness of the program. A basic preservation program should be easily integrated into the archival program and should not require extensive additional resources. The program manager should review the archives' budget to determine if existing resources can be redirected to cover the expense of new or reengineered activities. Most archives are already spending funds for materials and activities that are closely aligned to preservation. For instance, the purchase of folders or storage boxes is clearly an activity related to holdings maintenance. Often a change in type of materials purchased with already existing funds and some retraining of staff are all that is necessary to reengineer an activity to conform to preservation standards at little or no additional cost.

Having determined which activities to include in the preservation program as well as their associated costs, the manager must decide how each activity will be executed and in what order. Because it is unlikely that resources will be available to support all recommended activities, priorities must be set. High-priority activities are those that are required to meet critical needs and therefore *must* be funded. Other high-priority activities might be those that cost nothing but are important, as well as those that are essential to the future of the program. Priorities should not be chosen solely on the basis of cost or ease of implementation. Priority-setting depends on several factors: benefit or impact of the activity; cost of the activity in terms of time, staffing, and other resources; time frame of the activity; and significance of the activity as a building block for the rest of the program.

After realistic priorities have been established, the program planning and design process is completed and the program is ready to put in place. At this point, the institution has a comprehensive program design that is customized, based on clearly defined needs, and designed around a plan whose goals and strategies address those specific needs. The program also incorporates only those elements and associated activities that will attain the specified goals, and it realistically reflects the resources and financial climate of the institution.

Preservation is a basic archival function. But preservation is not, and cannot be, a series of unrelated activities carried out in response to problems as they occur. In order to address creatively, cost-effectively, and efficiently the range of preservation problems facing archives in the modern age, the institution must make a commitment to supporting a comprehensive preservation program that focuses on preservation needs across the institution and on preserving information throughout the entire collection. Preservation is critical to the future of archives and fundamental to the archivist's ability to ensure long-term continuing access. It is at once the most basic and yet the most valuable, essential, and significant thing that archivists do.

Suggested Readings

Bradsher, James Gregory. "An Introduction to Archives." In *Managing Archives and Archival Institutions*, edited by James Gregory Bradsher, 1–17. Chicago: Univ. of Chicago Pr., 1988.

Dalley, Jane. *The Conservation Assessment Guide for Archives.* Ottawa: Canadian Council of Archives, 1955.

Garlick, Karen. "Planning an Effective Holdings Maintenance Program." *American Archivist* 53 (1990): 256–264.

Gwinn, Nancy E. *Preservation Microfilming: A Guide for Librarians and Archivists.* Chicago: ALA, 1987.

Jones, Norvell M. M., and Mary Lynn Ritzenthaler. "Implementing an Archival Preservation Program." In *Managing Archives and Archival Institutions*, edited by James Gregory Bradsher, 185–206. Chicago: Univ. of Chicago Pr., 1988.

Kaplan, Hilary A., and Brenda S. Banks. "Archival Preservation: The Teaming of the Crew." *American Archivist* 53 (1990): 266–273.

LaRose, Michele. "Conservation Planning and Programs." In *Proceedings of Conservation in Archives: International Symposium, Ottawa, Canada, May 10–12, 1988*, pp. 297–307. Paris: International Council on Archives, 1989.

Lyall, Jan. "Disaster Planning for Libraries and Archives: Understanding the Essential Issues." *Provenance, the Electronic Magazine* 1, no. 2 (March 1996).

Marelli, Nancy. *Implementing Preservation Management: A How-To Manual for Archives.* Quebec: National Library of Quebec and National Library of Canada, 1996.

McCarthy, Paul H. *Archives Assessment and Planning Workbook.* Chicago: Society of American Archivists, 1989.

National Association of Government Archives and Records Administrators. *NAGARA GRASP: Guide and Resources for Archival Strategic Preservation Planning.* Atlanta: NAGARA, 1990.

———. *Preservation Needs in State Archives.* Albany, N.Y.: NAGARA, 1986.

National Research Council. *Preservation of Historical Records.* Washington, D.C.: National Academy Pr., 1986.

Piggot, Michael. "Conservation." In *Keeping Archives*, edited by Anne Pederson, 219–251. Sydney: Australian Society of Archivists, 1987.

Ritzenthaler, Mary Lynn. *Archives and Manuscripts: Conservation, A Manual on Practical Care and Management.* Chicago: Society of American Archivists, 1993.

Ritzenthaler, Mary Lynn, Gerald Munoff, and Margery S. Long. *Archives and Manuscripts: Administration of Photographic Collections.* Chicago: Society of American Archivists, 1984.

Schellenberg, T. R. *The Management of Archives.* New York: Columbia Univ. Pr., 1965.

United States. National Archives and Records Service. *Intrinsic Value in Archival Materials.* Staff Information Paper 21. Washington, D.C.: NARS, 1982.

Wright, Sandra. "Conservation Program Planning at the National Archives of Canada." *American Archivist* 53 (1990): 314–322.

4

■■ ■ ■■

Programs, Priorities,
and Funding

■ ■ ■

MARGARET CHILD,
with the assistance of LAURA J. WORD

Many individuals, institutions, and organizations have actively contributed to the development and growth of efforts to save America's intellectual heritage as documented on paper and other media. The preservation movement in the United States has been neither centralized nor systematically organized, but has instead been spontaneous, opportunistic, flexible, and multifaceted. The primary propellants of its expansion and forward movement have been individual initiative, hard work, and something approaching messianic fervor. The availability of funding, both public and private, has both stimulated and sustained its growth. If there is something that deserves to be called a "national preservation program," it is the totality of all the distinct and distinctive preservation activities that have developed from grassroots efforts across the country. This program is typically American in its openness to change and in its ingenuity in devising new practical and conceptual solutions to the problems it confronts. Moreover, despite the organizational variety and broad geographic dispersal of the multitude of preservation programs currently under way, they share another characteristic: a commitment to cooperation growing out of their members' common goal of furthering the cause of preservation.

This chapter can only skim the surface of the many layers and types of endeavors that form the backbone of the national preservation program. We will begin at the top simply because it is easier to provide a broad overview of all levels and kinds of preservation activity if the relevant national programs and organizations are described first. This is not meant to imply any hierarchical relationship between what is going on at the national level and regional or local preservation activity. There are, however, important links between some national programs and regional and local programs. In particular, much of the available funding comes from federal sources or from national foundations. Their goals and priorities have inevitably shaped the kinds of projects and programs that could be undertaken. In addition, two of the major centers of scientific research on the preservation and conservation of books, paper, and other documentary media, and therefore of reliable information, are federal institutions.

In the past decade, preservation in the United States has been engulfed by the digital revolution. This has markedly affected program priorities as administrators have tried to exploit the benefits of digitization in providing access to materials, to test its potential for long-term preservation, and to devise systematic methodologies to preserve the ever-increasing amount of information created in digital form. Recognition of this sea change has been incorporated insofar as possible throughout the chapter, but its underlying perspective is now historical rather than current.

National Program

Federal Funding Agencies

The three principal federal sources for preservation grants are the National Endowment for the Humanities (NEH) Division of Preservation and Access, the National Historical Publications and Records Commission (NHPRC), and the Institute of Museum and Library Services, which administers the Library Services and Technology Act (LSTA) and National Leadership Grants. Although none of these agencies could or would claim to be a cooperative program in the strict sense of the word, to differing degrees the programs they administer have in fact been shaped in cooperation with the constituencies they serve.

This is particularly true in the case of the NEH's Division of Preservation and Access, which supports preservation microfilming of brittle books and serials, arrangement and description of archival collections, preservation education and training, and research and demonstration projects that seek to improve institutional practice and the effective use of technology for preservation and access. The division also administers two major cooperative initiatives—the Brittle Books Program and the United States Newspaper Program—and is a partner with the National Science Foundation (and others) in the Digital Libraries II initiative. The system of peer review by external reviewers and panels used by NEH to evaluate applications provides a regular channel for comment from the field. Reviewer evaluations do not focus only on the particulars of a specific application but also deal with its underlying principles and how it fits into the broad spectrum of national preservation activity. Panel meetings often devote considerable time to policy issues raised by one or more proposals, and consensus from one or more panels can lead to a change in the Division Guidelines. In addition, many projects introduce innovations in practice, new standards of performance, and other developments that are in turn incorporated into NEH models of a typical project. There is thus in place a structure to facilitate an ongoing dialogue among NEH staff and applicants, reviewers, and panelists, which provides a real opportunity for the preservation community to influence how NEH interacts with the evolving national program.

At the same time, the National Council on the Humanities, a body of prominent scholars, citizens, and educational administrators appointed by the president, provides guidance to each agency division on policy issues. In addition, the chairman of NEH must approve any redefinition of requirements or shifts in direction by any program. And each NEH division must be able to justify changes in its program to both the agency administration and to Congress at budget time. Despite these checks on staff independence, the relationship between the NEH programs that have provided support for preservation projects and the constituencies they serve has traditionally been collaborative.

NHPRC also uses external reviewers to advise on the merits of the applications it receives. In addition, it relies on historical records advisory boards in each state to work with prospective applicants to develop solid proposals. These boards are usually chaired by the state archivist and reflect a broad range of archival activity within the state. In addition, the commission itself is composed of one representative each from the U.S. Supreme Court, the Senate, the House of Representatives, the Departments of State and Defense, and the Library of Congress; two presidential appointees; and one representative each from the American Historical Association, the Organization of American Historians, the American Association for State and Local

History, the Association for Documentary Editing, the National Association of Government Archivists and Records Administrators, and the Society of American Archivists. This broadly representative group is chaired by the Archivist of the United States. It, too, is concerned with policy issues to ensure that grants truly meet the changing needs of efforts to preserve and provide access to the historical record in all its manifestations. In June 1997, NHPRC adopted a new strategic plan that shows increased attention to the challenges of preserving electronic records and improving access to a wide range of historical materials. The three equal strategic goals include completing publication of the Founding Fathers papers, collaborating with state historical records advisory boards to "strengthen the nation's archival infrastructure and expand the range of records that are protected and accessible," and providing "leadership in funding research-and-development on appraising, preserving, disseminating, and providing access to important documentary sources in electronic form."

Federal library programs once administered by the Department of Education were transferred to the Institute of Museum and Library Services (IMLS) in fiscal year 1997. Legislation renewed and reorganized the Library Services and Construction Act (LSCA) and Title II of the Higher Education Act into the Library Services and Technology Act (LSTA). Block grants to states encourage all types of libraries to "use technology to bring information to people in new and interesting ways, and to assure that library service is accessible to all—especially those who have difficulty using the library." Although preservation is not specifically mentioned in the IMLS guidelines for LSTA support, the overall focus on access implies a commitment to maintaining collections so that they can be used. States, therefore, are continuing to use LSTA funds for such projects as preservation surveys.

IMLS also offers National Leadership Grants that are intended to "enhance the quality of library services nationwide and to provide coordination between libraries and museums." These grants "mark a new opportunity for libraries to address pressing needs in education, research, and preservation and for libraries and museums to work together to address community needs, expand audiences, and implement the use of the most efficient and appropriate technologies." In the first round of applications received, more than one-quarter were for projects to preserve unique library resources or address challenges of preserving and archiving digital materials. It is not yet clear what types of projects will be most competitive. Nonetheless, some of the impetus built up during the last years of Title IIC, especially for major microfilming and other reformatting projects to preserve the full range of information media, has been lost. Like both NEH and NHPRC, external reviewers play a major role in selecting the projects to be funded by IMLS.

The National Libraries and NARA

Four other federal agencies play a significant cooperative role in the national preservation program: the Library of Congress (LC), the National Archives and Records Administration (NARA), the National Library of Medicine (NLM), and the National Agricultural Library (NAL). Again, they are not in themselves cooperative undertakings, but they cooperate with and contribute to preservation programs of all kinds throughout the country. The first two support research programs that address some of the basic scientific questions of the preservation field, such as the chemical and physical characteristics of all types of information media and the mechanisms of deterioration. Over the years they have produced data that, in turn, have provided the basis for the formulation of a wide range of national standards relating to preservation. Library of Congress scientists have also worked to develop a method of mass deacidification, which could attack the preservation problem at its source by providing a cheap, effective way to neutralize the acid in paper before it begins to deteriorate. The diethyl zinc (DEZ) process showed great promise, but was judged by the contractor not to be commercially viable, resulting in the closure of the pilot treatment plant. The library is now using the liquid-based technology called Bookkeeper that impregnates books with magnesium oxide particles that both neutralize the acid in paper and leave behind an alkaline buffer.

The National Archives research and testing section supports the work of its conservation staff by making recommendations on such problems as the optimum relative humidity at which to store various types of photographic materials. The section also does quality-assurance testing of materials used for housing archival collections (boxes, folders, plastic, storage furniture, exhibit cases, and other materials) and to ensure that they meet National Archives specifications. For example, they have tested the long-term effect of shrink-wrapping deteriorating bound volumes. Results of the work of the research and testing section are published in the "Technical Information Paper" series or as in-house reports. Librarians, archivists, and preservation professionals throughout the country may request a list of products that have been tested and then ask for the relevant report. Funds are also available to contract with the National Institute of Standards and Technology to undertake long-term research projects that eventually produce published reports. As a public service, NARA sponsors an annual conference on topics of interest to preservation administrators and conservators, such as preservation of machine-readable records or reformatting visual materials in a digital world.

Both the Library of Congress and the National Archives also serve as sources of last resort for technical information that cannot be found elsewhere. Like NARA, LC disseminates conservation and preservation information by means of publications and has also created audio-visual presentations that have been shown throughout the country. During the 1980s, the LC National Preservation Program Office sponsored a series of conferences that did much to raise the consciousness of library administrators about the importance of preservation and provided a forum for discussion of specific issues, such as statewide preservation planning and the preservation of serial literature.

Reflecting its more targeted mission and narrower collecting scope, the National Library of Medicine has assumed responsibility for the preservation of its holdings of biomedical literature by means of a multifaceted preservation program. This includes library binding, minor book repair, disaster prevention and recovery, monitoring storage environments, and staff and user preservation education. In 1986 NLM also began a massive program to microfilm its own collections. In order to film complete runs of serials, it has relied on cooperation from a large number of American and foreign libraries to loan volumes missing from its collection. NLM permits purchase of microfilm copies of the titles it has filmed without copyright restriction. While aware of the attraction of improved access offered by digital imaging, NLM is not planning to convert from filming to scanning brittle materials on a large scale "until costs are better defined, experienced vendors are available, standard procedures are established, and a program is in place to refresh files and migrate to successive generations of hardware and software to ensure that the information remains accessible over time."

The other prong of NLM's preservation initiative has been a campaign to attack the problem at the source by encouraging the use of acid-free paper for scientific and medical publications. By 1995, as a result of NLM's activities as well as similar efforts by other libraries and organizations plus changing economic incentives within the paper industry, 91 percent of the most recent issues of the U.S. Index Medicus titles tested were acid-free compared to 4 percent in 1985.

The NLM Preservation Program is currently exploring the issues related to preservation of nonpaper materials, especially those issued in electronic form. This involves "examining such complex topics as intellectual property, longevity of storage formats, the frequency with which data must be refreshed, obsolescence of hardware and software, and migration costs." This process is intended not only to address NLM's own problems but to provide useful information to the biomedical library community in general on the issues related to preservation of electronic publications.

The National Agricultural Library (NAL) is pursuing a different path to ensure the survival of publications in its discipline. While NLM determines its priorities on the basis of the degree of embrittlement of its own holdings, NAL has organized a cooperative effort to identify and preserve the "core literature" of the history of agriculture and rural life in the United States between 1820 and 1945. Nine land grant universities representing a cross section of states are using a methodology first developed and implemented at Cornell University in cooperation with the New York State Library to identify, rank, and preserve the most important literature on agriculture and rural life in their states held by repositories throughout each state. Both scholars and librarians are involved in this effort whose goal is ultimately to preserve the top-ranked 25 percent of titles identified.

Professional Associations

Three professional associations have been very active during the past twenty years in promoting the cause of preservation: the Preservation and Reformatting Section (PARS), a recent merger of the Preservation of Library Materials Section (PLMS) and the Reproduction of Library Materials Section (RLMS) of the American Library Association (ALA); the Association of Research Libraries (ARL); and the Society of American Archivists (SAA). All have provided training opportunities, published many key works in the field, lobbied both for federal and state funding and for legislation, and worked in many other ways to shape and sustain preservation in this country.

Indeed, a case could be made that much of the driving force behind many of the cooperative efforts undertaken to preserve U.S. library materials has been generated at meetings of PARS and its predecessors. Over the past two decades, PARS has grown from a mere handful of pioneering preservation administrators to several hundred members. Through its committee meetings, conference programs, institutes, preconferences, and publications, it has been a vital channel for the dissemination of reliable information on preservation. PARS meetings have also provided the occasion for extensive networking, brainstorming, and the generation of innovative ideas and approaches that practitioners could then apply to the problems confronting them. The willingness to share information, to mentor newcomers, and to work together to address issues of common interest that has characterized PARS has done a great deal to set the tone of collegiality and cooperation that has come to characterize the profession of preservation administration.

To a large extent, preservation administration in the United States is a field that invented itself to meet a need. Initially, few, if any, reliable publications existed to provide answers to operational questions. Often, there simply was no answer until a group of interested practitioners got together, often at PARS, to share experiences and information in order to find an answer or devise a plan for finding one. Because so many practitioners have for so long been essentially self-taught or have come into the field through an apprenticeship or internship, both mentoring and networking have been critical to professional development. Even today, much information, especially about new developments, is exchanged by word of mouth, telephone, or, increasingly, through e-mail and electronic bulletin boards, most notably CoOL (Conservation OnLine), a project of the Preservation Department of Stanford University Libraries. The Internet is therefore now providing to an ever-greater extent the links in the vast spiderweb of individual and organizational connections that constitute our national preservation program.

Although it does not provide an opportunity for periodic meetings of preservation professionals, the Association of Research Libraries has made substantial contributions to the cooperative development of preservation administration in this country. Its development and sponsorship of the Preservation Planning Program (PPP), administered by its Office of Management Studies (OMS), laid the foundation for the establishment of preservation programs at a number of major research libraries. An important consequence of the PPP was to provide job opportunities for preservation administrators, and it thus indirectly but substantially shaped that profession. The association has also published a useful series of information kits on preservation topics drawn from policies and procedures in use at member libraries. It has involved preservation administrators in further refinement of the PPP as well as in the preparation of other publications.

Another major ARL contribution was to manage a series of cooperative projects, funded mainly by NEH, to create more than 579,000 online records for monographic and serial preservation microform masters that were listed in the National Register of Microform

Masters. The Library of Congress, where the master file was located, made substantial contributions of technical assistance and staff for quality review throughout the project. Online Computer Library Center (OCLC), the contractor for most of the life of the project, also made critical and sizable in-kind contributions on behalf of research libraries. LC, Harvard University, and the New York Public Library provided significant staff support during the serials phase. The decade-long cooperative effort was completed in December 1997, and the records are now available online both nationally and internationally, where they serve to avoid duplication of effort in all subsequent refor-matting projects.

In addition, since 1988–1989, ARL has collected and published annual statistics on preservation personnel, expenditures, conservation treatment, preservation treatment, and preservation microfilming at its member libraries. These data show that since 1993, preservation expenditures have begun to level off, and 1995–1996 figures indicated a slight decline. This decline affected total preservation staff and in-house conservation activities as well as microfilming activity. Congressional cuts in the NEH budget in the mid-1990s resulted in less money being available for microfilming grants under the Brittle Books Program, many of which had gone to research libraries. But the decline in preser-vation expenditures at ARL libraries also probably reflects a shift in focus on the part of library administrators from traditional library activities, including support for comprehensive preservation programs, to managing the transition to the digital library. Indeed, despite the lack of defined cost data, standards, reliable vendors, accepted pro-grams for refreshing files and migrating data over successive genera-tions of software and hardware, not to mention standard operating procedures, hope seems to spring eternal in the administrative breast that digitization will ultimately solve the preservation problem rather than further complicate it.

The Society of American Archivists (SAA) has also been active in the preservation field. A series of NEH grants allowed it to offer inten-sive workshops in both basic preservation and photographic preserva-tion to archivists in the early 1980s. As part of the same effort, it published *Archives and Manuscript Conservation* in 1983 and *Archives and Manuscripts: Administration of Photographic Collections* in 1984, both in its Basic Manual Series. The former was revised and greatly expanded by Mary Lynn Ritzenthaler for publication by the Society in 1993 as *Preserving Archives and Manuscripts*. It remains one of the most com-prehensive and useful publications available. The spring 1990 issue of the quarterly journal, *The American Archivist*, was devoted to archival preservation and conservation. In the early 1990s, SAA developed a new series of workshops on a somewhat different model that were offered in various regions of the country, again with NEH support. Each workshop consisted of three weeklong sessions at six-month intervals to train archivists as preservation administrators by incorporating basic elements of preservation program development, such as preparation of institutional disaster plans and collections surveys, as required assignments.

As preservation has become an increasingly important part of archival administration, the SAA Preservation Section has become more and more active. It publishes a newsletter, organizes sessions at conferences, and makes an annual publication award of which the first winner was *Preserving Archives and Manuscripts*. The efforts of SAA to promote preservation awareness and institute programs have been complemented by those of regional archives associations.

Like that of PARS and ARL, SAA's attention has increasingly been shifting during the past several years to digital technology. Archivists were affected by the digital revolution even earlier than were librarians because of their need to manage the electronic records generated by the governments and institutions for which they were the repositories. This focus is clearly reflected in the SAA position paper, *Archival Roles for the New Millennium*, published in August 1997. The society's efforts to maintain a balance between archivists' old and new responsibilities are reflected in its list of fundamental archival roles and responsibilities. The first of these is to "manage cost-effective archival programs for the selection, retention, and use of both electronic and paper documentary materials." The sixth is to "preserve information and evidence in a protective environment and in a format or media that will remain usable over time."

All three associations have been very active in lobbying both the U.S. Congress and state legislatures for preservation measures, such as permanent paper legislation. They also can be counted on to provide expert testimony and a flood of constituent letters in support of the budgets of the federal agencies funding preservation projects. Similarly, they make themselves heard on the state level on behalf of bills to provide local preservation grant funds or programs to preserve local government records.

Other Organizations

Although neither a federal agency nor a membership organization like those described earlier, the Council on Library and Information

Resources (CLIR), a merger of the Commission on Preservation and Access (CPA) and the Council on Library Resources (CLR), continues CPA's role as an effective catalyst in moving forward the preservation agenda both in the United States and abroad. CLIR has particularly focused on widening the circle of those involved in cooperative efforts to deal with the deterioration of the documentary record by persuading scholars and university administrators that preservation is as much their problem as it is that of librarians and archivists. Most recently, in conjunction with the American Council of Learned Societies, it has convened five task forces to discuss the changes that technology will bring to research and scholarship and how we can assure that libraries and archives continue to serve the research needs of scholars and students in the face of technological transformation.

The council has also steadfastly maintained that preservation of documentary resources is not only an American concern but a crucial international issue deserving organized, cooperative international attention. Two of its three program officers deal with international issues. In the late 1980s and early 1990s, CLIR actively (and successfully) encouraged national and other libraries in Europe to participate in an international cooperative microfilming effort to save the information content of their countries' published materials. At the same time, it insisted that, in order to prevent duplication of effort and to encourage access, bibliographic records for master microforms be made available in a standard machine-readable format so that the data are readily available worldwide.

CLIR also issues requests for proposals to encourage technological innovation or to speed up the application of existing technology to preservation problems. In recent years, it has been particularly active in stimulating the development of projects to test both the capabilities and limitations of digital technology. While recognizing the potential of digitization to provide greater ease of access to materials preserved through filming or conservation treatment, CLIR is well aware that "digital formats have not yet established themselves as trustworthy preservation media." It therefore supports such projects as one at the Cornell University Library to assess the risks associated with pursuing a digital migration preservation strategy for a number of digital object types.

Making reliable information widely available and creating broader awareness of preservation issues have long been concerns of CLR, CPA, and now CLIR. Its series of reports on technical issues form the backbone of any collection of preservation literature. Its newsletter keeps readers up-to-date on a broad spectrum of issues and activities.

It was the organizing force behind the production of a film, *Into the Future*, which was broadcast during the winter of 1997–1998, as a sequel to *Slow Fires*, which, in the mid-1980s, had first alerted the American public to the brittle-paper disaster. *Into the Future* "explains clearly the perils to both the general public and the scholarly community of having information exist solely in digital form."

Although not so often thought of as a key player in the national preservation program, the National Information Standards Organization (NISO) has for years provided a mechanism for organizing cooperative efforts to advance the preservation cause. Its work is cooperative in the best sense of the word. Standards are developed by volunteer committees composed of librarians, conservators, preservation professionals, scientists, engineers, and others professionally concerned with the topic of the standard under development. The community itself usually identifies the need for a standard in a given area. Drafts are circulated and recirculated to a broad spectrum of interested parties. Once consensus has been reached, the standard is published as a formal U.S. standard. Over the years, a series of standards have been hammered out and issued that provide the basic scientific and technical underpinnings for much day-to-day practice. In addition, U.S. standards often serve as de facto international standards or form the basis for international standards promulgated by the International Organization for Standardization (ISO).

Another trailblazing and influential participant in the development of a national preservation program has been the Research Libraries Group (RLG), which was established initially to facilitate the cooperation of large research libraries in a number of areas, including automation and collection management. It was only natural that a preservation committee was organized in the late 1970s, comprising the preservation administrators of member libraries, to develop a cooperative preservation program. Led by a staff member responsible for preservation programming, the committee developed the first of a series of projects to film exceptionally strong or "great" collections. The first project was focused on Americana, but subsequent ones were much more diverse, with each participating institution selecting one or more subject or language areas in which it had built a notable collection. Not only did this become the model for organizing most subsequent filming projects by repositories of all types, but it was the seed that eventually blossomed into the NEH twenty-year brittle-books plan.

Because RLG included many of the major university libraries with staffed preservation programs, its preservation committee also constituted a critical mass of the most experienced preservation professionals in the country. Working through the committee, they developed procedures and standards, especially in respect to preservation microfilming, that served as de facto national guidelines. Meetings of the committee also provided a useful forum for discussing issues related to the management of institutional preservation programs. The information developed for and exchanged at such sessions was then often disseminated to the rest of the preservation community at ALA/PARS meetings, in conference presentations, and in workshops.

So effective was the Research Libraries Group's preservation effort and so useful was it to a preservation administrator to participate in the RLG preservation program that a number of efforts were made to try to find a way to serve libraries that belonged to OCLC rather than to RLG. For example, in 1991, RONDAC, the organization representing all the OCLC regional networks and OCLC itself, accepted a consultant's report that suggested a number of possible organizational structures that might be set up to deliver preservation information and services to all OCLC member libraries. In particular, it was felt that it was important to provide a mechanism to funnel information and services to areas of the country where there are no regional field service programs or no university library preservation program or state library able to provide information and leadership. Unfortunately, the followup to the report failed to secure funding, and the initiative was dropped. To some extent the vacuum has been filled by existing regional preservation field services, by state-based self-help efforts, and by the great expansion in information available electronically from such sources as CoOL.

Regional Preservation Programs

The regional preservation field service program that has become such an important segment of the national preservation scene was to all intents and purposes invented by the Northeast Document Conservation Center (NEDCC) in 1980. NEDCC was itself established in 1973 in Massachusetts to provide cooperative conservation services to libraries, archives, historical societies, museums, and other repositories of documentary materials in the six New England states. It was initially supported by annual contributions from the New England Library Board, representing the library agencies of the six states. It has since expanded its membership and services to include New York, New

Jersey, Maryland, and Delaware. NEDCC has from the beginning also obtained grants from private foundations and, beginning in 1980, from NEH for the field service program. In practice, because it is the nation's largest and most comprehensive conservation center serving libraries and similar institutions, and because there are huge areas of the country without access to such services locally, NEDCC is in many ways a national institution. Many of its workshops, too, such as the School for Scanning, are now offered throughout the country.

NEDCC differs markedly from the regional preservation programs offered by SOLINET and AMIGOS, which are based on regional bibliographic networks, because its original focus was and to an extent remains on conservation treatment. Its laboratories continue to provide professional treatment for paper, books, maps, architectural and other oversized drawings, parchment artifacts, photographs, and art on paper for institutions both within and outside of its region. It also offers a microfilming service that specializes in "difficult" materials, such as manuscripts, scrapbooks, brittle newspapers, and fragile books that cannot be processed on an assembly-line basis. Another service is duplication of historical photographs, especially nitrate negatives. From its inception, the center has also provided disaster assistance for its region and, when severe emergencies occur, will send experienced staff anywhere in the country. Over the years, it has also provided a full range of expert advice internationally—for example, after the Leningrad Academy of Sciences Library fire or, more recently, on basic preservation measures for Cuban repositories.

In 1980 an NEH grant enabled the center to add a field services program that has been in operation ever since. The program emphasizes the prevention of deterioration by providing a telephone reference service, workshops, and on-site consultation to survey both the physical environment in which materials are housed and the collections themselves and how they are managed. Recommendations are submitted to the client to help develop a long-range preservation plan. NEDCC conservators are also available to make site visits to advise on the treatment needs of individual objects or special collections. The field services program has had a very high rate of success over the years in assisting institutions to address their preservation needs systematically with the benefit of reliable professional preservation advice. It has been particularly helpful to small institutions that will never have staff who are professional preservation administrators but who must nonetheless care for their collections responsibly. Institution-specific assistance has been combined with a broad range of workshops to provide such staff with basic preservation expertise. This in turn has greatly accelerated the "trickle down" of practical preservation information from the national and research libraries, where sophisticated programs are in place, to ordinary public libraries or small historical societies that surprisingly often hold hidden treasures.

In 1992 NEDCC collected the Technical Leaflets it had been distributing for years, updated and revised them, and added new ones for publication in *Preservation of Library and Archival Materials: A Manual*, which was edited by the center's then director of book conservation, Sherelyn Ogden. A further revised and expanded edition was published in 1994 with contributions and expert advice from a wide range of conservation and preservation professionals in this country and abroad. The manual continues to be the source many practitioners reach for first when confronted with a new preservation issue or problem, and has been particularly effective in providing reliable information to the grass roots of the preservation movement.

A similar regional program resides at the Conservation Center for Art and Historic Artifacts (CCAHA), established in 1977 in Philadelphia. Like NEDCC, it offers an NEH-funded field service program based on a conservation laboratory that treats a full range of paper-based materials and photographs. It too provides workshops, on-site consultations and reports, and emergency assistance in case of disasters. CCAHA is a membership organization open to all nonprofit, tax-exempt institutions, including museums, archives, libraries, historical societies, academic institutions, state agencies, cooperative conservation programs, and private foundations. Its members are concentrated in the mid-Atlantic states. In the early 1990s, with support from the William Penn Foundation, CCAHA undertook a three-year project to improve the preservation of collections in the Philadelphia area by upgrading collection care and assisting in the development of a comprehensive preservation plan at sixty institutions. The center simultaneously provided classroom and hands-on experience in collection care to fourteen history museum professionals, again with a grant from the Penn Foundation.

The newest field service program began only a year ago at the Upper Midwest Conservation Association. Like NEDCC and CCAHA, this is an organization whose core activity is conservation treatment. Until recently, the association, based in Minneapolis and serving Iowa, Minnesota, North and South Dakota, and Wisconsin, was oriented primarily toward museums, for which it provided centralized conservation services. Thanks to an NEH grant, it has hired Sherelyn Ogden, formerly of NEDCC, to expand its range to libraries, archives, and historical societies and to shape and manage its field services. The association plans initially to offer two basic preservation workshops in each state of its region and two advanced workshops funded by the Institute of Museum and Library Services centrally in each biennium. Like its fellows, it will also provide general needs assessment surveys and collection-specific surveys, technical assistance, and disaster preparedness and response as well as mentoring.

Another model for preservation field services was created by the Southeastern Libraries Network (SOLINET) in the mid-1980s when it initiated its program, again with NEH funding. It includes all the services provided by NEDCC and CCAHA except those requiring the expertise of a professional conservator. It has, however, put much less emphasis on individual institutional surveys and has instead organized and managed a series of massive cooperative projects to microfilm endangered materials in Southern Americana and Latin Americana from its ten member states.

In 1990 the Southwestern Bibliographic Network (AMIGOS) received NEH support to replicate the SOLINET program to serve Texas, Arizona, New Mexico, Arkansas, and Oklahoma. Its focus has been primarily information dissemination, disaster preparedness and recovery, and preservation training. Because of the paucity of preservation services west of the Mississippi (except for California), the AMIGOS program has on occasion provided moral support, advice, and training to other states in that region that were beginning or developing preservation initiatives. AMIGOS has also been a leader in the effort to coordinate the work of the various field service programs more closely in order to reduce duplication of effort in the production of informational material and specialized workshops. For example, it cosponsored a workshop on the preservation of architectural records that was given by CCAHA in 1998 in Austin, Texas, then repeated in New Orleans, where it was cosponsored by SOLINET.

The several field service programs have recently organized the Regional Alliance for Preservation (RAP) to provide a formal structure for cooperation. Periodic meetings and a shared newsletter have promoted greater coordination, especially of training resources and publications. The effort got off the ground with an initial one year's support from CLIR, but has subsequently moved to an even more cooperative mode with AMIGOS publishing the newsletter and SOLINET hosting its World Wide Web site. The group has expanded slightly beyond the organizations already mentioned by including the Museum Management Office of the National Park Service and its far-flung and innovative preservation program.

State Preservation Programs

During the 1980s and early 1990s, statewide preservation programs began to function in a number of states. Several different models were developed, reflecting the varying political and economic circumstances of each state: a grant program for library preservation projects funded by state appropriations and administered by the state library (New York, New Jersey); a grant program for the preservation of local government records funded by a surtax on registration of real estate transactions and administered by the state archives (New York, Virginia); a program administered by the state library using LSCA funds to pay the salary of a coordinator to provide preservation training and services to the state (Massachusetts, Connecticut, Florida); a coalition of volunteers, including preservation professionals from research libraries and historical societies, who run workshops and serve as consultants while working toward getting state funding or other support (South Carolina, Nebraska, Oklahoma, Colorado, Arizona, Ohio, Rhode Island); a consortium of institutional members, both archives and libraries, which contribute funds for the salary of a full-time director, and one of which provides space and clerical support for a program of education and outreach (North Carolina). A number of these as well as other states have carried out a statewide preservation planning project and produced a formal state plan, usually with funding from NEH. Most of these initiatives have been subject to political and economic factors irrelevant to preservation, which makes their long-term survival unpredictable. The one notable exception is the state of New York whose two programs appear to have built a broad and enduring spectrum of support.

Despite the seemingly constant ebb and flow of state programs, the variety of funding sources they seek to tap, the range of organizational models they adopt, and the different programmatic missions that they represent, a few generalizations can be made. The programs that have been most successful in achieving a measure of stability have displayed many of the following strengths: high-quality administrative leadership, be it a paid staff person or a committed volunteer; dependable funding, even if small in amount, so that resources are available to hold meetings, organize workshops, and, in some cases, provide grants to repositories in the state; locally available, professional-quality expertise in preservation; the genuine support of key library and archival leaders in the state, such as the state archivist, the state librarian, and the directors of major research libraries, historical societies, and museums; a small nucleus of committed workers; and a sustaining infrastructure that provides space, telephone and other communications support, equipment, and perhaps clerical assistance.

After lack of funding, the greatest danger confronting state programs, especially in parts of the country without a regional field services program to consult, is lack of knowledge and experience. Both conservation and preservation are developing very rapidly as professional fields. A great deal of unmonitored information is available on the Internet. Both theory and practice can change suddenly and dramatically, as research results are published or experience demonstrates the benefits or dangers of certain practices. It takes considerable effort and professional sophistication to keep up with and interpret new information correctly. Fortunately, as the University of Texas library school preservation administration training program (originally at Columbia University) continues to graduate students, more and more staff are available with a solid foundation in preservation basics.

Conclusion

It is difficult to make generalizations about such a diverse patchwork of institutions, agencies, organizations, and associations as constitute the U.S. national preservation program. Each has its own agenda, which is frequently reshaped by both external and local political and economic factors, new technological developments, and individual capabilities and goals. Just as there was no inspired vision of what an American national preservation program should be in the mid-1970s, so in the intervening years its development has followed an ever-shifting course that has on occasion reversed itself or wandered down blind alleys. Without central direction or systematic coordination, and with no professional certification or standards for evaluation of performance, both individual and institutional players have been free to define their own areas of expertise and often their programmatic boundaries.

The principal control on such autonomy has been financial. The guidelines of federal funding agencies, the program descriptions of private foundations, and the provisions of state appropriations bills are the main sources from which are derived formal definitions of the extent and character of the preservation projects seeking support. Competition for the finite amount of funding available also standardizes and even limits the range of preservation activity because applicants tend to look for successful model projects and replicate them. The recent decrease in the amount of federal funding available because of congressional budget cuts in addition to the ever-present effects of inflation has further dampened new initiatives, with the exception of a few experimental digital projects. The NEH Division of Preservation and Access, for example, has been concentrating its reduced resources on maintaining the preservation infrastructure and core programs developed over the preceding two decades. Applicants, too, are self-limiting because preparing an application to a federal agency requires a great deal of work and would probably not be undertaken for a project that ploughs totally new ground for which there are no precedents for funding. Reduced funding has also meant that there is more internal competition at large institutions among potential applicants who know that it is unlikely that more than one or two proposals from the same institution will be successful. Again, this tends to damp down creativity and innovation and encourage the tried and true.

These constraints have reinforced some long-standing characteristics of preservation practice in this country, such as a steady adherence to the pragmatic rather than the visionary. The search for ad hoc solutions has led to an openness of mind, a willingness to experiment, and a lot of creative plagiarism as one practitioner rapidly adopts elements of practice that have worked for someone else. This "can do" attitude has encouraged individuals both to collaborate with others whenever that seems useful and to work independently without following a grand design or needing direction from some higher or central authority. At the same time, it has been accompanied by a firm belief in the importance of standards and the need to create them, which has gradually led to an accretion of research reports, guidelines, manuals, and formal standards that have come to define acceptable practice. It is perhaps significant that all the rather tentative efforts that have been made to date to impose greater coordination on preservation activity in this country in order to get everyone moving more or less in the same direction have not gone very far. The national preservation movement remains too multifaceted, too amorphous, too diverse to be united by more than the wholehearted commitment to cooperation that has powered its success to date.

5

Planning for Preservation in Libraries

JUTTA REED-SCOTT

The large-scale deterioration of library collections that we are witnessing is historically unprecedented. Careful analytical studies confirm that one-fourth of all volumes held by research libraries are brittle and at risk of disintegration, and nearly 80 million books in American research libraries are threatened with destruction. Archives and manuscript collections as well as libraries face major challenges in preserving nonbook media. Condition surveys repeatedly reveal that deterioration of library collections exists not only in the older, large research libraries, but in all libraries with historical collections. The long-term survival of collections is directly related to the question: Can libraries halt the slow fires in the stacks? The answer to that question depends, in no small part, on how well libraries craft a coherent, comprehensive, and aggressive preservation strategy.

The Preservation Need

The preservation problem is long term and requires long-term responses. It is a problem that is manifested in many ways. For the library administrator, it is the pressure and competition for resources and the intensified struggle to distribute finite resources across seemingly infinite tasks. For the library user, it is the unavailability of a book that is so brittle its pages can no longer be turned. For the collection development librarian, it is the instability and deterioration over time of portions of the collections that represent not only a major intellectual but also a capital investment.

It is generally agreed that we have more deteriorating and endangered materials in our collections than we can preserve. Choices must be made. Libraries currently face the intellectual problems of determining what should be preserved and what should be allowed to deteriorate. Preservation problems are pushing collection managers into a more activist role, in which they must make crucial preservation decisions—or decide by not deciding what to preserve.

Growing awareness in the past decade of the magnitude of the preservation problem has resulted in a steady increase of preservation programs within research, academic, and public libraries. Preservation planning was and continues to be an important managerial tool in shaping new programs and improving existing preservation policies and practices.

Developing a Preservation Plan

Planning a library's preservation program helps to ensure the systematic maintenance of and access to the library's information resources. Planning provides a rational process to analyze needs systematically to minimize the problems and maximize the opportunities. It is the means to identify local needs and priorities. Equally important, preservation "planning efforts [serve] an important function in educating a broad spectrum of staff about preservation and [create] an environment in which actual program development subsequently [can] take place."[1] Preservation planning is based on the fundamental assumption that a library can improve the care of its collections when the staff involved recognize the seriousness of the situation, expand their knowledge and skills, and take into their daily work a new preservation awareness as well as specific preservation knowledge and skills. A systematic planning process gives the basic framework for understanding preservation needs. It is only then that effective preservation strategies and actions can be fashioned.

Nature of Preservation Planning

The development of a preservation plan will enable the library to take needed steps to retard the damage and deterioration of library materials to ensure their continued serviceability. The elements of effective preservation programs depend on careful planning and thorough understanding of the nature and present condition of the collections, the user groups, and the institutional context. Central planning components are:

Identifying and assessing preservation needs

Relating preservation needs to the library's mission and setting appropriate priorities

Identifying and examining existing preservation activities

Defining needed preservation functions and determining the overall organization of preservation activities

Determining and allocating resources

Creating a formal plan to improve the library's preservation program

Developing an implementation strategy

The benefits of a formal planning study include:

Raising awareness of the library's preservation problems

Focusing on identifying major preservation needs and on determining priorities for the library preservation program

Assisting in allocating financial resources, developing implementation strategies, and taking actions to address specific preservation priorities

Strengthening institutionalization of the preservation process and increasing knowledge among library staff of issues in preservation

The planning cycle consists of three steps: defining the library's preservation issues and needs, identifying potential solutions, and developing and implementing a plan of action.

Defining the Preservation Needs

The first step in the planning cycle is an investigation of the library's preservation issues. At the center is the recognition of the library's preservation needs. The dimensions and scope of the problem will vary but the central ingredient is the collections and the types of materials collected by the library: books, newspapers, maps, photographs, manuscripts, slides, and a myriad of other formats, increasingly including electronic resources. Within these disparate types of materials will be some that are rare and valuable and must be preserved in the original format; others will have a more limited life cycle, but must be maintained in usable condition for many years. The vast majority of the materials constitute the library's information resources, and their deterioration must be retarded.

The investigation focuses on key questions: What is the current condition of these materials and what materials predominate? What are the environmental conditions under which the collections are housed and how do these conditions compare to standards for housing collections? What preservation activities, such as binding, basic repair, or collections maintenance, are performed and by whom? Where does preservation fit into the organizational structure? What are the current expenditures for preservation activities? What strategies can the library pursue for controlling the preservation problem? The answers to these questions and analysis of data will define possible priorities.

Shaping the Preservation Program

The second step is to identify potential solutions and to evaluate the viability and feasibility of specific solutions suited to the institution's collections and service goals. The general approach to preservation differs in each library, but no matter what the particular organizational structure and what the level of the preservation program is, preservation will require consideration of several options. A useful guide is *Preservation Program Models*, published by the Association of Research Libraries (ARL) in 1991. The report describes the ten components of a comprehensive preservation program and provides benchmarks for selected core activities.

The preservation of collections takes place on several different levels. The first level treats collections as a whole and focuses on housing and maintaining collections in controlled environments. The single most important preservation action is to store collections at properly controlled temperature, humidity, and air quality. Optimal environmental conditions will buy time and will increase the life span of all materials in the collections.

The second level focuses on ways to identify endangered or deteriorated materials. The dominant strategy is demand or use driven. Frequently the deteriorating condition of a specific title is evident when the book is circulated and forces a decision; that is, the book's condition requires action on an ad hoc basis. In contrast to the demand-based strategy, the collection-centered approach links collection strengths to preservation priorities. Such a strategy for identifying deteriorating materials will focus on specific subjects and their value to both local academic programs or local user needs and the national scholarly world.

The third level of collection preservation is the actual preservation option chosen for individual titles: the action taken to preserve the item through reformatting, physical repair, or other appropriate action.

The most viable solution will effectively integrate an array of preservation strategies into a systematic preservation program that matches the institution's resources and needs. In a small special library, priorities may be identifying and repairing those materials that are in immediate danger. In a large research library, the activities will be designed to establish a well-organized operating program. The components of an effective preservation program are diverse. Jan Merrill-Oldham grouped preservation components into two general categories: the first involves such operational activities as bindery preparation, preservation replacement, and stack maintenance, and the second includes the administrative components, such as environmental control, disaster planning and response, preservation-related staff and user education and advocacy, and integration of preservation activities with other library activities.[2]

Plan of Action and Implementation

The final step is the development of a preservation plan of action together with a mechanism to see that recommendations are carried out. Central to developing a preservation plan is establishing the goals for the library's preservation program within the institutional context. These program objectives provide the framework for setting priorities for improvements in the care and handling of library materials. The plan will provide a statement of current and prospective preservation activities that will seek to balance resources and needs. The plan needs to outline central control strategies. Facility improvement is often the single most important step in order to provide an environment with controlled and stable temperature and humidity levels. Although upgrading environmental conditions requires significant capital expenditures, a library can take many steps to improve its preservation program with a more modest investment. The use of acid-free materials and staff training in appropriate repair techniques are two such steps. A strong administrative component is essential to expand the library's preservation efforts into a formal preservation program. A preservation plan is most likely to succeed when there are clearly defined priorities with doable targets and assigned responsibilities for accomplishing the tasks. Implementation of the plan will then build on tangible results.

Models for Preservation Planning

Interest in planning has gained momentum in recent years, and several approaches are available for planning for preservation program development.

Staff-directed Preservation Planning Model

For research libraries, an effective tool is the Preservation Planning Program (PPP), which exemplifies the library-based planning model. Developed by the Association of Research Libraries' Office of Leadership and Management Services with support from the National Endowment for the Humanities, the PPP helps libraries review systematically the variety of challenges related to preservation. A typical library takes from six to nine months to complete the program, which involves the participation of twenty-five to thirty staff members. The result is a comprehensive, three- to five-year action plan to develop, improve, and expand the library's preservation program.

Over almost two decades, twenty-nine ARL libraries have completed the program and a significant additional number of member libraries have used its resources. Designed to assist academic libraries in developing local preservation programs, the PPP provides self-help tools that enable staff to develop long-term plans for preserving library materials.

The self-study begins with the naming of a study team of four to seven staff members, who are charged with conducting an investigation of the library's preservation situation. Task forces are then appointed by the study team to carry out investigations of specific preservation needs at the library. Usually, about five task forces will be involved.

A preservation administrator serves as consultant and assists the study team and task forces. The consultant, who is available throughout the study period, makes periodic visits to the library and provides an outsider's perspective on the findings and plans.

Seven major areas usually are examined: the physical environment in which materials are housed; the physical condition of the collections; the library's preparedness for disasters that might damage the collection; the administrative, organizational, and operational components of the library's preservation activities; the resources that are currently allocated and additional funding needed for an expanded program; staff and user education; and interinstitutional cooperation. However, it is possible to conduct more limited studies, selecting only a few areas of interest.

In the final phase, the study team develops a phased plan for responding to preservation needs in a step-by-step process whereby the library can create a comprehensive preservation program over a three- to five-year period. The plan, with all its supporting documents, is then presented to the library administration as the final report of the self-study.

The Preservation Planning Program offers a comprehensive process to assist self-study and encompasses extensive training and assistance. Many libraries, however, have adapted the program's resources and methodology and employed some of its techniques in analyzing local preservation needs. These planning efforts may differ in the scope of data gathering and analyses, but they share the fundamental commitment to staff participation in charting a library's preservation program.

Computer-assisted Self-study Model

To accelerate the process of assessing preservation needs, several organizations have developed special computer programs. One early effort was the Preservation Program (GRASP) developed by the National Association of Government Archives and Records Administrators. The self-study manual and software support preservation planning by government archives and historical records repositories.

A second example is the Calipr automated preservation needs assessment program. The Calipr software and manual were developed by the Conservation Department of the University of California–

Berkeley. Many professionals in the field of library preservation reviewed and tested the preservation needs assessment instrument, which was automated in 1991 and upgraded in 1997. Calipr has been designed to allow institutions without preservation expertise on their staffs to determine the preservation needs of their collections. Calipr generates a series of management reports that can be used to identify the subset of the collection needing the highest-priority attention.

Although special computer programs can assist in a library's preservation needs assessment efforts, they alone cannot form the basis for long-term preservation planning.

Consultant-driven Planning Model

A third category is the special survey conducted by an outside consultant. A number of organizations provide field services, including the well-known preservation survey programs of the Northeast Document Conservation Center (Andover, Massachusetts), the Conservation Center for Art and Historic Artifacts (Philadelphia), AMIGOS (Dallas), and SOLINET (Atlanta). Using a preservation specialist to assess the institution's preservation needs, identify broad areas of problems, and recommend strategies for addressing them is a cost-effective alternative for organizations that lack staff with preservation expertise. The steps the consultant follows are similar to those discussed in the staff-conducted preservation planning model. One key difference is that there is less opportunity for involving and educating the institution's staff. However, many field surveys increasingly make efforts to build staff commitment to the preservation plan. The function of the survey as conducted by an outside consultant is to enable the institution to focus on improving the preservation of its collection and to build on outside expertise.

Cooperative Preservation Planning Model

Preservation activities at the statewide and regional levels have multiplied rapidly. Cooperative preservation planning can enhance individual library efforts by pooling information and resources, serve as a catalyst for strengthening local efforts, and provide the organizational structures and services for achieving collective action. Coordinated preservation planning can also enable libraries to share scarce technical expertise and to acquire expensive equipment.

A number of states and regional groups have conducted systematic preservation planning projects. An early landmark study is the exhaustive study of historical records conditions in New York State. *Our Memory at Risk* resulted from this three-year effort to analyze preservation needs of libraries and archives in the state.[3] In the early 1990s, the National Endowment for the Humanities' Division of Preservation and Access awarded grants to eleven states for statewide preservation planning projects. These projects resulted in the creation of statewide preservation plans and served as catalysts for projects in other states.

Frequently a major undertaking of these projects is the development of a preservation needs assessment project to determine preservation needs in the state's public, academic, and special libraries, historical societies, and archives. These efforts not only provide a comprehensive picture of preservation needs in an array of libraries, but also help to raise preservation consciousness. For example, the California State Library conducted a statewide preservation needs assessment survey, and the results were used in the preparation of the California Preservation Plan.

Condition Surveys

Regardless of the specific preservation planning model that an institution employs, a central component of preservation planning is development of reliable data about the condition of the collections. Condition surveys investigate the physical condition of a subset of the collections and collect information about the extent of deterioration based on a random sample of volumes. The underlying assumption was well articulated in the pioneering Stanford survey: "If a reliable random sample can be taken in a research collection, and books selected can be graded in an objective and accurate manner, the percentage of deterioration can be determined."[4] Condition surveys are important tools for answering questions about the collections: What portion of the collection is in good condition and what portion has suffered minor damage that can be repaired? What portion of the collection is badly deteriorated and must be replaced? What is the extent of the brittle-book problem? What is the extent of mutilated portions of library materials? Sample-based condition surveys are also often important tools for planning preservation programs for nonbook media collections.

A growing number of surveys have been conducted by libraries during the past several years. Options include conducting a large-scale condition survey; a limited condition survey; or an informal, subjective evaluation. The most comprehensive condition survey was undertaken at Yale University Library with funding from the National Endowment for the Humanities. This large-scale study assessed the physical condition and extent of deterioration of books in a sample of 36,500 volumes that included all types of materials. The survey was designed to provide information on the preservation needs of distinct collections that varied in age, size, use, and housing condition. The results brought the extent of preservation needs into sharp focus. In the Yale University collection, numbering at that time more than 7.7 million volumes, 12.8 percent needed immediate repair and 37.1 percent were printed on brittle paper.[5]

In contrast is the small-scale condition survey based on the methodology developed by Stanford University in 1979, which uses a random sample of five hundred volumes and a limited set of questions. This methodology has been adopted by numerous libraries.

Condition surveys reveal that preservation problems exist not only in the large research libraries, but in all libraries. In some libraries, the brittle-books problem will be daunting while in others the number of embrittled books may be small but the number of deteriorated bindings may be overwhelming. Table 1 is based on sources listed in the Suggested Readings and summarizes several studies. It is not intended

Table 1
Selected Collection Condition Surveys

DATE OF STUDY	LIBRARY	SAMPLE SIZE	FINDINGS
1979	Stanford University Library	500	27% of books were brittle
1982	Yale University Library	36,500	37.1% of books were brittle
1984	Library of Congress	1,200	90% of volumes contained acidic paper

(continued)

Table 1 *(continued)*

DATE OF STUDY	LIBRARY	SAMPLE SIZE	FINDINGS
1985	Syracuse University Library	2,548	12% of books were brittle; 86% were acidic
1985	National Library of Medicine	384	8.8% of books were brittle
1986	Northwestern University Library	664	30% of books were brittle
1987	University of Illinois	384	37% of titles were brittle
1989	Washington Research Library Consortium	5,021 books (11 participating libraries)	44.9% of volumes need repairs
1990	Brigham Young University Library	384	75.5% of books were acidic; 3.8% were brittle

to give the results of all library surveys but to highlight the range of approaches and the results.

Although the sample size and the nature of the collections in these examples varied substantially, successful condition surveys all share several common requirements: careful attention to designing the sample; detailed mapping of the collections; development and pilot testing of the survey form; training of surveyors to ensure consistent grading; and computer analysis of the results.

Sampling

Because it is usually impossible to survey all titles in a collection, sampling a representative portion of the collections is the most practical approach. Random sampling is the method used to select the titles in the condition survey. The size of the sample of volumes or other items to be included is an important decision in designing the sample. The larger the sample the greater will be the confidence level that the results are accurate. For example, typically a sample of four hundred volumes will have a 95 percent confidence level; that is, the final results will be accurate within a range of ±5 percent and could therefore vary by as much as 10 percent. Statistical formulas can be consulted to determine the degree of error that would apply to a given size sample in relationship to the size of the collections. It is important to note that in small samples the results will only describe the physical condition of the collection as a whole and will not provide information on specific parts of the collection. In all condition surveys a balance needs to be achieved between the accuracy of the results, the degree of information needed on subsets of the collection, and availability of staff to carry out the data collection.

Mapping

In order for the survey to be completely random, so that each volume in the collection has an equal chance of being included, special attention must be given to the sampling frame and how volumes are selected. Although some libraries have used the shelflist as the basis for selecting the random sample, a more accurate basis is a mapping of all the shelf ranges and selecting volumes on a random basis from the numbered stack ranges. Maps of the stacks housing collections must be prepared. These maps will show the ranges of shelving, the number of sections, and the number of shelves.

Survey Forms

Development of the survey form is often the most time-consuming step. Survey forms used in past condition surveys range from the concise questionnaire used in the Stanford study to the detailed set of questions investigated in the Yale study. The construction of the questionnaire must achieve the appropriate local balance. The questions should reflect the variables to be studied and be clearly stated to avoid different interpretations. It is essential to pretest the questionnaire to make sure that it can be completed accurately and consistently. The questionnaire itself may be precoded to make data analysis easier.

Data Collection

Careful attention must be given to training the staff in conducting the survey to guard against missing, inconsistent, or inaccurate data.

Careful monitoring of the staff and screening of the completed questionnaires are equally essential.

Data Analysis

The results from the survey must be summarized, compared, and synthesized. The rich literature on condition surveys provides examples of tabulations. Analysis of the data will document the collection characteristics and the condition of the collection, and establish preservation needs. Understanding the needs of the collections is the key step in addressing the major problems identified. The data provide persuasive documentation for crafting the preservation plan.

Conclusion

Libraries have made substantial investments in collections and must maintain access to these resources. Preservation planning is the means to accomplish this task. There are many preservation planning models available that can be adapted to local requirements. Planning for preservation will assist libraries in their efforts to shape local programs that will preserve the institution's collections for current and future use.

As Pamela Darling noted, "Planning is not the solution to the preservation problem, but it is an essential tool for drafting responses to the preservation challenge."[6] The series of preservation planning efforts already completed, chiefly from major research libraries, have produced a rich literature of planning studies. Additional libraries throughout the United States, building on the foundation of this experience and information, are initiating preservation planning efforts.[7]

These efforts have played a critical role in improving existing practices and in shaping effective library preservation programs. Typically the results of a systematic assessment include:

- Improved collection maintenance
- Upgraded environmental control
- Increased disaster preparedness and prevention
- Enhanced staff and user education
- Improved book repair and library binding operations
- Enhanced opportunities for planning cooperative projects
- Leverage for additional resources

Notes

1. Pamela W. Darling and Sherelyn Ogden, "From Problems Perceived to Programs in Practice: The Preservation of Library Resources in the U.S.A., 1956–1980," *Library Resources & Technical Services* 25 (1981): 9–29.

2. Jan Merrill-Oldham, "The Preservation Program Defined," in *Meeting the Preservation Challenge*, edited by Jan Merrill-Oldham (Washington, D.C.: Association of Research Libraries, 1988), 19–25.

3. *Our Memory at Risk: Preserving New York's Unique Research Resources. A Report and Recommendations to the Citizens of New York by the New York Document Conservation Advisory Council* (Albany: New York State Education Department, 1988).

4. Sally Buchanan and Sandra Coleman, "Deterioration Survey of the Stanford University Libraries Green Library Stack Collection," in *Preservation Planning Program Resource Handbook*, compiled by Pamela W. Darling and Wesley L. Boomgaarden (Washington, D.C.: Association of Research Libraries, Office of Management Studies, 1987), 189–221.

5. Gay R. Walker, Jane Greenfield, John Fox, and Jeffrey S. Simonoff, "The Yale Survey: A Large-Scale Study of Book Deterioration in the Yale University Library," *College & Research Libraries* 46 (1985): 111–132.

6. Pamela W. Darling, "Will Anything Be Left? New Responses to the Preservation Challenge," *Wilson Library Bulletin* 56 (November 1981): 177–181.

7. Wesley Boomgaarden, "Preservation Planning for the Small Special Library," *Special Libraries* 76 (1985): 204–211.

Suggested Readings

Bond, Randall, et al. "Preservation Study at the Syracuse University Library." *College & Research Libraries* 48 (1987): 132–147.

CALIPR: Preservation Planning Software. Sacramento: California State Library, 1997. <http://sunsite.berkeley.edu/CALIPR/>

Chizastowski, Tina, et al. "Library Collection Deterioration: A Study at the University of Illinois at Urbana-Champaign." *College & Research Libraries* 50 (1989): 577–589.

Commission on Preservation and Access. *Report on the Preservation Planning Project: University of Pennsylvania Libraries*. Washington, D.C.: Commission on Preservation and Access, 1991.

Darling, Pamela W. *Preservation Planning Program Resource Notebook*. Revised edition by Wesley L. Boomgaarden. Washington, D.C.: Association of Research Libraries, Office of Management Studies, 1987.

Darling, Pamela W., and Duane E. Webster. *Preservation Planning Program: An Assisted Self-Study Manual for Libraries.* Expanded 1987 ed. Washington, D.C.: Association of Research Libraries, Office of Management Studies, 1987.

Drott, M. Carl. "Random Sampling: A Tool for Library Research." *College & Research Libraries* 28 (1987): 119–125.

Eveland, Ruth A. "How a Medium-Size Public Library Tackled the Preservation of Its Collection." *Bookmark* 45 (spring 1987): 156–160.

Hazen, Dan C. "Preservation in Poverty and Plenty: Policy Issues for the 1990s." *Journal of Academic Librarianship* 15 (1990): 334–351.

Lowell, Howard P. *Planning for Library Conservation: A Needs Assessment Manual.* Denver: Colorado Conservation Study, 1981.

National Association of Government Archives and Records Administrators. *NAGARA Preservation Program Guide and Resources for Archives Strategic Planning.* Albany, N.Y.: NAGARA, 1990.

Nickerson, Matthew. "pH: Only a Piece of the Preservation Puzzle: A Comparison of the Preservation Studies at Brigham Young, Yale, and Syracuse Universities." *Library Resources & Technical Services* 36 (1992): 105–112.

Schmude, Karl G. "The Politics and Management of Preservation Planning." *IFLA Journal* 16 (1990): 332–335.

"Survey of Book Condition at the Library of Congress." *National Preservation News: A Newsletter of the National Preservation Program Office* 1 (July 1985): 8–9.

Walker, Gay R. "Preservation Planning and Perspective." In *Meeting the Preservation Challenge,* edited by Jan Merrill-Oldham, 43–47. Washington, D.C.: Association of Research Libraries, 1988.

6

Issues in Digital Archiving

■ ■ ■

PETER S. GRAHAM

This chapter deals with the preservation of digital information as distinct from preservation of print materials through digitization. Though terminology is not yet fixed, the former (our subject) is often referred to as digital archiving, or preservation of digital information, to distinguish it from the latter, often known as digital preservation.

Our concern is with the preservation of digital information that takes place within a digital library, for which the Digital Library Federation (DLF) has provided the following definition:

> Digital libraries are organizations that provide the resources, including the specialized staff, to select, structure, offer intellectual access to, interpret, distribute, preserve the integrity of, and ensure the persistence over time of collections of digital works so that they are readily and economically available for use by a defined community or set of communities.[1]

Such a verbose, clumsy definition is necessary because of the constantly changing technological and social environment surrounding traditional library activities. The DLF quite rightly points out that other organizations may invoke one particular concept from this definition to call their project a digital library (for example, the National Science Foundation focus on databases in its Digital Libraries project);

yet without the related concepts, the library service provided will be narrow and insufficient.

The mission of libraries has long been to acquire information, organize it, make it available, and preserve it. This has been their significant, distinctive, and successful role with print and other artifactual materials for the past several hundred years. The mission has not changed in the digital environment, but the inflated DLF definition is currently necessary to make clear to others what we believe a digital library should be about.

Most libraries are now trying to provide an ever-increasing volume of scholarly electronic information to their clienteles. Research libraries have taken on the provision, organization, and preservation of information with the same long-term commitment made for print materials. It is an expensive, uncharted, and difficult task.

Until the long-term commitments are undertaken, many current digital proposals will have only temporary effects. Cataloging of networked resources will necessarily remain tentative until the objects being cataloged have a permanent network presence, whether at fixed or virtual locations. Otherwise the cataloging that points to them will itself have an ephemeral quality. (Cataloging for some transitory electronic materials will always be necessary.) Similarly, the expensive products of recent valuable digitizing demonstration projects, from microfilm to digital form and vice versa, will be at risk after only a few years if tools and commitments are not in place for the preservation of what has been achieved.

Most importantly, the ability of the scholarly community to give serious weight to electronic information depends upon its trust in such information being dependably available, with authenticity and integrity maintained. Changes in scholarly publishing that might alleviate the serials crisis, for example, are (in North America) bound up with the prestige of electronic journals in the academic tenure process. The ability of the academic to count on long-term, secure existence of electronic scholarly work will be an important determinant of the success of academic electronic publishing. Libraries and universities have a stake in helping electronic publishing to succeed and, therefore, have an interest in establishing secure, persistent, and authoritative digital research libraries.

Users will continue to want information that is reliably locatable, so that when they go there (whether personally or on the Net) they can expect to find what they're looking for. Users will expect information to be available that was placed in the library's care a long time ago, and they will expect that the integrity of the information they get from the library will be assured.

The requirements of digital technologies will change the way most librarians work throughout research libraries. As it happens, professional librarians are uniquely qualified to take up the technological challenge. But if we do not, we will contribute to the stagnation of our own profession as well as fail in our responsibility to civilization.

Preservation in libraries has until now been largely a matter of preserving the artifact which provides the work inherent in it, thereby preserving the work itself. Electronic documents, by contrast, not only require the preservation of the objects, but also require the preservation of the information contained in those objects that is now so easily separable from them.

Barry Neavill deserves credit for writing presciently fifteen years ago that no one had yet "addressed the issue of the long-term survival of information. . . . The survival of information in an electronic environment becomes an intellectual and technological problem in its own right."[2] If we want to assure permanence of the intellectual record that is published electronically, he said, then it will be necessary consciously to design and build the required mechanisms within electronic systems. We are still in need of those mechanisms.

This chapter sets out some of the major issues in providing these user needs. In fact, the primary requirement for a digital research library is that from the beginning it be committed to organizing, storing, and providing electronic information for periods longer than human lifetimes. Implementation of a digital research library will require accomplishing specific tasks and undertaking several commitments. In what follows, the tasks are given the most space, yet, as technical problems, tasks are probably the easiest to solve. The institutional commitments described in a later section will be much more difficult to achieve.

The Tasks

Preservation of electronic information encompasses three distinct tasks: medium preservation, technology preservation, and intellectual preservation. What is new about preservation in the digital environment is that digital information must now be dealt with separately from its medium. A crude analogy might be to place a book on a closet shelf and close the door for five hundred years. At the end of that time, broadly speaking, one can open the door and read that book. With an electronic resource, we can't be confident after even ten years that the information is intact: The device on which it is recorded may deteriorate, the technology for its use is liable to be obsolete, and the contents may have easily and invisibly changed.

Medium Preservation

Over the years the recording medium of tapes flakes off its support, or the support itself gets brittle. CD-ROMs are still not considered to have a dependable life of over fifteen years—if air enters through the plastic coating, the metal reflective layer quickly corrodes. Aside from proper environmental and handling controls, the solution has been to "refresh" the information; that is, to copy it from the potentially deteriorating medium to another, fresher medium of the same or a similar kind. Except for device-dependent formatting, the information itself is not changed in any way detectable by the user or its application program.

Technology Preservation

The preservation of the medium on which the bits and bytes of electronic information are recorded is an important concern. But such solutions will inevitably be short-term and will not in themselves be the means of preserving information over long periods. Michael Lesk in 1992 urged that the greatest attention should instead be directed to the obsolescence of technologies rather than simply of the media.[3]

Lesk describes the rapid changes in the means of recording, in the storage formats, and in the software that allows electronic information to be of use. Urging what might be called technology preservation, he asserts that for digital data, "preservation means copying, not physical preservation." That is, the preservation of electronic information into the indefinite future requires its being "migrated" from old to new technologies as they become available and as the old technologies cease being supported by vendors and the user community.

It is becoming clear that information migration, or technological preservation, is the most problematic of the digital archiving challenges. One evident technical problem is how to assure forward compatibility of information files within subsequently developed application programs, given the short life span of program versions and of their supporting corporate creators. The logistical question is this: Should information be migrated forward in time as new programs supersede old, or should information only be migrated forward to a new program when it is specifically needed? Is it necessary to preserve the technology that supports all details of the target information (for example, formatting of text) or only its essentials—and what, of course, is the "essential" part? Jeff Rothenberg and Clifford Lynch have addressed these problems. Rothenberg in 1999 discussed the strategy of "emulating" the software environment of a digital object.[4] In speeches, Lynch has proposed the analogy of textual editions and film versions of books to suggest that the goal of perfect information migration may not need fully to be achieved in order to satisfy future needs.

Intellectual Preservation

Intellectual preservation addresses the integrity and authenticity of the information as originally recorded. Preservation of the media and of the software technologies will serve only part of the need if the information content has been corrupted from its original form, whether by accident or design. The need for intellectual preservation arises because the great asset of digital information is also its great liability: The ease with which an identical copy can be quickly and flawlessly made is paralleled by the ease with which a change may undetectably be made.

Clifford Lynch has noted that

> it is very easy to replace an electronic dataset with an updated copy, and . . . the replacement can have wide-reaching effects. The processes of authorship . . . produce different versions which in an electronic environment can easily go into broad circulation; if each draft is not carefully labeled and dated it is difficult to tell which draft one is looking at, or whether one has the "final" version of a work.[5]

Donald F. McKenzie, in his 1992 Centenary Lecture for The Bibliographical Society (London), wrote, in urging a new direction for the society, that

> it's the *durability* of those textual forms [books] that ultimately secures the continuing future of our past; it's the *evanescence* of the new ones that poses the most critical problem for bibliography and any further history dependent upon its scholarship. . . . As the late Northrop Frye said, "Society, like the individual, becomes senile in proportion as it loses its continuous memory," and [electronic] texts are now part of that memory, significant products of our civilisation. . . . [There is] a new urgency with the arrival of computer-generated texts. The

demands made . . . by the evolution of texts in such forms, the speed with which versions are displaced one by another, and the question of their authority, are no less compelling than those we accept for printed books.[6]

The problem may be put in the form of several questions that confront the user of any electronic document (whether it is text, hypertext, audio, graphic, numeric, or multimedia information):

How can I be sure that what I am viewing is what I want to see?

How do I know that the document I have found is the same one that another used and made reference to in a footnote?

How can I be sure that the document I now use has not been changed since the last time I used it?

How can I be sure that a document is what it purports to be?

We properly take for granted the fixity of text in the print world. The printed journal article I examine because of your footnote is the same text that you read. Therefore, we have confidence that our discussion is based on a common foundation. With electronic texts we no longer have that confidence.

Three possibilities for change in electronic texts confront us with the need for intellectual preservation techniques:

accidental change

intended change that is well meant

intended change that is not well meant; that is, fraud

Note that backup is not the issue or the solution. In question is how we know what we have (or don't have).

A document can sometimes be damaged accidentally, perhaps by data loss during transfer or through inadvertent mistakes in manipulation; for example, data may be corrupted in being sent over a network or between disks and memory in a computer. This no longer happens often, but it is possible. More frequent is the loss of sections of a document, or a whole version of a document, because of accidents in updating.

At least two possibilities exist for intended change that is well meant. New versions and drafts are familiar to us from dealing with authorial texts, for example, or from working with successive book editions, legislative bills, or revisions of working papers. It is desirable to distinguish bibliographically between one version and another. Readers are accustomed to visual cues to indicate when a version is different. In addition to explicit numbering, one may observe the page format, the typography, the producer's name, the binding, the paper itself. These cues are not available or dependable for distinguishing electronic versions.

Structural updates (changes that are inherent in the document) also cause changes in information content. A dynamic database by its nature is frequently updated: *Books in Print*, for example, or architectural drawings, or elements of the Human Genome Project, or today's *New York Times* on the Web. How may one identify a given snapshot and authenticate it as representing a certain time?

The third kind of change that can occur is intentional change for fraudulent reasons. The change might be of one's own work, to cover one's tracks or change evidence for a variety of reasons, or it might be damage to another's work.

In an electronic future the opportunities for revision of history will be multiplied. An unscrupulous researcher could change experimental data without a trace. A financial dealer might wish to cover tracks to hide improper business, or a political figure might wish to hide or modify inconvenient earlier views. Consider the consequences if political opponents could modify their own past correspondence without detection. Then consider the case if each of them could modify the other's correspondence without detection. Society, as well as each opponent, needs a defense against such cases.

The need is to fix, or authenticate, a document so that a user can be sure of the unaltered text when it is needed. Such a technique must be easy to use so that it does not impede creation or access. It must also provide generality, flexibility, openness where possible but document security where desired, low cost, and—most of all—functionality over long periods.

Digital time-stamping and various forms of digital signatures are among solutions available for the electronically novel problem of intellectual preservation. There are likely to be others, each with their own assets and liabilities. The preservation community must keep abreast of potential solutions and urge implementation of ones most broadly suitable; most of all, those responsible for preservation must be aware that the problem exists and that it requires a solution beyond the important preservation of the media and the technologies.

Commitments

Much of what has been described so far is merely technical, so to speak, and the outlines of solutions are emerging even if the details remain to be worked out (setting aside here the nontrivial matters of cost). More difficult will be the social compacts—that is, the agreements on standards, intellectual property, and access modes. But most difficult of all to achieve, if electronic preservation and access are to be accomplished on any significant scale, will be the long-term commitments to these goals by institutions. Nothing makes clearer that a library is an organization, rather than a building or a collection, than the requirement for institutional commitment for electronic information to have more than a fleeting existence.

Organizational Commitment

The organization of libraries is already changing as electronic information increasingly becomes part of their charge. Most research libraries have had substantial systems departments that maintain infrastructures while the librarians take on more and more digital information responsibilities. Some libraries locate the responsibility for electronic information distinctly from that for print. Most libraries are coming to see the forms as inseparable and include digital responsibilities along with artifactual responsibilities in assignments for collection development, cataloging, and public service.

Shortly we will see the permanent assignment of staff responsibility for the long-term maintenance of electronic information within a library. There is no obvious artifactual parallel for this responsibility; for print it is now shared by circulation, stack maintenance, preservation, and physical plant departments. Nor are there present parallels in academic computing centers, where staffs typically focus on technological advance and availability, leaving data to the users. The electronic preservation responsibility will be focused as it will require technical expertise likely to be located in a single functional area.

It is unlikely that this functional area will be what we used to call the library's systems department. As libraries move more into the electronic environment, the historic tripartite division of libraries into public services, technical services, and collection development continues functionally but in more fluid arrangements. In addition, the need for consortial activity has become evident both for provision and preservation of digital information. People who combine bibliographic understanding, problem-solving abilities, negotiating skills, and process orientation will be needed throughout libraries; such staff will take on the demanding new technical, collection, and service responsibilities for long-term support of digital collections.

Fiscal Commitment

The permanent existence of a digital research library will require assured continuity in operational funding. Almost any other library activity can survive a funding hiatus of a year or more. Acquisitions, building maintenance, and preservation can be suspended, or an entire staff can be dispersed and a library shut down for several years, and the artifactual collections will more or less survive. But digital collections, like the online catalog, require continual maintenance if they are to survive more than a very brief interruption of power, environmental control, backup, migration, and related technical care.

Online catalog maintenance costs have reached roughly a steady state, and the capital costs for new OPACs are decreasing relative to the capabilities provided. The catalog size will continue to increase, but catalog records are small relative to the information to which they refer. Digital collections, however, as a proportion of the library's supply of information, will grow for the foreseeable future, and the quantity of information requiring care will become considerable (and much larger than the catalog). Unit costs of storage are likely to continue falling for some time, which may make the financial burden manageable. (Staffing costs are not expected to increase, only because most libraries now recognize that overall staff growth for any reason will not be allowed for some time; reassignments, however, are likely.)

Long-term funding will be required to assure long-term care. Libraries and their parent institutions will need to develop new fiscal tools and use familiar fiscal tools for new purposes. Public institutions, usually constrained to annual funding, will have particular difficulties, but existing procedures for capital or plant funding may provide precedents. One familiar technique is the endowment. It has been difficult to obtain private funding for endowments of concepts and services rather than books and mortar, but it is possible. Institutions might also build endowments out of operating funds over time.

Some revenue streams associated with digital research libraries may be practical. Consortial arrangements may allow for lease or purchase of shares in a digital collection. Shorter-term access might be provided to other institutions on a usage basis. Access could be sold to certain classes of users, for example, businesses, nonlocal clienteles, or specific information projects. New relations with publishers, currently difficult to perceive through the miasmic fog rising from intellectual property concerns, might provide income for storage of electronically published materials during the copyright lifetime in which publishers collect usage fees. With commitment and imagination, long-term fiscal tools will be found.

Institutional Commitment

The organizational and fiscal commitments just discussed are instrumental means of accomplishing the greatest requirement, that of conscious, planned, institutional commitment to preserve that part of human culture that will flower in electronic form. While museums preserve artifacts, often beautiful, that embody information, libraries preserve information that—until now—has been embedded in artifacts (only occasionally of aesthetic interest in themselves). The advent of electronic information will accentuate the difference between these roles as libraries take the responsibility for the preservation of information in nonartifactual forms.

For the past century, most research libraries have been associated with universities, and this connection seems likely to continue. Whatever the governance structure, an institution wishing to benefit from electronic information will have to make a conscious commitment to providing resources. Michael Buckland, of the University of California–Berkeley, has distinguished between a library's role and its mission.[7] Where the role of a library is to facilitate access to information, its mission is to support the mission of its parent institution. One can extend this to understand that if a university wishes to continue gaining support for its mission from its library, it will have to make commitments to the library's role. In the electronic environment, this means new, long-standing financial commitments that the library and university together must identify and accomplish.

The commitment will have to be clearly and publicly made if scholars and other libraries are to have confidence that a given digital collection is indeed likely to exist for the long term. It is essential that guidelines or standards be established defining what is meant by a long-term commitment, and defining what electronic repositories of data can qualify to be called a digital research library. Just as donors of books, manuscripts, and archives look for demonstration of long-term care and commitment, so too will scholars and publishers as they create digital information that requires a home.

Current Activities

Describing current activities in digital archiving is best done by describing efforts undertaken by various national groups. This approach has the advantage of emphasizing the importance of consortial activity. As 1999 began, progress in digital archiving was strikingly international, but it was unevenly distributed around the globe.

Australia

Work in Australia originated in 1993 on an explicitly national basis, with funding both from the government and from the national library. It can be described as a top-down approach, aiming first at principles and goals before proceeding to implementation. PADI (Preserving Access to Digital Information) is headed by an officer of the National Library of Australia, has an office and a budget, and has developed statements of vision, goals, and objectives. PADI maintains strong links between the library and archives communities. Its *Statement of Principles on Preservation of Australian Digital Objects* reflects an early achievement of national consensus, and it has been followed by reports attempting to deal with location of responsibilities, definitions of how digital information is to be preserved, and the likely costs over time of digital archiving.

United Kingdom

The Follett Commission of 1993 stimulated electronic library ("eLib") activity on a broad front in the United Kingdom, supported by millions of pounds annually and managed by the Joint Information Systems Committee (JISC) of the Higher Education Funding Councils. After several national workshops on digital archiving, in 1997 JISC inaugurated a specific program through CEDARS (CURL Exemplars in Digital Archives, where CURL is the Council of University Research Libraries of the United Kingdom). I am a member of this project's advisory board. The CEDARS participants comprise Cambridge, Leeds, and Oxford Universities.

> The main deliverables of the project will be recommendations and guidelines as well as practical, robust and scalable models for establishing distributed digital archives. It is expected that the outcomes of CEDARS will influence the development of legislation for legal deposit of electronic materials and feed directly into the emerging national strategy for digital preservation currently being developed through the National Preservation Office of the British Library.[8]

Another JISC-funded eLib project is the Arts and Humanities Data Service, which has responded to specific requests of JISC's Digital

Archiving Working Party by developing strategic policy framework statements for creating and preserving digital collections.

United States

Activity in the United States contrasts with that of Australia and the United Kingdom in that several centers of activity exist that don't seem to have much relation to one another, nor are any of them very explicit as to what they are about. First, it is important to note that the substantially funded NSF Digital Libraries projects have focused primarily on large database construction (round one, in the mid-1990s) and on social implications (round two, now under way). Emphasis is always on "innovative applications"; archiving is mentioned in passing, but so far not funded.

Digital Library Federation: The DLF has now been in existence for several years, but remains opaque to external observers. A coalition of about twenty libraries, it has developed some brief broad strategic outlines of proposed activity but has been silent as to actual projects within member libraries. In early DLF statements, digital archiving was listed as one of three main priorities; more recently, it is an "other" priority, with preeminent place given to user authentication and authorization matters. Donald Waters, the primary author of the important 1996 report from RLG and the Commission on Preservation and Access, has been the DLF director since 1997.

Research Libraries Group (RLG): The ARCHES (Archival Server) project, begun in 1996, is specifically intended by RLG to address digital archiving. In its first instance it is intended both to support a specific repository and to create a software environment that will make long-term archiving possible. Details of the digital archival commitment being made by the project are unclear, and in its beginnings the project appears to have been subordinated to the specific content repository created for it on marriage and law in the nineteenth century.

OCLC: This largest library utility is well placed to create and provide archiving services, for it has readily available both the financial and intellectual capital to do so. In 1997 it committed to archiving e-journals on behalf of its subscribers and bravely included a commitment to technological migration. However, it has remained silent on details of how it intends to achieve this goal, and has not yet had to come through with this commitment in any specific instance. Also, OCLC has included the statement that it will migrate digital objects "at its discretion," presumably depending on the degree of difficulty.

Though in practice perhaps such a stipulation is always implied, its unqualified emphasis so early does not add to the confidence one wishes in such a project.

Canada

The Canadian Initiative on Digital Libraries began work in 1997, but to date has shown little emphasis on digital archiving. On the other hand, many Canadian libraries are members of United States consortia (for example, OCLC and RLG) whom they may count on to act in their behalf.

The commonwealth tradition of national planning and initiative (in spite of Thatcherism and similar antipodean free-market emphases) appears in strong contrast to the fragmented, nongovernmental activities in North America. It remains to be seen which approach will generate the optimal and broadly exploited archiving technologies that are needed. However much one can wish from the outset that the United States groups were more communicative about what they are doing, and in particular that they would coordinate their efforts with one another, to date there is little evidence that they do so.

It is notable, however, that regardless of where digital archiving investigation is going on, it is in consortial activity. There is uniform recognition that digital archiving is not a matter solvable by individual institutions, whether for collection reasons or for technological reasons.

Conclusion

Why should librarians undertake the difficult job of digital preservation? Why bother with this troublesome task? The answer should be self-evident: It is what we librarians do. The paradigm of librarianship taught in library school is to acquire information, organize it, preserve it, and make it available. This has been useful and instructive in dealing with print materials, and it continues to be useful and instructive as we consider digital information.

It is the preservation imperative that is particularly important for readers of this volume. In research libraries, and not only in special collections, the consideration of long periods of time is more important than in other library fields. It is our particular responsibility to see that library materials are preserved and organized for use not only by our generation but by succeeding generations of scholars and students. No one else has this specific responsibility; it is what we do. If we do not do it, no one else will do it.

Pessimistically speaking, it is possible that the job cannot be done. We may be swimming against the tide. Sociologically, much of our society is obsessed with the present and uncaring of the past and therefore of its records. Technologically refined tools are now available that not only allow but encourage the quick and easy modification of text, of pictures, and of sounds. It is becoming routine to produce ad hoc versions of performances, and to produce technical reports in tailored versions on demand. The technology that allows us to interact with information is itself inhibiting us from preserving our interaction. In addition, society will have to allocate significant resources to the preservation of digital information.

However, there is cause for optimism. In our house there are many mansions; there will continue to be people who want history, who care about the human record, and who will support our efforts to serve them. Some aspects of electronic preservation are already being dealt with by other communities. The financial and business community, for example, has a stake in authentication of electronic communication. The business and computing communities in general are interested in protecting against the undesired loss of data in the short term. The governmental and business communities have an interest in the security of systems.

But there is no other professional group dealing with the combination of all these issues—authentication, security, and protection—as complicated by the length of time in centuries that research librarians contemplate, and by the need to provide organized access to what is preserved.

Some librarians may draw back from the apparent complexity of the technologies that support electronic information. But these technologies should present no difficulty to minds that can easily deal with corporate authorship and with the acquisition of monographic continuations. Our ability to create and use the MARC record is now adequate to the task of setting standards for electronic preservation. Providing valid electronic authentication techniques is no more intractable than designing holdings statements for works in multiple formats. Many librarians are very aware of the technology and increasingly aware of how we need to manage it.

And it is managing that is necessary. There are technical people aplenty who can grapple with the bits and bytes of these issues if librarians give them proper direction. The need is for people to articulate the requirements for the electronic preservation of the human record and to lead our profession in making it happen. That is the professional requirement, and it is the professionals reading this—you—who are the most capable of assuring that it does happen. There is a kind of back-to-basics quality to our now confronting the electronic environment: to grapple with the ephemerality of electronic information is to answer the abstract question of why we are librarians.

Most of us know that we like books; readers of this volume are likely to appreciate books as physical objects and to enjoy reading. But back to basics. Our social value as librarians comes from our provision of information—our locating it, organizing it, and preserving it. Libraries, and technical services, will change. The changes will be affected by how well we propose to carry on professional activities. If we continue to emphasize only the physical objects we know as books, important as they are, then a largely museum role becomes increasingly likely as we become marginalized from the real scholarly communication now going on.

Alternatively, we can continue to emphasize our professional obligation to preserve and make available the human record, regardless of its form. Then we can lay claim to being a part of the very current affairs of our society and of our universities. We can then lay very effective claim to the resources we need to carry out this obligation; and finding ways to do that is also our professional requirement.

Establishing a digital research library continues the research library role. To do so should be considered as natural as acquiring the next book or cataloging the next journal. Not to do so would be an abdication of that role. The tasks call not so much on new knowledge nor on new techniques, but upon informed commitment—that is, upon will. For librarians wondering what is to come of their profession in the electronic age, here is their challenge.

Notes

1. <http://www.clir.org/diglib/dldefinition.htm>

2. Gordon B. Neavill, "Electronic Publishing, Libraries, and the Survival of Information," *Library Resources & Technical Services* 28 (1984): 76–89.

3. Michael Lesk, *Preservation of New Technology: A Report of the Technology Assessment Advisory Committee to the Commission on Preservation and Access* (Washington, D.C.: Commission on Preservation and Access, 1992).

4. Jeff Rothenberg, *Avoiding Technological Quicksand: Finding a Viable Technical Foundation for Digital Preservation* (Washington, D.C.: Council on Library and Information Resources, 1999).

5. Clifford Lynch, "Accessibility and Integrity of Networked Information Collections" (Office of Technology Assessment, Congress of the United States, July 5, 1993), 68.

6. Donald F. McKenzie, *What's Past Is Prologue*, The Bibliographical Society Centenary Lecture, 14 July 1992 (n.p.: Hearthstone Publications, 1993), 21–22, 27.

7. Michael Buckland, "Electronic Information: What Is It and How Do We Organize It? Putting It Together: The Principles of Information Access" (paper presented at ALCTS Institute on [the] Electronic Library: Administrative Issues for Organization and Access, October 30, 1994).

8. Kelly Russell, "CEDARS: Long-term Access and Usability of Digital Resources," *Ariadne*, no. 18 (December 1998) <http://www.ariadne.ac.uk/issue18/cedars/>.

Examples of Digital Library Projects

AUSTRALIA

PADI: Preserving Access to Digital Information
<http://www.nla.gov.au/padi/>

CANADA

Canadian Initiative on Digital Libraries (CIDL)
<http://www.nlc-bnc.ca/cidl/aboute.htm>

UNITED KINGDOM

British Library Research and Innovation Centre Digital Library Research Programme
<http://www.ukoln.ac.uk/services/bl/>

eLib: Electronic Libraries Programme
<http://www.ukoln.ac.uk/services/elib/>

CEDARS: CURL Exemplars in Digital Archiving
<http://www.leeds.ac.uk/cedars/>

Arts and Humanities Data Service (AHDS)
<http://ahds.ac.uk/>

UNITED STATES

Digital Libraries II
<http://www.dli2.nsf.gov/>

Digital Library Federation
<http://www.clir.org/diglib/dlfhomepage.htm>

OCLC Archiving Solution
<http://www.oclc.org/oclc/eco/archive.htm>

RLG ARCHES Project
<http://www.rlg.org/strat/projarch.html>

Suggested Readings

Beagrie, Neil, and Daniel Greenstein. *A Strategic Framework for Creating and Preserving Digital Resources.* London: Library Information Technology Centre, South Bank University, 1998. (eLib Supporting Study p3) Also available at <http://ahds.ac.uk/manage/framework.htm>.

Commission on Preservation and Access and the Research Libraries Group. Task Force on Archiving of Digital Information. *Preserving Digital Information.* Washington, D.C.: CPA, 1996. Also available at <ftp.rlg.org> or <http://www.rlg.org/ArchTF/index.html>.

Graham, Peter S. "Building the Digital Research Library: Preservation and Access at the Heart of Scholarship." Follett Lecture Series, Leicester University, 19 March 1997 <http://www.ukoln.ac.uk/services/papers/follett/graham/paper.html>.

Michelson, Avra, and Jeff Rothenberg. "Scholarly Communication and Information Technology: Exploring the Impact of Changes in the Research Process on Archives." *American Archivist* 55 (1992): 236–315. Also available in the Rand Reprint Series under the same title as RAND/RP-187 (1993).

Mohlhenrich, Janice, ed. *Preservation of Electronic Formats: Electronic Formats for Preservation.* Fort Atkinson, Wis.: Highsmith, 1993.

Rothenberg, Jeff. "Ensuring the Longevity of Digital Documents." *Scientific American* 272, no. 1 (1995): 42–47.

7

■━ ■ ━■

Environment and Building Design

■ ■ ■

PAUL N. BANKS

Providing a suitable environment is the most fundamental means of preserving library and archive collections. This is so obvious that we forget it: We place books and other records that we want to preserve in the shelter of a building and assume they are protected from nature's processes of decay. We may also forget that books and other records, unlike living organisms, have no regenerative powers, and that deterioration of books, whether mechanical, chemical, or biological, is cumulative and irreversible. Thus, if we want records to last longer than a human life span—that is, indefinitely—we may have to undertake protective measures more stringent in some respects than we take for ourselves. Even for records for which indefinite preservation is not currently desired, controlling their environment may be a cost-effective way to attain their desired service life.

The environmental factors discussed in this chapter are temperature, relative humidity, airborne pollutants, and light. These factors will be considered primarily in connection with storage of books and other records. Although the effects of environment on records during use in reading rooms or elsewhere should not be ignored, records spend most of their lives in stacks or other storage areas.

The influence of environment on records is complex, as is controlling that environment. The best that a single chapter can do is to alert you to some of the major issues and factors involved in controlling or improving the environment for conservation.

The Effects of Environment on Collections

Books, manuscripts, maps, photographs, magnetic tapes, and virtually all other forms of records found in libraries and archives are composed almost wholly of organic materials. Although it is true enough to be useful to say that all organic materials will deteriorate over time, the rate of deterioration varies greatly. Some World War II–era paper, for example, has become so brittle in fewer than fifty years that it shatters when handled, while five-hundred-year-old paper usually comes down to us in sturdy condition. The dyes in some color photographs fade in a few years, while the polyester film used in some records is expected to last for centuries.

Temperature

The speed of most chemical reactions increases with higher temperature, and the most serious form of paper deterioration in most American libraries, the progressive embrittlement that occurs even when records are not being used, consists of chemical reactions.[1] It has been estimated that a reduction of temperature from 77°F to 68°F, for example, will increase by 2.4 times the time required for "good-quality" paper to lose half its useful properties, and the benefit of reduced temperature for acidic paper may be even greater.[2] Although it may be misleading to overgeneralize about specific rates of deterioration of different kinds of paper (and other records), one broad generalization can safely be made: The lower the temperature, the longer records will last. Rates of biological attack are also slowed by storage at lower temperature.

Relative Humidity

The role of relative humidity (RH) in the deterioration of records is more complex and less precisely understood. In fact, it is not the humidity in the surrounding air that affects the chemical, mechanical, or biological deterioration of materials, but the moisture content ("equilibrium moisture content" or EMC) of the book or other record itself.

Most of the materials of records are hygroscopic; that is, they take up and give off moisture in response to the ambient relative humidity.

The EMC of any given material (a particular type of paper or adhesive, for example) is affected in part by the degree of hygroscopicity of the material itself, in part by temperature, but mainly by the relative humidity of the surrounding air. In any case, it is not feasible to control the moisture content of each record individually, so all we can do is try to control the RH of the space in which the records are housed.

Within certain limits, increased moisture content accelerates chemical deterioration of organic materials, and very high humidity (above 65–70%) encourages insect and fungal deterioration. Also, many organic materials shrink as their EMC diminishes, and lose flexibility at very low humidities (below perhaps 30%) so that they are more vulnerable to fracturing. Some materials undergo irreversible molecular changes at these low humidities. Composite objects, such as books, that were fabricated at one humidity warp when placed in a significantly different level.

Fluctuations in relative humidity appear to be even more damaging than constant humidity in the middle range. Three types of modern paper studied by Shahani et al. deteriorated significantly faster when cycled at twelve-hour intervals between 40 and 60% than when kept at a constant 40, 50, or 60% for the same period.[3]

It has been widely asserted that the optimum RH for preservation of books and manuscripts is 50 or 55%. However, lower humidity can significantly increase the longevity not only of paper, but also of photographic and magnetic materials. At the same time, evidence is growing that low humidity (at least down to about 30%) has less adverse effect on the flexibility and other mechanical properties of materials even when they are being used than has previously been contended.

The conclusion that seems increasingly inescapable is that records should be stored at lower humidity than has previously almost universally been recommended.

Pollutants

Airborne pollutants are categorized as particulates—that is, particles or minute droplets—or gases. The obvious damage from particulate pollutants is dust accumulations and soiling. The handling entailed in cleaning dust accumulations (large particulates) from books is costly and incurs wear and tear. Fine, sooty particulates are disfiguring and virtually unremovable. Both types may cause subtler and less well understood damage, such as encouraging mildew and chemical deterioration.

Gaseous pollutants, such as sulfur dioxide, ozone, and oxides of nitrogen, cause far more serious damage. These pollutants can irreversibly break down the molecules from which paper, fabrics, and leather derive their mechanical strength, and they can cause the fading and discoloration of photographic materials, including microfilms, and of some pigments and dyes. Vegetable tanned leather and paper containing mechanical wood pulp are particularly vulnerable to sulfur dioxide, which they take up readily.

Internally generated pollutants, such as ozone (generated indoors by, for example, photocopiers and laser printers), volatile organic compounds (VOCs) including formaldehyde, and tobacco smoke, are also increasingly of concern. Although there has been little research on the effects of these pollutants on library or archival materials, they can generally be assumed to be harmful to collections.

Pollutant gases are particularly insidious because they are not evident to people, and their damage is irreversible and cumulative over the entire time that records are exposed to them, even though the levels in the air are so small that they are difficult to measure and control.

Light

Light is energy that also can accelerate deterioration on the molecular level. Ultraviolet (UV) radiation, visible light, and infrared (IR) radiation are adjacent regions of the continuous electromagnetic spectrum (see figure 1). Understanding the continuity of this spectrum is

Figure 1
Portion of the Electromagnetic Spectrum

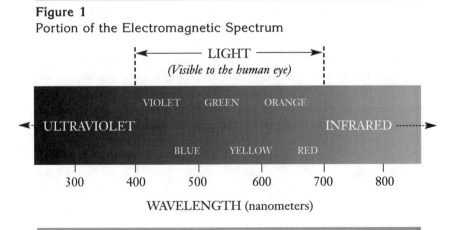

important; there is no basis in physics for sharp distinctions between adjacent regions. The only difference (as the term "visible light" for the middle region suggests) is the sensitivity of the human eye. Other things being equal, the shorter the wavelength of the radiation, the greater the potential for damage to collections, so that UV is more damaging than violet light, blue light is more potentially damaging than green, and so on. (It isn't really quite this simple, because radiation must be absorbed to do damage, but this is a useful practical generalization.)

The primary effect of infrared radiation is to heat objects that absorb it. It is of concern in two contexts: solar heat gain and the local heating of objects being exhibited. Solar gain through windows causes erratic heating of the space, and IR from either the sun or incandescent lamps can cause local warming and desiccation of objects that it falls on.

Ultraviolet radiation is widely understood to be damaging to the collections of libraries, archives, and museums. The potential for damage from visible light, especially light at the bluer (shorter wavelength) end of the visible spectrum that lies next to the UV region, is not so widely appreciated. In other words, elimination of UV reduces the most serious potential for light damage, *but eliminating UV alone does not eliminate light damage.* Reducing the intensity of visible light or the length of exposure, or both, are also necessary to reduce light damage. (Damage from visible light can also be almost totally eliminated by filtering out the blue end of the spectrum, but this creates an overall yellow or orange color and is not normally practical.)

The mechanisms of light damage are rather complex, but the result is irreversible damage, such as the fading or other color change in inks and dyes, or reduction of strength of such materials as paper, textiles, and leather.

Of the common lighting sources, direct sunlight contains very high intensities all across the spectrum. Daylight, although lacking IR, actually has a higher proportion of UV than direct sunlight. Most incandescent lighting emits relatively small amounts of UV, but in some situations IR heating can be a serious problem. Fluorescent tubes emit little IR, but vary widely in the amount of UV they produce. Some types have built-in UV filters, but most produce potentially damaging levels. It should be noted that while ordinary glass filters out the most energetic and damaging shorter wavelength UV (shorter than about 325 nanometers), the quartz envelope of quartz-halogen lamps does not.

Economic Considerations

Providing optimum environment is the only preservation strategy that can help prolong the life of *entire* collections. It is to be sure expensive both in initial cost and in ongoing operating costs. Persuading resource allocators of the importance of providing optimum environment is a challenge, but examination of alternatives may make the case more persuasive: Commercial library rebinding costs $10 per volume or more, is an option only for books whose paper has not yet seriously deteriorated, and may need to be repeated; microfilming to preservation standards for deteriorated books may cost $50 to $100 per volume; and competent conservation treatment of irreplaceable volumes costs from several hundred to several thousand dollars.

Donald Sebera's concept of *isoperms* is a method for visualizing the effects of temperature and relative humidity on the rate of deterioration of modern paper.[4] It is based on assigning room conditions (20°C, 50% RH) as an isoperm of 1, and representing graphically the rate at which longevity will be increased or decreased by varying the temperature or relative humidity or both. As an alternative to rigid standard set points, Sebera's approach permits some tinkering with temperature (T) and RH in response to local conditions in order to achieve a level of longevity established as a matter of policy by the institution.

The isoperm method predicts life expectancy of a material at constant T and RH, but does not indicate the cumulative effect of varying conditions. Because deterioration, once it has occurred, cannot reverse itself, the life expectancy of a material is necessarily reduced by any period of poorer conditions, even though it may have spent much of its life in "good" conditions. By considering the isoperm for a given combination of T and RH as a *preservation index* (PI), the Image Permanence Institute (IPI) devised a system for integrating varying conditions into a *time-weighted preservation index* (TWPI).[5] The TWPI can serve several practical uses, especially in situations in which there is limited environmental control. An example given in the IPI publication is choosing among a hypothetical attic, closet, and basement for storage of records. (The longer period of lower temperature of the basement wins—not necessarily the intuitive choice.) The system can also be used by preservation managers to support arguments to resource allocators for improved environment, and to visualize the effects of fluctuations in a controlled system on rates of deterioration.

When an end point can be established, such as the point at which embrittlement of paper requires that a book must be microfilmed (or otherwise copied), or when the least-stable dye in a color photograph has faded by 30 percent, and the costs of alternatives can be estimated, the isoperm and TWPI models can be the basis for cost-benefit studies. Such a study was undertaken at the U.S. National Archives to determine whether providing optimum environment or copying is the most cost-effective approach for preserving cellulose acetate–based photographic materials.[6]

In addition to economic benefits, providing optimum environment also helps to preserve visual values that cannot be fully reproduced and artifactual values that can never truly be restored once they have deteriorated.

The costs of environmental control can to some degree be contained by careful planning and engineering, especially when the opportunity arises (or is created) to begin with a new building. Some specifics will be given later in this chapter.

Norms and Standards

It is both important to state specific quantitative environmental standards for preservation of collections and perilous to do so. Formal, published standards are important because those responsible for preserving collections need authoritative support to back up their claims. Specific numbers are necessary because the people who design and operate buildings and heating, ventilating, and air-conditioning (HVAC) systems are quantitative people, and equipment control systems must have actual numbers set into them. However, if they are to serve a useful purpose, standards must be flexible enough to be applicable in different climatic, technical, economic, and functional situations. Under any circumstances, standards that are—or are perceived to be—too rigid or idealistic are likely to be simply ignored, perhaps even without the benefit of the informed discussions necessary to arrive at the compromises least damaging to collections.

If, on the other hand, formal standards are too loose, it can be predicted that those responsible for projects will opt for the least stringent of the choices offered because it is cheaper or the least unpopular (for example, putting windows in stacks). Because of design, construction, or operating limitations, systems often do not maintain initial design conditions, so if the standards are loose to begin with, actual conditions may wind up even farther away from an optimum conservation environment.

It is important to note the phrase "in a given situation." The environmental standards that are appropriate in New Orleans may not be feasible to maintain in Minneapolis. Conditions that are appropriate for a modern building constructed for a specific purpose may be quite inappropriate in a historical society housed in an adapted private residence. Conditions that are feasible in a deposit library may not be so in a heavily used open-stack collection. For these reasons wisdom dictates some caution about too-specific numbers that are meant to be applicable to all situations.

It is also important to understand what the numbers in environmental standards mean. For most parameters, there is a rough correlation between the size of the dose and the degree of damage. In other words, most of the cited numbers are arbitrary; they are not "magic numbers" above which there will be damage and below which there will be no damage. (Relative humidity is the partial exception to this.) This is also a reason that differing standards exist; the numbers depend in part upon the judgment of the people or bodies that developed them.

Having mentioned the pitfalls of specific numbers for preservation environments, it is now time to cite some, primarily for books, manuscripts, and other paper-based records.

Temperature

The lower temperature limit in libraries, and to a lesser extent archives, is dictated by three factors: cost, comfort, and condensation.

Water vapor in the air (that is, humidity) will condense as liquid water on a surface that is below the dew point of the air, which is controlled by the amount of moisture in the air. The dew point of air at 75°F and 50% RH is about 55°F. This suggests that (depending on rates of use and conditions in reading areas) 60° or 62°F may be a reasonable minimum storage temperature from the standpoint of condensation.

Human comfort is often the factor controlling minimum storage temperature for collections. This is one of a number of reasons that, to the extent that long-term preservation is a goal, staff and user functions should be separated as much as possible from the stacks in which research collections are housed.

The cost of maintaining cooler temperatures will depend on a number of factors, among them climate, season, thermal quality of the building, and local energy costs. Maintaining lower temperature in winter can partially offset the higher energy cost of lower summer temperature. This principle is being applied in some storage libraries in which comfort can more easily be ignored.

For collections that can be separated from users (except, of course, for retrieval), 62–65°F may be a good target. For storage collections with very low rates of use, even lower temperature would be desirable if affordable. Where stacks cannot be separated from users, 68–70°F is probably the lowest that will be politically acceptable.

It is technically easy to maintain temperature within relatively close tolerances, at least in well-designed buildings. Although temperature fluctuations per se are not seriously damaging to collections, stable temperature is helpful in maintaining stable relative humidity.

Relative Humidity

As indicated earlier, there are a number of constraints—primarily climate, season, and the nature of the building envelope—on the overall *levels* of RH that can feasibly be maintained in a given situation. However, every effort should be made to maintain daily and weekly *stability* of RH.

Reasonable extreme limits of relative humidity in light of current understanding of its effects on materials are 50% maximum and 30% minimum. Because of the growing evidence of the seriousness of fluctuations on deterioration, minimizing fluctuations seems to be more important than the precise level, as long as the level is within the outer limits of 30% to 50%. A level that can be maintained with well-designed systems is ±3%.

If seasonal variations are necessitated by such constraints as inability of the building envelope to tolerate higher humidity in cold climates, the set point should be changed gradually, say, 5% a month.

In other words, if RH can be maintained within ±3%, a set point between 33% and 47% should be selected, the set point varying with the season if necessary. If the RH cannot be maintained within 3% of the set point, the outer limits may have to be closer together.

Pollutants

Remembering that all such numbers are arbitrary, several plausible sets of figures have been given for maximum gaseous pollutant levels. These limits are given in figure 2. It should be noted that HVAC engineers sometimes try to use the limits established by the Environmental

Figure 2
Commonly Cited Gaseous Pollutant Levels and Norms

	TYPICAL URBAN CONCENTRATION [1]		RECOMMENDED CONTROL LEVELS [2]	
Pollutant	ppb	µg/m³	ppb	µg/m³
Sulfur dioxide	84	240	≤0.4	≤1
Nitrogen dioxide	25	51	≤2.5	≤5
Ozone	19	40	≤1	≤2

1. From *1989 ASHRAE Handbook: Fundamentals.*
2. Various sources.

Protection Agency for human health, which are too high for continuous and permanent exposure of collections.

Standards for particulate pollutants are perhaps most practically set in terms of the efficiencies of the filters used to remove them, because that is how they are specified by mechanical engineers (see figure 3).

Light

Because the potential for light damage from a source having a given spectral distribution is a function of both intensity and time, a meaningful standard for exposure to visible light must be stated in terms of total dose—that is, lux hours or footcandle hours (fch). (One lux equals about 11 footcandles.) Three months is often used as the maximum safe duration for exhibitions, and 50 lux (about 5 fc) is widely accepted as the upper limit for extremely sensitive objects, such as watercolors and dyed leather. This translates into a total dose of about 42 kilolux hours (42,000 lux hours) per year. Thus, sensitive objects could be exposed continuously for an entire year at about 6.3 lux, or, at 55 lux (5 fc), exposure could be 1,000 hours per year or about 20 hours per week. Although there will presumably not be watercolors exposed in general library stacks, there may well be dyed leather bindings that might become rare books in the future, and this limit is certainly appropriate for rare book stacks.

Figure 3
Particulate Standards

SYSTEM FILTER LOCATION	ASHRAE WEIGHT ARRESTANCE EFFICIENCY	ASHRAE ATMOSPHERIC DUST SPOT EFFICIENCY	MIL-STD 282 DOP EFFICIENCY
Prefilter (For outside or makeup air)	≥80%	≥30%	≥5%
Intermediate filter (For outside and recirculated supply air)	≥95%	≥80%	≥50%
Fine filter (For outside and recirculated supply air)	N.A.	≥90%	≥75%

From Norbert S. Baer and Paul N. Banks, "Conservation Notes: Environmental Standards," *International Journal of Museum Management and Curatorship* 6 (1987): 207–209.

If a policy decision has been made that some fading or other slight damage to the exteriors of books can be tolerated, a limit of 165 kilo-lux hours per year may be appropriate (about 19 lux continuously).

Ultraviolet radiation is not needed for use of records, and the widely stated (if rather arbitrary) standard is 75 microwatts per lumen (µW/l). This figure requires some explanation; it is important to understand that it is a measure of the *proportion* of UV to the total light falling on a surface. The total UV energy at 75µW/lumen with a total illuminance falling on the object of 100 lux (a maximum level often recommended for sensitive paper objects) is 7,500 µW/m^2. But (to give an extreme example) direct sunlight might give 60,000 lux, so the total amount of UV energy falling on the objects could be 4,500,000 µW/m^2, six hundred times the accepted limit, even though the 75µW/lumen standard was in fact being met! Thus, this standard is appropriate only as long as it goes hand in hand with a suitable standard for total light level.

Several formal environmental standards and recommended practices for nonbook media have been published by the American National Standards Institute and others, and an important overview of handling and preservation of magnetic media has been published by the National Bureau of Standards. Citations may be found at the end of chapter 18, Preservation of Information in Nonpaper Formats.

Methods of Controlling the Environment

Building Factors

Although we may think of the environment of a library or archives being controlled primarily by HVAC systems, in fact, the indoor environment is a product of interaction among the outdoor environment (reflecting the local climate), the building envelope, internally generated thermal and pollution loads, and, finally, HVAC systems. Clearly the building itself is fundamental to the ability to provide an environment suitable for prolonging the life of collections, and especially to provide it at affordable cost.

In recent years, the bright, open, people-oriented designs that are attractive for public and school libraries have unfortunately been applied also to research libraries, for which long-term preservation is a fundamental part of their mission. Unless collections storage is reasonably confined and isolated from people activities (except, of course, for retrieving and replacing books), it is at best uneconomic and at worst impossible to provide a reasonable preservation environment. The guiding principles are (1) to be effective, space should be designed for preservation, and (2) there should be the most effective barrier possible between the collections and noncollection areas, including the outdoors.

Several strategies are available for reducing the effects of outdoor temperature conditions on internal temperature and humidity conditions. A massive building envelope (for example, many older monumental masonry library or archives buildings) provides a measure of thermal inertia, although in approximate inverse ratio to the amount of fenestration. This strategy has been revived in some recent archives buildings in Germany. Another strategy is to create a double-wall structure, as was done with the 1981 book-stack building at the Newberry Library in Chicago. A simple and conceptually elegant method is to store collections only in internal spaces, with staff and user functions around the perimeter of the building. Columbia University's 1934 Butler Library is an excellent example of this approach. This provides both the conditions needed for preservation of collections and the desired windows for staff and users. If groundwater can be effectively controlled, underground storage may provide the greatest stability at least cost.

Windows are fundamentally inimical to collections preservation. Not only do they let in damaging light, but they make it difficult to maintain stable temperature and humidity as well. Thermal window technology is improving, but really effective ones are expensive, and if collections to be preserved are separated from user and staff areas, as they should be, why are windows needed anyway?

An important building consideration is its *permeance*, the degree to which water vapor can pass into and through the building envelope. Most building materials are porous to some degree or another. Water vapor (like heat) tries to move from regions of higher vapor pressure to regions of lower, and when there is a significant difference between the humidity levels on the two sides of a wall or roof, moisture will migrate through the wall. If there is also a significant temperature difference, the water vapor may condense inside the envelope and it may also freeze if the outdoor temperature is low enough. Thus, in most climates, there needs to be a vapor retarder on the *warm* side of the building envelope. Unfortunately, it is often difficult to install an adequate vapor retarder in existing buildings, and in some historic buildings it may be impossible to do so without an unacceptable degree of alteration to the building. This may limit the amount of humidification possible during cold weather in cold climates and perhaps the amount of cooling possible in very hot, damp climates without potentially serious damage to the building envelope.

Needless to say, there are a great many considerations in achieving a conservationally sound building that cannot be covered here. The following points exemplify conservation thinking about space:

Avoid windows in collections areas.

Avoid cooling towers on roofs over stacks.

Avoid piping through or over stack areas.

Avoid shelving against exterior walls, which can lead to condensation, insect infestation, and mildew.

Avoid carpeting, which can emit pollutants, disguise infestations, and hold water in a flood.

Avoid dropped ceilings, which hide incipient leaks and make maintenance operations more difficult, among other problems (this may affect the design of the HVAC system—some systems use a dropped ceiling for return air).

Central HVAC Systems

Unfortunately, perhaps the only means of achieving relatively steady temperature and relative humidity, and of removing both gaseous and particulate pollutants, twenty-four hours a day, 365 days a year, is through full central heating, ventilating, and air-conditioning (HVAC) systems. I say unfortunately because there is no denying that effective systems are expensive to install and operate.

HVAC systems are complex, and (in part because of strategies to save energy consumption) becoming more complex. The basic *functions* that a central HVAC system needs to provide are:

Uniform distribution of treated air throughout conditioned spaces

Bringing in at least the minimum necessary outside air

Cooling during hot weather and to overcome internal heat loads (such as lighting and people)

Heating during cold weather

Adding to or removing moisture from the air as needed to maintain steady relative humidity

Reducing gaseous and particulate pollutants in the conditioned space

As shown in figure 4, the typical major *components* of a central HVAC system are:

A source of heat, which may be steam from a local or central boiler, hot water, or occasionally electricity

A source of cold; in larger systems this is almost invariably chilled water from a local or central chiller, and in smaller systems it may be a *direct expansion* unit of the type found in refrigerators and window air conditioners

Air cleaning equipment, including filters to remove particulates and adsorber beds for removing gases

Figure 4

Primary Functional Elements of a Conservation Environment
HVAC System

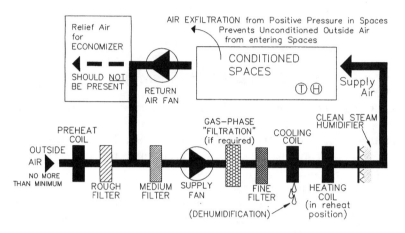

(c) 1990. William P. Lull, Garrison/Lull

Air handling units (AHUs), large sheet metal housings containing
fans to move air, most or all of the coils through which heat is
exchanged with hot or cold water, and the air cleaning equipment

Ducts to move air to and from conditioned spaces; ducts from each
AHU may be subdivided into zones, which are characterized by
some final control equipment for each zone

Control systems, increasingly computerized, to sense temperature,
humidity, and other conditions and to move valves, switches,
dampers, and so on to respond to sensed conditions

There are many types and variations of HVAC systems. Although
it is not appropriate to describe them here, a few features that can affect
the ability to maintain suitable conservation conditions should be
mentioned:

Constant volume of treated air should be supplied to conditioned
spaces.

Reheat should be provided to permit dehumidification in cool, damp weather.

The system should maintain positive pressure in conditioned spaces to prevent infiltration of untreated air, insects, and so on.

The system should be designed for maximum recirculation and minimum outdoor (makeup) air at all times in order to reduce pollutant levels, which means, for example, that it should not have an air-side economizer cycle.

Controlling Temperature   Temperature is both the easiest parameter to control within moderately close tolerances, and the parameter that is most likely to be controlled because humans are most sensitive to it. Temperature sensors and thermostats, the devices that actually control the functioning of equipment, are relatively sensitive and reliable, although, like all types of sensors, they need to be recalibrated periodically.

Controlling Relative Humidity   It will be noted that the list of HVAC system components does not include any separate equipment for humidity control. This is because the usual way to dehumidify is to cool air below its dew point as it passes over the chilled coils in the air handling unit, and drain off the resultant water. The air is then warmed to the desired temperature to deliver it to the conditioned space. In other words, cooling and dehumidification are usually part of the same process. It is important to be aware of this, because it means that the degree of dehumidification that a system can achieve is to a large extent designed into the system. In other words, there is no dial that says "humidity" that can be simply turned down if the humidity is too high.

A problem arises when, as is often the case, adequate reheat is not provided or when central chillers are turned off for the winter. When there is damp weather in the spring or autumn, there will be no means of dehumidifying. If possible, the library or archives should have its own source of chilled water so that the chiller can be kept in operation more of the year than is typical with central units, unless there is an assured year-round supply of chilled water.

Another method of dehumidification is the use of desiccant machines, which contain a material that readily absorbs moisture, and which have a mechanism for discharging the absorbed water outdoors. Desiccant machines are most often appropriate in the (increasingly common) cool, dry storage facilities designed for photographic and magnetic media because the amount of dehumidification that can be achieved by cooling below the dew point is inadequate.

Humidification is both simpler and easier to control. Some sort of device will be installed, usually in the air handling unit, to add moisture to the air. The type of humidifier that is generally the most satisfactory is one that injects steam into the airstream. However, it is important that the steam be clean; central boilers may have chemicals added to the feedwater that become an internally generated pollutant when the steam is injected into the air and that can be damaging to collections. Various kinds and sizes of "clean steam" generators are available, some of which use central plant steam as a source of heat to convert clean water to steam for humidification.

Controlling Pollutants   Multiple strategies are necessary to reduce pollutants to acceptable levels at affordable cost.

Particulates are usually removed from the airstream with various grades of mesh and fibrous filters. Electrostatic precipitators can be highly efficient in removing fine particulates, but may generate ozone, and are not desirable for libraries or archives. Removing gaseous pollutants requires adsorbers typically consisting of beds or canisters of activated carbon or activated alumina that is impregnated with an oxidant. Particulate filters are ineffective for gaseous pollutants.

Cleaning the air with filters and adsorbers as it passes through the air handling unit is essential for libraries or archives in polluted regions, but because cleaning equipment is expensive to install and operate, it is equally important to reduce the load of pollutants that the cleaning equipment must remove. In some cases, the load can be reduced by the location of the makeup air intakes; for example, they should be placed on the side of the building away from local pollution sources, such as busy streets or highways. The strategies mentioned in the next section are also essential for effective and economical pollutant control.

Ventilation, Air Circulation, and Pressurization   It is obvious that optimally treated air is only helpful to the degree that it actually reaches every object in the collections, and conversely that untreated air does not reach them. In order to achieve this, the system must be designed to deliver uniformly a constant volume of treated air.

People consume oxygen and emit carbon dioxide, and the supply of oxygen indoors must be replenished to maintain a healthful level. But the smallest amount of outdoor makeup air possible should be introduced into the space; the more air that is recirculated, the less treating, including cleaning, the equipment normally has to do. This requirement precludes *economizer cycles* that are designed to save energy by bringing in 100 percent outside air when outdoor conditions are moderate.

In order to prevent untreated air (as well as insects and small debris) from infiltrating into storage spaces, it is important that slight positive pressure be maintained in them.

Less than Central HVAC Systems

If it is not possible to have a full system, can an optimum environment be achieved? Probably not, but improvements can usually be made. For small and closely confined spaces, "package" HVAC units are available now that can control all the desired parameters, including gaseous air cleaning. Such units have been recommended for small rare-book or archives storerooms.

Conventional window air conditioners provide cooling, some dehumidification, and reduction of indoor pollutant levels compared with what they would be if windows were left open. However, it is important that window units be left on twenty-four hours a day, not turned off when staff goes home! The daily cycling of RH caused by using air conditioners only during working hours may actually cause more deterioration to collections than warmer but more stable conditions.

Portable domestic humidifiers and dehumidifiers can help to control humidity in certain situations, but they have a number of serious limitations that should be taken into account in deciding whether they can actually improve conditions. All too often their only effect is to give the illusion of doing something constructive. First, their capacity must be matched to the task. The extreme case of inadequate capacity is using humidifiers in centrally air-conditioned spaces; the six or so air changes per hour typical in such spaces will simply carry off most of the moisture produced. Second, they require constant maintenance: careful cleaning to avoid problems with dust and pathogens, and frequent filling or emptying as the case may be. Third, because they are likely to reach capacity and shut off at night or on weekends when no one is present to service them, they may cause damaging cycling of relative humidity (assuming that they have the capacity to effect significant change in the first place). Sometimes the problem of filling or emptying can be alleviated by plumbing them to a water source or drain.

If independent air conditioners or humidity control units are used, it is even more important than usual to watch their actual effects through careful environmental monitoring.

Lighting

Three fundamental strategies are available for reduction of light damage to collections: controlling spectral distribution (that is, reducing or eliminating more damaging wavelengths), reducing the intensity of light, and reducing the length of exposure of collections to light. The best way to control light damage to collections is to exclude it. Archives have an advantage over libraries in that archive collections are typically kept in a box or other opaque container, which, of course, is not feasible for general library collections.

In practical terms, by far the most beneficial single tactic for reducing light damage to collections is to avoid windows in collections storage areas. Tinted or reflective window glass can be beneficial where there must be windows in storage areas, but it is important to obtain from the manufacturer curves of total light and UV transmission for solar-control glass because glass that may be effective against solar heat gain is not necessarily as effective in reducing UV transmission.

Solar-control films for existing windows are sometimes recommended, but with these also it is important to examine transmission curves if a false sense of security is to be avoided, and to consider carefully their life expectancy in relation to their initial cost.

In an effort to provide users with exterior views while controlling solar heating effects, architects often specify shades or blinds over windows. Their effectiveness is high and proven *as long as they are closed*. This is the problem, however; people want more light or an unobstructed view and open the blinds. Moreover, it may be too much to expect personnel to be rigorous about closing blinds before leaving at the end of the working day, thus allowing morning sunlight to pour in before anyone is there to close the blinds. Fixed exterior louvers or awnings may overcome this fatal limitation of operable blinds.

Artificial lighting is more easily controllable than natural, by controlling the spectral distribution or by limiting the total dose to which collections are exposed, or both. Conventional incandescent lighting is considered (somewhat arbitrarily) to have suitable spectral distribution (that is, low in UV and blue), but because of its high energy consumption and heat output, it is now rarely specified. Fluorescent lighting may produce damaging levels of UV, but brands and types of tubes vary widely. Low-UV tubes are available, but are expensive.

The most widely used (and a potentially effective) deliberate method of reducing UV from fluorescent lamps is to enclose them in sleeves of UV-absorbing plastic. These may represent a significant investment, however, for a space that has hundreds or thousands of lamps. In addition, the sleeves, whose purpose is not self-evident, may be discarded when the library is relamped, an operation increasingly done by contractors when the facility is closed, so staff members may not even be aware of the loss. Luminaires containing titanium dioxide pigment in their finishes or having polycarbonate lenses emit lower than expected levels of UV, which may obviate the need for UV filtering sleeves.

A subtle potential hazard of UV filtering sleeves is that they create a false sense of security about having eliminated light damage—people forget that visible light is potentially damaging also.

The costs and limitations of relying on UV filtering sleeves strongly suggest that they should be specified only where they can make a real difference. Sleeves may not be needed in stacks where total exposure can be limited by such means as timed switches (a better way of limiting light damage—and saving energy costs also), or in reading rooms unless important materials are exhibited there.

Careful design is important to make lighting functionally effective at relatively low levels.

Energy Conservation versus Collections Conservation

A major preoccupation of facilities managers is energy conservation for cost savings. Many measures taken to reduce energy consumption also help conservation of collections, but others are potentially destructive. The helpful measures, such as better temperature control to avoid wasted heating or cooling and installation of thermal windows, are likely to be evident, while those that are detrimental to collections may not be obvious, especially without a systematic monitoring program carried out by conservation personnel. Detrimental measures include:

Raising chilled water temperature, which can sometimes be done with little apparent effect on space temperatures, but which is likely to reduce the ability to dehumidify

Turning systems off at night or on weekends. Because most air-conditioning is for human comfort, an obvious energy-saving strategy is to allow conditions to drift when people are absent. Collections, of course, are present and deteriorating around the clock.

Designing systems with economizer cycles

Removing or disabling humidifiers

Building and Renovation Planning

For a building or renovation project to meet reasonable conservation goals, both a commitment to conserving the collections and specific technical knowledge about means of achieving it must be present from the beginning of and throughout the planning process.

A carefully planned building or renovation project will begin with a *program*, an extensive document that spells out the functional requirements of the client. Obvious elements in a program document are such things as the space needed for present and projected collections and numbers of seats for users. Environmental requirements suitable to the particular collection, climate, and so on should also be included at this stage, because they will influence the basic character of the building. At the same time, preservation personnel should be thinking about what compromises can be made with the least damage to the collections, because compromises almost invariably have to be made.

As pointed out earlier, no single set of specifications is universally applicable; one cannot simply hand an architect a published standard and say "here, follow this." Even if a particular set of standards is widely agreed upon, climatic, technical, fiscal, or functional constraints will almost always require compromises from the ideal, and it is crucial that informed people be involved throughout the planning process to try to achieve the compromises least detrimental to the collections.

If an institution hopes to achieve a reasonably conservationally sound building, it must not leave the environmental considerations to the design architects and engineers. They have different agendas, and they are not specialists in conservation of collections. Most buildings are residential, commercial, or industrial, and many architects and HVAC engineers have little or no experience with buildings that are to house and protect cultural property, whose requirements are significantly different. Keep in mind that even the majority of libraries are not research libraries for which preservation is a basic part of their mission, and that architects win awards for architectural statements and public spaces, not for conservationally sound book stacks.

It may be helpful to try to find an architect—and certainly an engineer—who has relevant experience, and, because museums are more concerned with preserving cultural property than most libraries, it may be better to find an architect with museum experience rather than school or branch public library experience.

Consultants have a potentially important role in planning library or archives buildings or renovations. A good general library building consultant will have necessary information and planning techniques about many crucial aspects of library buildings, but his or her knowledge about conservation requirements and how to achieve them may be inadequate or out of date. If at all possible, a conservation environment program consultant should be on the planning team.

Operation, Maintenance, and Monitoring

Relations with Facilities Departments

Most libraries and archives are parts of larger organizations, and the department that operates the physical facilities almost always falls on a different branch of the organization chart. Such departments (as, for example, in a university or a state government) have many responsibilities; are under constant pressure to save money, especially on energy; and may have little knowledge of or interest in the special requirements of preservation. In many cases, the library or archive will be able to establish a good working relationship with capable and conscientious facilities people, but constant effort is required, and success will largely depend on the knowledge and credibility of the conservation personnel.

The most common complaints that facilities people deal with are about discomfort, and they often develop defensive mechanisms against such complaints. Thus it is important to educate facilities people to understand that the library or archive is concerned with long-term preservation of a major institutional asset, not just chilly drafts.

At the same time it is imperative that conservation personnel use accurate and credible data in their relations with facilities personnel (see "Monitoring" later in this section); and that conservation personnel understand the capabilities and limitations of existing buildings and systems, so that their demands are realistic and are directed to the appropriate people in the institution. If a building cannot be humidified in winter because it does not have adequate vapor retarders, there is no solution short of major alterations or a new building, which facilities managers cannot effect. If, on the other hand, problems stem from clogged filters or from humidistats that have not been recalibrated, conservation personnel can reasonably press for improved routine maintenance.

Frequently Encountered Problems

Buildings rarely provide the environmental conditions that they were intended to. There are many reasons for this: poor design, poor construction, poor maintenance, poor understanding of original environmental design goals, changing personnel, alterations to the building, or deterioration of systems and equipment. (HVAC equipment is generally assumed to have only a twenty- or thirty-year life expectancy.)

Diagnosis of environmental problems must remain primarily in the hands of facilities personnel or specialist contractors, and a useful diagnostic scheme would require an entire manual. However, it may be worth pointing out a few frequently encountered problems:

> *Disabled humidifiers:* Humidifiers require a high level of maintenance, and when they become too troublesome, facilities personnel are apt to simply disconnect them.

> *Clogged filters:* Rising temperatures in the cooling season and poor air circulation may be caused by filters that have not been changed.

> *Unchanged adsorbers:* There are no immediately obvious consequences from gaseous pollutant systems whose capacity has been exceeded; there is no simple routine monitoring method for pollutants, and recharging adsorber beds is expensive. Thus particular vigilance is required.

> *Uncalibrated sensors:* System controls are only as effective as their sensors, and all sensors drift with time. Recalibration of thermostats, humidistats, and other sensors is the kind of maintenance job that is easily, and all too often, put off.

> *Open doors and windows:* HVAC systems can maintain desired conditions only when air pressures and volumes are kept at their design levels.

> *Unused blinds:* Blinds and drapes can be effective in reducing light damage and solar heat gain, and, in fact, the capacity of an HVAC system may be designed taking blinds into account. Obviously if they are left open, they are not functional.

Monitoring

Humans are relatively insensitive to the environmental factors other than temperature that accelerate the deterioration of records. Thus there is no way really to know how severely detrimental to records environmental conditions are or whether they are within accepted limits except to monitor them with suitable instruments. It is very frequently the case that conditions are far from what they are claimed or assumed to be.

The Monitoring Program It is important that monitoring for preservation environment be carried out by conservation rather than facilities personnel. Conservation of collections is the primary responsibility of conservation personnel; the primary responsibility of facilities personnel is to operate systems as economically as possible. There are techniques, instrumentation, and a body of knowledge about monitoring for collections conservation that conservation personnel are familiar with and that facilities personnel may not be. Moreover, occasionally facilities personnel try to gloss over their ignorance or incompetence; the question conceptually becomes one of the fox watching the chickens.

The issue of independent monitoring is becoming slightly more problematical with the increasing sophistication of HVAC control systems, of which newer installations are usually *direct digital control* (DDC). This means that many aspects of a building's (or sometimes even a group of buildings') mechanical systems are monitored and operated from a computer in the facilities manager's office. Conservation personnel should carefully consider the extent of independent monitoring that is needed in such a building, which should depend upon how well the central system is designed (including whether there are enough sensors to give a good picture of the collections environment), and how close and cooperative the working relationship is between the library or archive and the facilities department. There may be a psychological barrier to undertaking redundant monitoring, but keep in mind that (1) "high-tech" systems are only as good as the people who design and maintain them, and (2) that the primary aim—the hidden agenda, one might say—of such systems and the people who operate them is *energy* conservation, not *collections* conservation.

The unfortunate truth is that *believable, meaningful* environmental monitoring is a fussy and tedious operation. Environmental data must be believable—accurate—because we must normally rely on facilities people to implement our requests, and data that are not accurate and defensible will not only weaken our immediate case but, more seriously, our credibility. Similarly, monitoring must be thought of as a *system*, not just casual, isolated readings, if it is to help in identifying and diagnosing problems.

It is a corollary of this—and a truth that needs to be stated—that a great deal of monitoring data are not worth even the limited amount of effort that goes into collecting them because they are simply inaccurate, or because they do not help to identify causes.

Because of the practical limits on the amount of temperature and humidity data that it is feasible to gather and process, only a small sample of the conditions in all parts of a building can be recorded. It is thus crucial that the monitoring system be carefully designed to provide the most useful information. Recognizing that environmental conditions in a given space within a building will vary with

- time of day,
- season,
- weather conditions,
- which air handling units and zones serve the space,
- condition and settings of mechanical equipment serving the space, and
- nature and amount of use (people present, lights on, equipment running), a useful monitoring program might consist of placing a hygrothermograph or temperature and humidity logger for at least one week in each zone during each season.

The resulting data need to be analyzed in order to show trends and to be able to localize problems and point to causes. A pile of hygrothermograph charts is in itself useless. The obvious way to do this is with a computer, probably using a spreadsheet for extracting, manipulating, and graphing data. With manual systems, entering each day's high and low temperature and RH permits graphing to show trends by location and by season. An obvious advantage of electronic systems is that the data can be fed directly into a computer for analysis.

Monitoring Methods and Equipment   Two fundamental principles of monitoring the environment are important to understand if monitoring is to be worth the effort involved. First, the sensors of most instruments, especially humidity sensors, can be seriously inaccurate, initially or as they age. This means that most such instruments need recalibration against an instrument of known greater accuracy (see figure 5).

Second, except for such parameters as artificial lighting that are relatively constant, individual spot readings are of little value and can indeed be seriously misleading. Temperature and humidity readings taken on a balmy day in May may indicate acceptable conditions, when in fact relative humidity may vary 20% or more per day and 70% or more from season to season. Similarly, readings taken during the working day might be acceptable, but when the HVAC system is turned off at night and on weekends, perhaps even unbeknownst to conservation staff, conditions can seriously deteriorate.

Temperature and Humidity   Many types of equipment monitor temperature and relative humidity, ranging from simple thermometers to sophisticated electronic instruments, and they may be *recording* or *nonrecording*. For most purposes, recording temperature and humidity instruments are essential for getting a useful picture of environmental conditions.

The primary such instrument has been the *hygrothermograph* (see figure 5), which has temperature and humidity sensors connected to pens that draw lines on a paper chart that is attached to a cylinder that

Figure 5
Environmental Monitoring Instruments

Photo courtesy Minnesota Historical Society

Clockwise from top: Hygrothermograph, aspirating psychrometer, UV meter, blue wool fading cards, visible light meter, dial thermohygrometer, cobalt salt humidity cards, electronic humidity meter; *center:* sling psychrometer.

is driven by a wind-up or quartz clock. The instrument thus provides continuous lines on the chart for temperature and humidity for (most commonly) one week. With this kind of record, conditions at night and at other times that the building is closed can be taken into consideration.

Mechanical hygrothermographs are temperamental devices subject to large inaccuracies, which can be caused by jarring (as when the chart is changed or the instrument is moved from one place to another), deterioration of the human hair bundle that is usually used to measure relative humidity, or exposure to pollutants or extremes of humidity. Because of these vulnerabilities, hygrothermographs need to be handled carefully and with some understanding of their pitfalls. They also need periodic maintenance and replacement of the hair bundles, and regular recalibration against a more accurate measuring instrument: Recalibration frequency can be learned only from experience with a particular model of instrument and with the circumstances of its use. You may discover that the instrument stays in calibration for several months, or that it may have to be reset every two or three weeks. *Once again, unless necessary maintenance and recalibration are done, the instruments may be worse than useless because they will give false readings.*

Electronic instruments are gradually gaining over mechanical hygrometers and hygrothermographs. Such equipment has several advantages: readouts are digital and calculations are programmed into a microchip, reducing potential misinterpretation; they are relatively insensitive to vibration and shock; they require much less frequent recalibration; and readings may be downloadable into a computer for analysis. Potential disadvantages are cost (although electronic instruments are tending to become cheaper than manual ones) and a deceptive appearance of precision and accuracy that may discourage needed recalibration. The Achilles' heel of electronic instruments is their humidity sensors; the most common type is easily thrown off by exposure to contamination, and the more rugged one has poor response at low humidities.

There are many types of hygrometers, instruments that measure but do not record relative humidity. The most familiar is the dial hygrometer that can be bought in hardware stores. All such instruments lose accuracy, most have limited accuracy to begin with, and most cannot be recalibrated. Such instruments are worse than useless because they are almost invariably misleading.

A type of humidity instrument that is capable of giving relatively accurate readings is the psychrometer, which consists of a pair of thermometers, one of which has a cotton wick on it. To use, the wick is dampened with distilled water and the psychrometer swung in a circle to obtain rapid air circulation over the wick. When the "wet bulb" temperature has fallen as low as it will go, the wet and dry bulb readings are compared with a chart or slide rule to determine the relative humidity. This "sling" psychrometer is both annoying to use and difficult to obtain accurate readings from. A significant improvement is the "aspirating" psychrometer, which has a battery-operated fan that draws a steady stream of air over the wet and dry thermometer bulbs. Even with this type, there is considerable margin for error when reading the temperatures and converting them into RH, and the cotton wick must be kept meticulously clean.

Electronic hygrometers may be on balance the most satisfactory instruments to use for recalibrating conventional hygrothermographs as long as they are themselves adequately calibrated.

Pollutants   It is doubly unfortunate that no simple way exists to monitor pollutants, especially gaseous pollutants, because there is so little measured experience with the effectiveness of different systems of pollutant removal, and most data on removal systems originate from their manufacturers. Most crucially, there is no easy and obvious way to determine when gaseous pollutant cleaning systems have reached their capacity and need to be replaced.

Instruments for measuring pollutants are not normally feasible for libraries and archives. At least one manufacturer of adsorbents, Purafil, provides a service based on measuring rates of corrosion on polished metal "coupons," but the service is expensive and does not yet represent a generally useful method for routine monitoring.

Light   It is relatively easy to obtain meaningful information about artificial light exposure, because it can be assumed that its level is constant (although in fact there is some change in output of lamps and bulbs as they age). The intensity of daylight, on the other hand, varies with its direction, the time of day, weather conditions, and the season of the year, so that individual spot readings are of little meaning except in that they have been taken at peak times. In this case they may be useful as quantitative evidence that conditions need to be improved.

Relatively simple and inexpensive meters that measure visible light well enough for practical purposes are readily available; many photographers' light meters are also adequate. However, for integrated measurement of daylight—that is, a measure of the total cumulative dose of light to which objects are being exposed—a reasonably well established monitor of a sort is the "blue wool standards," cards containing patches of dyed textiles that fade at a known rate relative to each other. A more quantitative method is the use of a visible light meter that can be hooked up to a computer, but this level of sophistication is probably overkill when it is evident that sunlight is streaming in on collections.

Ultraviolet radiation is more problematical to monitor. There is currently only one practical instrument available, and it has several limitations. It can be dangerously misleading unless it is understood that the meter reads not the total amount of UV energy falling on the object, but the *proportion* of UV in the total amount of light (see the explanation in the section on "Norms and Standards" earlier in this chapter). A meter that measures proportional UV *must* be used in conjunction with visible light level readings.

There is no doubt that providing optimum conservation environment for archives, library, and historical society collections is expensive, but a rapidly growing body of evidence indicates that it is cost-effective in comparison with alternatives for long-term preservation of collections. Newer information media are especially vulnerable to environmental deterioration. Providing optimum environment requires thoughtful, specialized planning from the very earliest conceptual phases of a building or renovation project and throughout the project, as well as careful monitoring and maintenance throughout the life of the building.

Notes

1. In tropical climates, insect infestations and other biological damage may overwhelm chemical deterioration as a cause of the destruction of records, even though the latter will also be accelerated by poor environmental conditions.

2. Note that this is not the same as the almost universally cited statement that increasing the temperature 10°C (sometimes even given as 10°F) will double the rate of deterioration of paper. A specific temperature factor can be given for a single, specific chemical reaction, but the chemical deterioration of each paper involves a number of different chemical reactions, each of which has its own temperature dependency.

3. Chandru J. Shahani, Frank H. Hengemihle, and Norman Weberg, "The Effect of Variations in Relative Humidity on the Accelerated Aging of Paper," in *Historic Textile and Paper Materials II: Conservation and*

Characterization, edited by S. Haig Zeronian and Howard L. Needles, ACS Symposium Series 410 (Washington, D.C.: American Chemical Society, 1989), 63–80.

4. Donald K. Sebera, *Isoperms: An Environmental Management Tool.* (Washington, D.C.: Commission on Preservation and Access, 1994).

5. James M. Reilly, Douglas W. Nishimura, and Edward Zinn, *New Tools for Preservation: Assessing Long-Term Environmental Effects on Library and Archives Collections* (Washington, D.C.: Commission on Preservation and Access, 1995).

6. Steven Puglia, "Cost-benefit Analysis for B/W Acetate: Cool/Cold Storage vs. Duplication," *Abbey Newsletter* 19 (1995): 71–72.

Suggested Readings

General

Appelbaum, Barbara. *Guide to Environmental Protection of Collections.* Madison, Conn.: Sound View Pr., 1991.

Harris, Carolyn L., and Paul N. Banks. "The Library Environment and the Preservation of Library Materials." *Facilities Manager* 6, no. 3 (1990): 21–25.

Lull, William P., with the assistance of Paul N. Banks. *Conservation Environment Guidelines for Libraries and Archives.* Albany: New York State Library, 1991. (A revised edition is in progress.)

Thomson, Garry. *The Museum Environment.* 2d ed. London: Butterworths, in association with the International Institute for Conservation of Historic and Artistic Works, 1986.

Library Buildings and Systems

Cullison, Bonnie Jo. "The Ideal Preservation Building." *American Libraries* 15 (1984): 703.

Hilberry, John D. "What Architects Need to Know, and Don't Want to Hear." *Museum News* 61, no. 5 (1983): 54–61.

Rohlf, Robert H. "Library Design: What Not to Do." *American Libraries* 17 (1986): 100–104.

Stuebing, Lawrence D. "Climate Control: Architectural, Mechanical, and Electrical System Requirements." In APPA, The Association of Higher Education Facilities Officers, *Preservation of Library and Archival Materials*, 29–39. Alexandria, Va.: APPA, 1991.

Monitoring the Environment

Brown, Jonathan P. "Hygrometric Measurement in Museums: Calibration, Accuracy, and the Specification of Relative Humidity." In *Preventive Conservation: Practice, Theory and Research*, edited by Ashok Roy and Perry Smith, 39–43. Preprints of the Contributions to the Ottawa Congress, 12–16 September 1994. London: International Institute for Conservation of Historic and Artistic Works, 1994.

Lafontaine, Raymond H. *Recommended Environmental Monitors for Museums, Archives and Art Galleries.* Canadian Conservation Institute Technical Bulletin, no. 3. Ottawa: Canadian Conservation Institute, 1975.

Saunders, David. "Environmental Monitoring: An Expensive Luxury?" In Scottish Society for Conservation and Restoration and The Museums Association, *Environmental Monitoring and Control*, 1–15. [Edinburgh?]: SSCR, 1989.

Reference Works and Manuals

American Society of Heating, Refrigerating, and Air-Conditioning Engineers. *ASHRAE Handbook: Fundamentals. ASHRAE Handbook: Applications. ASHRAE Handbook: Equipment. ASHRAE Handbook: Systems.* Atlanta: ASHRAE, various dates. (Each volume is reissued every four years.)

Leighton, Philip D., and David Weber. *Planning Academic and Research Library Buildings.* 3d ed. Chicago: ALA, 2000.

Cost/Benefit Studies

Calmes, Alan, Ralph Schofer, and Keith Eberhardt. *National Archives and Records Service (NARS) Twenty-Year Preservation Plan.* NBSIR 85-2999. Washington, D.C.: National Bureau of Standards, 1985.

Hayes, Robert M. The Magnitude, Costs, and Benefits of the Preservation of Brittle Books. Report #0 on the Preservation Project. Washington, D.C.: Council on Library Resources, 1987.

8

Collections and Stack Management

DUANE A. WATSON

This chapter examines and defines collections and stack management and the role and responsibilities of the staff member or members in charge of these areas. *Collections management* is broadly defined to include all storage and access areas and activities that play a part in safely maintaining an item in good condition from the time it arrives in the institution until it is deaccessioned. The goal of collections management is to create an environment in which a balance is maintained between access today and access in the future.

It is important from the outset to distinguish collections management from both the collection development units that build collections in a library and the collection conservation units that treat materials. Collections management is the establishment of institutional policies addressing the needs of the collections by providing a safe, secure, and environmentally stable space for library and archival collections; assuring that materials in diverse formats are properly housed and shelved; training staff and patrons to handle, use, and store materials with care and sensitivity; supervising the maintenance and retrieval of materials; and monitoring any activity or event that may place the collection at risk.

Managing the Collections

The staff member who is responsible for the active care, handling, and protection of the collections from the time an item arrives in the stack area until it is withdrawn from the collection may or may not have the official title of collections manager, but he or she is certainly performing the collections management function. In open-stack libraries the head of access services, circulation, or public service is often responsible for the stacks though daily responsibility may be delegated to a member of the staff who reports to the head. Collection management is a shared responsibility in many institutions, especially those in which collections circulate. Management of the spaces in which collections are housed and accessed has traditionally been a shared responsibility. Also, in a wide variety of libraries responsibility for the "stock" may not be limited to the stack or storage facility. It may include materials housed and used in public access areas; off-site storage facilities; packing and shipping units for interlibrary and exhibition loan; book drops; and book conveyance systems such as book trucks, elevators, or other devices utilized in the movement of library materials.

Given the Herculean nature of overseeing the range of areas described above, shared responsibility is a necessary and practical approach. The collections manager, frequently a nonprofessional staff member, oversees the maintenance of the stacks, shelving, shifting, and retrieval, and trains the staff who assist in these tasks. Public service staff respond to patron requests and the return of materials to the shelves, and supervise the use of reference collections in reading rooms. In small research libraries and special collections with limited patron access, the professional librarians and nonprofessional staff often assume many of the responsibilities mentioned above because of limited staff or to maintain tighter security. Often there is little supervision of materials outside the stacks and public service areas, thus increasing the opportunity for damage or loss.

Institutional Policy

How the role of collections manager is viewed by the library or archives administration, staff, patrons, and the collections manager herself or himself depends on the philosophy of the institution and the policies it establishes. If the acquisition and retention policy—in short, the view of the collection—is that the items are expendable, the collections manager's task differs significantly from that in which a policy establishes that all acquisitions are made for retention in perpetuity. It is the definition of the role of the collection that guides the collections manager in preservation decision making. Inexpensive, short-term treatments that assure immediate access for a given length of time become appropriate decisions for some collections. A clearly defined and articulated policy is essential if time, staff, and money are to be used efficiently and effectively. Repair, rebinding, reformatting, rehousing, and replacement—essential actions to be taken with collections with long-term research value—may be unnecessary or vastly limited in a collection with a shorter shelf life.

An institution's policy regarding the anticipated longevity or useful life of its collection will aid the collections manager in planning a strategy for care and housing. A simple example is the book drop. Preservation administrators, conservators, and circulation librarians are aware of the damage these devices cause. In many libraries, book drops are freestanding metal containers much like postal drops, located outside the library or repository building to permit one to return a book or other item when the building is closed. Other institutions utilize a model that is inside a building but provides a door or slot for deposit. The items deposited may fall some distance to the bottom of the container or on top of previously deposited items. Some drops have a spring-loaded platform that is lowered by the weight of the books. This provides some protection by reducing the distance of the item's fall. Fragile materials are recognizably vulnerable and may suffer damage on the first drop. Newer, stronger items are jarred, dented, and abraded, weakening them and reducing their useful life. Should the returned item survive its fall and the effects of the other materials that fall upon it, it may be subject to uncontrolled temperature and humidity as well as the "joke" deposit—food, drink, carrion, a bomb, a firecracker, or an incendiary device—almost anything the human imagination can fit into the drop.

If book drops are as bad as this account purports, why, in the name of sane librarianship, are they tolerated? At this point we return to "policy" for our answer. If a collection is heavily circulated and highly in demand, and it is essential that the materials be returned promptly for others to use, a means of easy, economical return any time of day is important. Students use materials at all hours of the day and night. Their personal schedules and those of building service hours may not be compatible. So, the compromise is wear, tear, and possible loss for expendable materials or increased service time. Budgets have an immediacy about them and few are ample enough to provide twenty-four-hour service seven days a week.

Replacement of damaged materials is often impossible and likely to be costly. Addressing the problem of replacement of damaged materials requires planning and a policy that takes into consideration the expediency of using book drops, the cost and availability of replacement copies, and the inherent risk of damage to irreplaceable materials. The institution and the collections manager need to understand this and decide how they will address the problem. There is no doubt, however, that unless expendable material can be separated from items considered of long-term significance—a difficult, sometimes impossible task—book drops are to be avoided and policies established. The book drop is but one example of the necessity of policy when making practical, cost-effective preservation decisions. Security is another.

Security

Security is everyone's responsibility and should be so reflected in a security policy document. From the preservation viewpoint, security should aim toward maintaining the physical integrity of an item as well as assuring that it remains physically a part of the collection. To this end, vigilance by all staff is necessary to reduce vandalism—mutilation, page removal—and theft. Many security systems require the insertion of a detection strip in the spine of the book, between pages, or disguised in or under a bookplate. The process of sensitizing the books and materials endangers the binding structure, the adhesives may cause staining, and inserting the devices is both labor-intensive and expensive. Many titles are available from library book vendors with sensitizing devices already inserted. Some vandalism may also occur after the books are sensitized, when curious patrons try to discover the strips or remove them. It is important to know the risks, the advantages and disadvantages, and the nature of the collection, and to have an institutional policy. The decision for circulating collections may well be to go ahead with the security devices, the potential damage from them being outweighed by the reduction in loss.

The collections manager is concerned with every aspect of the security of the items in the stacks, storage facilities, reading rooms, and, to the extent possible, the work areas and offices in the institution. Security includes protecting the collection from theft, vandalism, endangerment by use, and damage or destruction from human-made or natural disaster. Preventing damage or breach of security of the collection, like so much of the collections manager's responsibility, involves working closely with others in the institution—security officers, fire officials, building maintenance and management, the personnel office, and all staff members who interact with the collection. Security issues are a vital part of the collection care and handling training program and should be coordinated with other security programs in the institution.

Processing Materials

If library and records materials are to be effectively managed, where and when should the process begin? To answer this question, it is useful first to trace the movement of a new acquisition through the system to its storage space and then consider how its storage and access may negatively or positively affect its useful life.

Library and archival materials arrive in different ways at various entry points in an institution. Standard orders of new stock are usually delivered by truck to a mail or receiving room, where they are sorted (and sometimes unpacked) and sent on to the acquisitions department or individual curators, bibliographers, or acquisitions librarians. Acquisitions staff may open the packing containers, log in receipts, and send the materials to individuals for examination and review or to an area where new receipts are temporarily shelved until the review and processing procedures are completed. Individuals may receive and open packages and provide temporary storage in offices and work areas. Special materials and gifts may appear at any time in any form of packaging and in any area of the institution, from the president's office to the back or front step. There is obviously no control over the unanticipated, but procedures for handling both expected and unexpected materials are necessary to assure that they receive careful handling and safe storage.

Assuming that the materials have arrived unscathed from their senders because, or in spite, of their packaging and transporting medium, and have further received good care in the shipping room and institutional distribution and unpacking system, the items enter the bibliographic arena for their baptismal rites. Processing an item, from the logging-in procedure in the acquisitions unit through review, cataloging, stamping, labeling, and shelving, is a rite of passage that is fraught with opportunities for physical damage ranging from torn pages and broken, marred, and weakened hinges and covers to soiled pages, defacement from property stamps or labels, and bumps and falls during transport. Materials sent to offices or other work spaces for review by curators, bibliographers, or other staff are confronted with other dangers, such as food and beverages, light, heat, water, even pets.

When the review and processing procedures are complete, the item is taken to its shelving area in the stacks, reading area, or other access point. During this process the item is handled, placed on a book truck, perhaps taken to another floor by elevator, and eventually shelved until it is requested for use. Or, it may be among those materials slated for shifting or off-site storage, all activities that present potential risks for library and archival materials. Processed, cataloged, and stored, the item is now available for patrons.

Access

The term *preservation and access* has become a rallying cry for libraries and archives in their quest for federal, state, corporate, and private funding. Although there is much talk about this union, institutional philosophy and the policies that govern its actions in fact show a disparity between "preservation" and "access." This should come as no surprise to anyone with a degree in library or information science or anyone who has worked in an archives or records center. As Paul N. Banks has noted, "the library profession, and its clients, are so imbued with the principle of immediate service—indeed service is the first tenet of the American Library Association code of ethics—that the idea of further sequestering some classes of collections is repugnant, regardless of the long-term consequences of unrestricted or inadequately restricted use."[1]

In order to present this issue fairly, we must look at the "access" services provided and again consider policy. The public services department is the first area to examine when determining an institution's preservation and access policy. The circulation staff in a library or archive, whether servicing items used in-house only or circulated outside, has more contact with individual items and their patrons than any other institutional staff. The attitudes, training, and example of these staff members have a greater and more immediate impact on patrons and the collection than most, if not all, preservation and collections management staff. The importance of their role cannot be overestimated in identifying preservation needs, providing proper handling and care both at the desk and in retrieval, instructing patrons, advising on use patterns that influence preservation decision making, and assessing the vulnerability of material requested.

Access staff are the interface with the institution's constituents— those for whom the professional principles demand service and for whom collections are presumably built. Circulation staff not only provide patrons with materials across the circulation desk, they also make interlibrary loans, use materials to meet fee-based service requests, and, in academic libraries, respond to the demands of the faculty. Addressing these requests requires an understanding of the physical nature of books and other types of materials, which collections managers are taught if trained by preservation or conservation staff. Public service training, however, is often far removed from preservation education, and thus public service staff are forced to make decisions based on little or no knowledge or understanding of the potential harm caused by uninformed access decisions.

The access process in closed-stack libraries generally works like this: A page or staff member receives a patron request and retrieves the item from storage, one hopes with care. The item is carried by hand, book truck, or conveyor to the reading area where it may be subjected to the checkout process, photocopying, patron handling, book drop return, the check-in process, and travel through and outside the library space. A request for an item located in an off-site storage facility is subject to the additional risk of multiple handling and transport. A frequently requested item may repeat this process monthly, weekly, even daily.

In open-stack libraries, access is much more direct. The patron removes the book from the shelf, whereupon the book is subjected to the same processes and risks as in a closed-stack collection. However, because of less handling control in the stack area, open-stack libraries must depend on vigilant staff, education of patrons, and the example of good housekeeping and good staff role models for collection care and protection. Developing a concern for the collection through patron education and a means of timely response to the needs of endangered materials, especially those identified by patrons, is essential. Care of the collections must become a partnership between the patrons and the staff.

How can the safety of library and archival materials be assured in an environment in which responsibility is shared and items must pass through many hands and spaces, a necessary but risky process, before they are safely housed and available for access? The answer lies in clearly established and articulated institutional policy and preservation education and training for all staff and patrons.

Education and Training

Education and training in collections care and management are essential to the preservation of a library or archival collection. Planning and coordinating an education and training program is the responsibility of the preservation officer or staff member in charge of the care and preservation of the collections. Three key groups need education and training: the professional staff, including public and technical services librarians, curators, bibliographers, and administrators; the shipping or mail room, acquisitions, processing, circulation desk, paging, and all stack maintenance personnel; and the patrons.

The collections manager, whether responsible for all areas where collections are housed and used or just for stack areas, is a key figure in an institutional education program. An educated collections manager is familiar with preservation and access issues and knows how and when to solicit the aid and advice of preservation and access professionals on staff. A knowledgeable collections manager knows how to address the needs of patrons and assure the longevity of the collection. This requires not only an understanding of preservation issues and the needs of patrons but also an ability to work with a variety of professional and nonprofessional library staff as well as building maintenance and security personnel. A successful education program is more likely if the collections manager understands the institutional mission as well as the needs, concerns, and responsibilities of the staff and patrons; they in turn understand that preservation education and training is clearly part of the collections manager's responsibility. The education and training program is strengthened by staff understanding of its importance and of who is responsible, and by the collections manager's ability to work with staff in all areas of the institution.

An ongoing training program for new and part-time staff and regular review and updating sessions for others are necessary to maintain preservation awareness and a cooperative and coordinated approach to the care and handling of the collections. Increasing staff interest, knowledge, and involvement in protecting the items they work with is well worth the time and effort expended in creating and maintaining a well-planned institutional education and training program.

Many of the following issues are discussed in greater detail in other chapters of this book, but all are important considerations for successful collections management.

Environment

The environment in storage areas is crucial to the preservation of the collection. Collections managers must be knowledgeable about the importance of maintaining an environment in which temperature and relative humidity fluctuations are controlled. Environmental monitoring may or may not be the responsibility of the collections manager, but if it is, training in the calibration and reading of hygrothermographs, data loggers, and other monitoring devices is essential as is the maintenance of records and statistics. If monitoring is the responsibility of another unit, an understanding of the process, the equipment, and the monitoring schedule along with a cooperative working relationship with staff in the responsible unit provides an additional safeguard for the collection. Awareness of changing conditions and immediate reporting prevent unsafe situations from arising. Collections managers need to be aware of air pollution, conditions fostering mold and mildew growth, pest infestations, and the deleterious effect of sunlight and unfiltered fluorescent lighting. In many cases an understanding of the phenomena and an awareness of who is responsible is sufficient; in others the collections manager is the person who monitors conditions and works with plant managers and maintenance staff to provide a stable environment for the collection. Vigilance on the part of the collections manager alone is not enough; all staff need to be trained to observe and report potential and existing environmental risks to the collections manager or the preservation officer.

Housekeeping

Housekeeping is a basic task, which may fall, like environmental monitoring, under the purview of the collections manager but be carried out in part by the institutional maintenance staff. It is the collections manager's responsibility to work with the maintenance staff on regular cleaning schedules and procedures that are safe for the collection. If floors are mopped, materials must be shelved high enough above the floor to ensure that items on the lowest shelves are not in the way of mops and thus subject to water damage or stains on their bindings. Whether or not a program of regular vacuuming and shelf cleaning is a responsibility of the collections maintenance unit, the preservation office, or the building maintenance staff, the collections manager is well advised to take an active role in any cleaning projects. The procedures and equipment used and the training given staff are issues that must be carefully addressed to assure the safety of the materials being cleaned.

Three collections maintenance activities that can have a significant impact on the preservation of a collection are care and handling, shifting, and shelving. Each of these activities maintains order and accessibility and each is potentially damaging to the collection unless collections maintenance staff are trained and supervised.

Shelving and Transporting Library Materials

Library materials usually consist of various types of paper, some in bound formats, others in folders or housings of many kinds and sizes. Materials may be strong and flexible or brittle and fragile, rare or common, intact or in pieces. The collections maintenance staff is charged with the shelving and safekeeping of these materials. How staff members handle, shelve, and move materials determines the shelf life of the items.

Staff must be trained in safe handling techniques, including the necessity for clean hands, how to remove a book from the shelf (push the books on either side back enough to grasp the desired book on each side before removing it; tip tightly packed books forward using the index finger on the top edge, not the head cap), and the use of sturdy bookends of a size proportional to the book being supported and wide enough to prevent the book from damage by being pushed onto it. Patrons should be made aware of the correct way to remove a book from the shelf through posters and information sheets. Shelvers and paging staff need to adjust and support books as they reshelve or retrieve materials. Proper support is essential to a well-maintained collection. Appropriate shelving requirements and the problems involved in handling special and oversized materials should be addressed in the staff training program.

Training in safely transporting materials by hand, book truck, book lift, or elevator is equally important for all staff. Even a short drop is harmful to all library materials and may cause total loss of a fragile item. Stack staff, as well as any contract movers, should be well trained in handling materials, loading them on trucks and transporting devices, and maneuvering these vehicles down aisles, and into and out of elevators and transporting vehicles. Materials to be transported to other locations in a building, including interlibrary loans, are safer if placed in a protective enclosure. A comprehensive care and handling program that includes mail service staff is wise and necessary.

The circulation desk and the reading room are areas where materials are constantly handled, and the circulation and professional staff need training in care and handling. Checkout and check-in procedures and temporary shelving methods and procedures should be designed to assure that materials are not endangered in the public service process. If checkout or check-in procedures involve stamping or the use of "light pens," improper handling may put the item at risk.

Patrons are positively influenced by staff who set a good example in their handling and protection of the collection. Book cradles, gloves, and book snakes (soft cloth tubes filled with pellets that hold a book open without damage) are necessary and appropriate for safe use of rare books and bound manuscripts and should be readily available. Pencils should be required for note taking in archives and special collections reading rooms, and readers should be shown how to handle fragile items. Oversized materials require adequate space and support, and patrons often need assistance to use them safely. Clear and conspicuous instructions and signage and a well-trained staff alert and willing to assist readers reduce risk to the collection.

Several audiovisual programs are available that clearly illustrate care and handling procedures. These programs are useful for staff and patron education. Illustrative signs, bookmarks, brochures, and informative exhibits as well as announcements and articles in institutional publications are also positive means of educating and heightening awareness. A screen on the online public access catalog with a message about care and handling and preservation is another venue for increasing patron awareness.

Staff offices and work spaces are final areas in which care and handling are of great concern. Mail room and shipping staff play a crucial role in the safety of library and archival materials. They need to be included in a training program and made aware of their important part in preserving the collection. The issue is more delicate when one is faced with changing the habits and procedures of professional staff, including directors and high-level administrators; curators; bibliographers; and acquisitions, technical services, and reference librarians. The success of a program in care and handling for staff at all levels will depend in large part on a sensitively planned approach that considers varied needs and concerns, support from the director, and an energetic, informed collections manager working closely with a preservation officer, conservator, or both.

Photoduplication

Photocopying and other photoduplication services are needed by staff and expected by patrons in most libraries and archives. Even with the least-damaging machines and staff trained to use them, photocopying endangers bound materials. The best that can be done, however, is to provide the best machines available within one's budget, to train staff to use them with care, and to provide mediated copying for patrons. In addition, staff and patrons must be aware that some materials will not survive even one copying. Identification of these materials and the decision to deny copying must lie with staff trained in recognizing endangered items. The collections manager, preservation officer, and conservator must serve as the trainers, and the administration must understand and support the staff who make the copying determination.

The reality, however, is that few institutions are able to provide mediated copying or the kind of supervision necessary to protect fragile general collections. Education and "collection friendly" equipment are the best preservation measures one can hope for.

Food and Drink

Although food and drink should have no place in areas where collections are housed or used, including offices and work spaces, prohibition is often effective only in archives and special collections reading rooms that are under more or less continuous staff surveillance. The nearly insurmountable problem of effective enforcement appears to be leading some general academic libraries to abandon the effort altogether. In fact, libraries are beginning to include coffee bars and small cafes in the library, perhaps in part on the theory that providing a place within the building where food is allowed will make enforcement of food and beverage prohibitions in other parts of the library easier. The understanding, in many but not all cases, is that library materials may be used in these areas. Although there is concern about pests being drawn by crumbs and spills, these risks can be reduced by good cleaning and maintenance.

Reading rooms, especially those in special collections and archives, are often the most attractive spaces available for group programs. Collection development officers, publicity staff, and administrators who must raise funds and cultivate prospective donors often present compelling reasons for serving food and drink in rooms that collections managers and preservation administrators consider sacrosanct. If no other spaces are available and financial reality overrules strict adherence to preservation ideals, the risks inherent in using these spaces may be reduced in part by controlling the type of food and drink served, by providing supervision of catering staff, and by cleaning the room immediately after the event. A compromise that involves minimal risk to the collections and that results in additional funds for their care and protection is worth careful consideration.

Disaster Preparedness and Recovery

Collections managers must be active participants in institutional disaster preparedness and recovery planning. They have responsibility for and knowledge about the collections and the spaces in which they are housed that is unavailable to most of the staff. If collections managers do not have training in disaster preparedness and recovery, they should be among the first to receive it. It is not necessary for the collections manager to be the coordinator, especially if a conservator or preservation administrator is on staff, but involvement in planning, training, and participation on the recovery team is essential.

Conclusion

Is it possible for a collections manager to know and do all the tasks outlined in this chapter? To a certain degree, the answer is yes. The qualifier is, of course, the level of effectiveness with which one person can realistically meet all the expectations set for this position. In the short term, it is more important to heighten awareness among staff and patrons; establish administratively supported policies, procedures, and routines that are conducive to good care, handling, and security of the collections; and to build a unified, cohesive, and collegial approach to addressing the needs of the collections and those who serve and use them.

Note

1. Paul N. Banks, "Preservation, Library Collections and the Concept of Cultural Property," in *Libraries and Scholarly Communication in the United States,* edited by Phyllis Dain and John Y. Cole (New York: Greenwood, 1990), 107.

Selected Readings

Columbia University Libraries. *Murder in the Stacks.* Videotape. New York: Columbia University, 1987.

Drewes, Jeanne M., and Julia A. Page, eds. *Promoting Preservation Awareness in Libraries: A Sourcebook for Academic, Public, School and Special Collections.* New York: Greenwood, 1997.

Feather, John. *Preservation and the Management of Library Collections.* London: The Library Association, 1996.

Foot, Mirjam. "Housing Your Collections: Environment and Storage for Libraries and Archives." *ILA Journal* 22 (1996): 364–365.

Harvey, Ross. *Preservation in Libraries: A Reader.* London: Bowker-Saur, 1993.

———. *Preservation in Libraries: Principles, Strategies and Practices for Librarians.* London: Bowker-Saur, 1993.

Hubbard, William J. *Stack Management: A Practical Guide to Shelving and Maintaining Library Collections.* Chicago: ALA, 1981.

Kohl, David F. *Circulation, Interlibrary Loan, Patron Use, and Collection Maintenance: A Handbook for Library Management.* Santa Barbara, Calif.: ABC-Clio, 1985.

Library of Congress. National Preservation Program Office. *Handling Books in General Collections.* Slide-tape presentation. Washington, D.C.: Library of Congress, 1984.

Ogden, Sherelyn, ed. *Preservation of Library and Archival Materials: A Manual.* Rev. ed. Andover, Mass.: Northeast Document Conservation Center, 1994.

Wells, Marianna S., and Rosemary Young. *Moving and Reorganizing a Library.* New York: Gower, 1997.

9

Preservation Management: Emergency Preparedness

SALLY A. BUCHANAN

Emergency preparedness is a component of preservation management that is often overlooked by librarians and archivists. Perhaps emergencies to collections are seen as unlikely or the recovery too difficult. Insurance companies, however, have long recognized the necessity for sound risk management and have encouraged cultural institutions to include such planning as part of their overall asset management. It is now an indisputable fact that sound emergency planning can prevent true disaster or ensure a cost-effective and timely recovery if collections are affected.

Collections in libraries and archives are especially vulnerable to damage caused by exposure to water, fire, environmental extremes, and infestations of mold and insects. Without intervention, this exposure can result in a disaster. More positively, hazards can be avoided and damage mitigated by a staff familiar with a comprehensive emergency preparedness plan.

Recovery from an emergency that could have been avoided altogether, or at the least responded to more competently, can often be nearly impossible. Even if funds can be found, many collections cannot be replaced because they are unique or are no longer published. Others are physically damaged to an extent that requires sophisticated and very costly intervention. Collections of note may never be restored to their former breadth and depth. Resources that could have been used in more positive ways must be channeled into recovery efforts. Access and service are disrupted. Public relations suffer.

Weather around the globe over the past decade has been extreme, resulting in hurricanes, floods, earthquakes, and fires. Political conflicts have caused the total destruction of libraries and museums. Concerned cultural organizations have collected sad statistics on the loss related to disasters. It is not clear whether there have been more disasters worldwide, or whether documentation and communication simply are improved. At any rate, the subsequent reduction in access to information and service for scholars and the public has been significant. The cost has been staggering. The American Library Association (ALA), UNESCO, the International Federation of Library Associations and Institutions (IFLA), and the International Council of Museums (ICOM), as organizations, are trying to educate members about the wisdom of emergency planning and preparedness.

Increasing numbers of professional librarians and archivists acknowledge the practical necessity for risk management. They are aware of the many case studies that document how small emergencies can be managed without damage to collections while even more serious ones can be resolved in a cost-effective, positive response. All that is necessary is a willingness to undertake onetime comprehensive and systematic planning and, once completed, a periodic review of the resulting document.

In the past twenty years, a great deal of research has been undertaken to improve recovery of a variety of library and archival media, including print, magnetic, photographic, and electronic, from exposure to emergency conditions. The result is numbers of publications, interactive computer programs, technical leaflets, and scientific papers devoted to successful emergency management and recovery methods. Included are steps to follow for writing an emergency plan, for responding to an emergency, and for choosing the best recovery methods. The Suggested Readings at the end of this chapter include only a small selection of these resources.

Emergency preparedness is simply another sensible action to undertake in library and archival asset management. The following are considerations for a planning process that will result in a comprehensive and usable collection emergency plan.

Organizing the Process

To be effective, emergency planning should be undertaken within the framework of the institution's goals, policies, and priorities. Staff, financial resources, politics, and any larger context, like a city government, within which the library or archive might exist need to be considered carefully. The completed plan must be not only specific, but also realistic and practical so it can be implemented if necessary. Therefore, the selection of the person responsible for the planning is crucial. That person must have enough management experience to understand all the implications of a planning process and to be objective enough to find creative solutions to the challenges that will inevitably arise.

Organizational administrators must also be committed to the concept of emergency management and planning and be prepared to support the planning process and its leadership with the necessary time and resources. Nothing is more deadly to staff commitment and morale than an organization in which large amounts of time are expended in good faith only to have the results ignored or overruled.

Once planning leadership and staff are named, reasonable project goals and a time frame can be negotiated. Administrators should make it clear within the organization that the planning process is part of a larger (named) goal and that cooperation at all levels will be appreciated and expected. Sound communication channels need to be established and clarified if necessary, and any secretarial or support staff assigned to help speed the process.

Understanding Priorities

The development of an emergency plan is less time-consuming, and the resulting document is more specific, if the committee can work with a collections management plan for the library or archives. Such a plan will contain clearly identified priorities and goals for obtaining, cataloging, establishing provenance, accessing, deselecting, and preserving overall collections. Knowing how materials are used, and by whom, and how this relates to the mission and goals of the institution, will assist emergency planners in setting realistic response and recovery guidelines that are sensible and acceptable to all members of the staff and the administration. In the event of an emergency, there will then be no need for "heroic" and costly attempts to salvage badly damaged materials if they are a low priority or can be replaced by another format acceptable to all.

Collection development and public services staff must be consulted at this stage of the planning process for they best understand questions related to collection priorities and use, both present and expected.

Identifying Risks

A well-managed emergency preparedness committee will take into consideration all the realistic risks to which a particular building and collection may be exposed. Asking experts to help assess building hazards, like fire potential or leaking roofs, is sensible. In addition, the committee will want to think about potential hazards related to circulation, rare and unique collections, and external challenges, such as the likelihood of severe weather or of flooding. Mechanical and electrical systems, fire prevention equipment or the lack of it, and other internal problems that may jeopardize collections must be taken into consideration as well. In some parts of the world, there are concerns about mold or insect infestations. Some librarians and archivists must think about war or terrorist attack. Although many hazards cannot be prevented, certainly the odds can be considered and plans made to counteract possible damage if the unthinkable should occur. The committee should balance concern with common sense, sometimes a hard assignment.

Guiding the Process

It is the job of the chairperson to guide the planning process to a successful conclusion. This often involves some deft management, allowing everyone to participate and communicate while keeping the goals and schedule in mind. Making use of available time and talent takes skill and a sense of humor. Organizing carefully even before committee members are chosen will provide a framework for everyone to gauge progress. Communication should be a high priority, with members of the committee representing significant management areas of the institution, including support and facilities staff.

Generally, members of the planning committee will need to be educated about emergency preparedness before they can help write an emergency plan suitable for a particular institution. This can be accomplished fairly easily by assigning reading from a selected bibliography and attending a workshop given by an outside expert. The workshop should not be about how to write a plan—that is the chair's job—but instead about what an excellent plan should contain. A workshop should also include instruction on what to expect in an emergency response and recovery operation. Many library and archival regional and professional organizations offer workshops periodically.

The administration of the organization must be kept informed with brief reports on progress. And they must be consulted if problems or uncertainties arise. Although the process sometimes can be confusing, it is often rewarding, as accomplishments become apparent. It is the chair's job to clarify progress and encourage members of the committee. If the institution is a large one, committee members may find that working in smaller task forces hastens things along, but meetings of the whole are important to avoid losing sight of the goal and of significant gains.

The chair can also often bring helpful insights related to other areas of the organization. For instance, apparent lack of cooperation from collection development staff may be because they are preparing a major exhibition. Sharing this information will prevent hard feelings from cropping up. Maintaining objectivity is essential in such an undertaking as emergency preparedness planning because it often calls into question practices that must be reconsidered or changed. The chair should expect this and be prepared to discuss and compromise when necessary.

Completing the Planning Process

As various components of a disaster preparedness plan are nearing completion, it is the chair's job to work with the various staff or task forces, analyzing the recommendations, asking critical questions, and filling in gaps. Are resources identified? Would even a volunteer be able to understand and use the plan? Is the plan useful and sensible? The chair must eventually write an introduction to the use of the plan as well as any transitions that are required between sections so the finished document is complete and comprehensible. It is the responsibility of the chair to ensure that the emergency plan is as foolproof and usable as possible. This may mean asking other experts to read it and respond as well as circulating the draft to selected staff within the organization.

Other critical management decisions concern implementing the completed emergency plan. Who will be responsible for training staff to use it? Should there be an emergency response team? If so, how will team members be chosen and trained? How are communication channels set up to be fail-safe if, for instance, an emergency happens on a holiday or when only facilities staff are in the building, or volunteers? The committee can raise a number of sensible questions to test their plan. Clarifying these issues ahead of time can mean saving hours of precious time in the event of an emergency.

Testing the Results

There is no better way to test a completed emergency plan than to stage a simulated disaster. The inevitable lapses will become apparent and can be assessed and guidelines or recommendations revised. Communication gaps can be repaired. The disaster response team will gain self-confidence. The rest of the staff will be educated and better prepared. Most positive of all will be the assurance that the collections will be as physically safe as the committee could realistically manage.

Conclusion

Emergency preparedness planning can be successful if care is taken to organize the process from its inception. Choosing a chairperson who is familiar with the planning process and who understands the need for open communication will ensure not only a thoughtful emergency plan, but also a process in which participants have learned a broad spectrum of skills. The planning committee and its chair, as a team, will feel a sense of accomplishment for a critical management task completed and implemented. The organization will benefit both tangibly and intangibly.

Suggested Readings

Association for Information and Image Management. *Disaster Recovery Planning and Resources for Records Managers and Librarians.* Silver Spring, Md.: AIIM, 1991.

Barton, John P., and Johanna G. Wellheiser, eds. *An Ounce of Prevention: A Handbook on Disaster Contingency Planning for Archives, Libraries and Record Centres.* Toronto: Toronto Area Archivists Group Education Foundation, 1985.

Buchanan, Sally A. *Disaster Planning: Preparedness and Recovery for Libraries and Archives.* RAMP Study. Paris: UNESCO, 1988.

Chartrand, R. L. "Emergency Preparedness and Response Challenges for Special Libraries." In *Geographic Information Systems and Libraries, Patrons, Maps, and Spatial Information.* Urbana-Champaign: University of Illinois Graduate School of Library and Information Science, 1996.

Eulenberg, Julia Niebuhr. *Handbook for the Recovery of Water Damaged Business Records.* Prairie Village, Kans.: Association of Records Managers and Administrators, 1986.

Fortson, Judith. *Disaster Planning and Recovery: A How-to-Do-It Manual for Librarians and Archivists.* New York: Neal-Schuman, 1992.

Illinois School Library Media Association. *School Library Media Center Disaster Response Plan Handbook.* [Canton, Ill.]: ISLMA, 1994.

Joseph, G. W., and G. W. Couturier. "Essential Management Activities to Support Effective Disaster Planning." *International Journal of Information Management* 13 (October 1993): 315–325.

Lee, Mary Wood. *Treatment of Mold in Library Collections with an Emphasis on Tropical Prevention and Climates.* RAMP Study. Paris: UNESCO, 1988.

Ogden, Sherelyn. "Emergency Management." In *Preservation of Library and Archival Materials: A Manual,* edited by Sherelyn Odgen. Andover, Mass.: Northeast Document Conservation Center, 1994.

Parker, Thomas A. "Integrated Pest Management for Libraries." In *Preservation of Library Materials,* edited by Merrily A. Smith, 2:103–123. Munich: K. G. Saur Verlag, 1987. (IFLA Publications 40, 41)

Smith, Richard D. "Disaster Recovery: Problems and Procedures." *IFLA Journal* 18 (1992): 13–24.

Standing Conference of National and University Libraries. *Working Papers on Disaster Management.* London: SCONUL, 1995.

Stielow, Frederick J. "Disaster Preparedness and Response Manual: A Common Sense Guide to Risk Management." *LLA Bulletin* 56 (summer 1993): 29–34.

Trinkley, Michael. *Can You Stand the Heat? A Fire Safety Primer for Libraries, Archives and Museums.* Atlanta: SOLINET, 1991.

10

Library and Archives Security

■ ■ ■

RICHARD STRASSBERG

In March 1990, the Federal Bureau of Investigation arrested Stephen Carrie Blumberg at his home in Ottumwa, Iowa, on charges of illegal transportation of nineteen tons of stolen rare books, manuscripts, and other library materials. Among those items are the property of more than 327 of the most prestigious libraries and archival repositories in forty-five American states and Canada. The Blumberg affair is merely the most spectacular in a continual series of revelations that libraries and archives are easy prey for the would-be criminal.

This problem, moreover, is not limited to research libraries, special collections, and archives, such as Blumberg frequented. Theft of library materials is also epidemic in public, college, and university libraries. A study on the Long Beach Public Library in California, for example, reported an 8 percent annual loss because of theft. The same library reported a 76 percent missing rate for Western American fiction produced in the years 1981–1987. An earlier study conducted at an urban university estimated that 8 percent of the student body of that institution was stealing library materials.

Unfortunately, book and especially periodical mutilation is as pervasive as theft in libraries. A nationwide sampling found significant mutilation of library resources in well over 60 percent of the American libraries studied. Another study, conducted in a single library, revealed a periodical mutilation rate of 15 percent.

Libraries are among the most welcoming and available of public institutions. Thus they are frequently seen as an easily available target for individuals or groups who nurture grudges against the library or its administrators, the public entity that supports it, or society at large. Such attacks have, on occasion, resulted in major catastrophes, such as the 1989 Los Angeles Public Library fire. Greed and impatience also play a role in mutilation in libraries.

Who are the criminals responsible for this theft and mutilation, and what are we to do about them? Those convicted inhabit every stratum of society. They range from the mentally ill to individuals whose motivation is purely financial. One university library study even concluded that academic competition was a primary motivating force for the mutilation of books and periodicals. Certainly this has frequently been the anecdotal explanation for such destruction in law and medical libraries. Scholars, novelists, clergymen, policemen, and lawyers number among the professionals who have been found guilty of significant crimes against archives and libraries. Most disconcertingly, many have been fellow librarians and archivists. Some commentators have suggested that as many as 75 percent of thefts in libraries and archives are "inside jobs." Although one would hope that this estimate is excessive, the proportion of professional colleagues convicted of such theft is still deplorably high.

Although it may be impossible for libraries and archives to be totally immune from theft and vandalism, far more can be done to minimize the opportunities. This can be done by building intrinsically more secure facilities, developing effective security policies and procedures, and by attempting to change the rather casual public attitude toward library and archival theft.

Facility Considerations

Architects who design libraries and archives sometimes do so without the awareness of real potential for theft and vandalism in such institutions. Although burglary certainly has been a source of concern in the design of rare book or special collections facilities, it seldom has been seen to be a serious issue in the planning of new or renovated public or academic libraries. In the future, both the security of library and archival collections and the safety of staff and users must be a paramount concern in facility planning. A security consultant should be part of the design team for every major new or renovated library or archives.

A thoughtful design will minimize the patron's ability to avoid passing through electronic object surveillance devices when removing library materials during normal library hours. Good design also means adequate and dependable alarm systems within the facility to detect and report unauthorized movement after hours with the minimum of false alarms. Architects love large windows, atriums, vistas, and a plethora of entrances and exits. But security demands limited use of windows, easily monitored spaces both for collection and user protection, and carefully controlled entrance and egress. The demand for such controlled egress, moreover, must conform to existing fire codes. Library and archival administrators should select architects who are sensitive to such contradictions and who can offer affordable suggestions on how to resolve them.

Electronic Security Systems and Key Control

Given the substantial and complex literature on the subject, an attempt to detail the requirements for electronic security systems would be pointless in a general essay of this type. Librarians and archivists should know that such systems can monitor the use of perimeter and internal doors or detect movement within designated portions of a facility or both when the security system is activated. A wide range of such systems is available, and their appropriate application is a matter of careful analysis of the actual threats facing a particular institution and its internal and external physical configuration. It is also important to note that the experience and reliability of the installer and ease of repair and maintenance of the equipment selected are critical factors in the successful operation of intrusion detection and access control systems. Before deciding which available equipment to purchase, it is essential to seek the advice of the police or security agency that will be responsible for responding to its alarms.

One relatively inexpensive program any facility can adopt is key control. The security of perimeter keys—that is, keys that can be used to open exterior doors—as well as keys to special collections areas obviously deserves the closest scrutiny. Exterior and special collections door locks should be rekeyed frequently, and some thought should be given to the use of the Sargent Keso, Medeco system, or some similar type that uses a high-security tumbler and a key or unlocking device that cannot be easily duplicated. The manufacture and control of excess keys and the keeping of an inventory and checkout forms should be the responsibility of a single staff member who also manages a locked key cabinet in which extra keys are secured.

Optimal door locking control is affordable to most libraries contemplating new or renovated structures. It involves the use of a computer-monitored door access system. Such systems allow their owners not only to control who can enter and exit a particular portal but also to limit the time of day and week such individual access is permitted. Such systems can also log entries and exits and permit the immediate cancellation of portal privileges. A magnetic card or a combination of card and keypad are currently the most common methods of activating such systems. Biometric technology, which allows the utilization of voiceprints, fingerprints, hand geometry, palm prints, retinal scans, or facial comparison scanning, is rapidly becoming cost-effective and will become much more common in door access systems in the next decade. This new technology is likely to first be applied in door access systems controlling rare book and manuscript vaults.

Security Policy and Procedures

Although proper facility design and electronic security are important to minimize theft, the attitude of the library staff to maintaining security is equally critical. It is crucial for staff to understand and support the institution's security program. What are the components in a good library or archival security program and how should such a program be implemented? A midlevel or senior staff member should be appointed to serve as the library or archive security officer. Initial policy should be developed by this individual working with an advisory committee. The committee, which will be responsible for developing both the security policy and the procedures to enforce it, should include the local police organization's crime prevention specialist, representatives of all levels of the staff, and at least one user.

The elements of a sound library security program include: the design and application of a physical security survey to the facility or facilities that house the library or archive; the design and application of a current security procedures audit to review present security practices within the organization; the development of a written library security policy; the development of written security procedures to implement this policy; and the development of a staff training program. Optional steps also might include the development of a crime prevention awareness program for users and a public relations campaign for the community.

Conducting a physical security survey is part of the standard operating procedures of most institutional security departments. It is best to have a trained specialist review lock hardware, alarm systems, perimeter security, the crime profile in the neighborhood, and similar issues, because such specialists probably will be able to do this in greater depth and more effectively than can the librarian or archivist.

Along with the survey, the library security officer can use library security literature or the advice of an outside security specialist, or both, to develop an appropriate current security procedures audit. The focus of such an audit will be on staff procedures, including opening, locking up, patron screening, property marking, and special collections security.

Based on the survey and audit, the security officer and advisory committee can draft a security policy. Such a policy defines violations, defines security procedures as they apply to users and staff, and specifies the action or response of library personnel in the event of a violation. After the draft security policy has been reviewed by the institution's administration, it must be widely circulated among the staff while it is still in its tentative form. Staff review and comment on the draft are essential if the final policy is to be workable and actually implemented. Following the staff's advice, it is essential for the appropriate administrator to seek final review of the proposed policy by institutional security consultants and, especially, legal counsel. While the document is being reviewed, the library security officer and advisory committee should be at work developing the procedures that will be used to implement the final policy. Library and archival literature on this subject, with models from different institutions, will be helpful here. Generally the procedures cover such matters as responding to a security alarm, actions for failure to return books, and antisocial behavior in the library. Frequently there is a set of more detailed procedures for special collections areas.

Following the development of these procedures, a workshop for library staff should be held. The workshop should focus on the implementation of the security plan, and might have as a guest speaker someone with experience administering such policies and procedures in a peer institution. The meeting will serve as a discussion forum for staff concerns and practical solutions. Only after the workshop's successful conclusion should the new security regulations be formally promulgated.

With the promulgation of a new security policy, library staff will have the moral obligation to attempt to enforce it. But moral obligations notwithstanding, the administration already has certain important legal obligations, including reasonable efforts to ensure the protection of the collection, staff, and users from the actions of disruptive users or criminals as well as protection of the civil rights of those suspected of theft and vandalism.

Unfortunately, institutional security policy and procedures, no matter how good, are hampered by the persistent unwillingness of society at large to see crimes against library and archival property as a serious issue. Ironically, the publicity surrounding the Blumberg case or the Los Angeles Public Library fire may do more to enhance effective punishment of crimes against libraries and archives than anything the custodians of such institutions have been able to do.

Mutilation and Vandalism in Libraries

The motivations of those who mutilate library materials are complex and range from simple irritation with library equipment failures to proclivities that are symptomatic of larger social ills. Whatever the cause, the substantial cost of finding replacements poses a great and growing dilemma for librarians. Some research indicates that a significant portion of the mutilation of library books and periodicals is acts of frustration, caused in particular by inoperative copying machines or an inability to pay because of lack of funds or of correct change for a coin-operated machine. Although mutilation of books and periodicals is never to be condoned, it is at least comprehensible in a library that fails to provide its users with simple, reliable, and inexpensive methods for photoduplication. Unfortunately, even if a library provides good and reasonably priced duplication services for its patrons, it may not be able totally to eliminate its mutilation problems. Investigators have found that a substantial amount of mutilation is caused not by frustration but by simple selfishness compounded by the beliefs that such activity is easy and that there is little risk of getting caught.

In recent years, librarians have looked to technology to help with their book and periodical mutilation problems. The reduction of paper periodicals to images that must be accessed electronically will certainly impede the casual thief and vandal, thereby lowering the incidence of mutilation. If the use of digitization and electronic images substantially raises the cost to the user of accessing information, however, the incidence of vandalism against the library's very expensive retrieval equipment may rise proportionately. The theft of a single article cut from a periodical, moreover, does not have nearly the impact on service to other library users that the theft of a compact disk containing several thousand articles or a server containing an entire run of a periodical might have.

Whatever the cause, library professionals must insist that individuals apprehended mutilating library materials be prosecuted or disciplined. However, the actual worth of the item will generally determine the penalty. If the item stolen or mutilated is of small monetary value, legal authorities will not be disposed to prosecute. Even though libraries and archival institutions may not always be able to influence the outcome of trials relating to library crime, they should attempt to vigorously prosecute such activities.

The librarian's only probable recourse in such instances is an education campaign that makes the enormous aggregate cost of the theft and mutilation of library property known to the public. In some states, active lobbying by librarians, archivists, and their supporters have resulted in legislation substantially increasing the penalties to convicted book and manuscript thieves or mutilators.

Employee Theft

There are important aspects of such criminal activity, moreover, in which a thoughtful library security program can have substantial positive effect. One of these is in the area of employee theft.

What motivates employee theft in libraries and archives? Because the great majority of library staff members are basically honest people, it is likely that the motivation for employee theft is not casual. Compulsive behaviors (such as bibliomania, drug dependency, or "conspicuous consumption") are obvious motivations to theft. In many cases, genuine need is a motivation to steal, as is true for someone facing impossible medical expenses, for example. Often these problems manifest themselves in patterns of behavior that appear clearly to a sensitive supervisor. Garnishments or inquiries by creditors, persistent borrowing, obvious extravagance, compulsive gambling, and sudden changes in personality are obvious examples. It probably does not need to be added that inquiries from creditors or any of the other problems enumerated above are hardly evidence that the individual in question is or ever will be a thief. It is just that such individuals may be exposed to excessive temptation under the circumstances. It is up to supervisors or fellow workers to help such colleagues through such hard times, if this is possible, or at least be sensitive to the affected individual's vulnerability.

The decision to hire someone is the most important decision that a supervisor makes that ultimately affects employee theft. Given the difficulty in terminating employees after their probation period in most institutions, the efforts that a supervisor makes to determine the general reliability and honesty of a potential employee are critical.

Employers need to be conversant with their state's regulations regarding the appropriate questions to ask as a part of the application and interview process. In New York State, for example, it is acceptable to ask, on employment applications or during interviews, whether the applicant has been convicted of a crime, but not whether he or she has ever been arrested. Likewise, in New York it is permissible to require fingerprinting as a condition of employment in public galleries and museums but not libraries unless they are part of such institutions.

If allowable by state human rights statutes, some employers use written "honesty" tests for prospective employees. Some authorities have questioned the reliability of such tests while others advocate them. Employers often turn to so-called information brokers who, for a relatively modest fee, will do a "criminal history" search on an individual's record in a particular state as well as an educational verification or employment verification. These services should be used with caution because such brokers do not necessarily guarantee the accuracy of what they provide. They have been known to report incorrectly such basic information as the gender of the individual being investigated.

Ultimately the best screening technique is to carefully validate references provided by potential candidates for employment. In this regard, applicants should be asked if they would agree to allow you to write and telephone for references from previous employers. Potential employers also should insist on complete lists of relevant previous positions and make sure that there are no substantial gaps in time between jobs that cannot be accounted for.

When writing for references, the inquiry should be framed in a way that informs the previous employer that the position in question is a responsible one involving access to valuable or confidential library materials (if this is the case), and the previous employer should be specifically asked if the applicant is suitable for such a position. If the response regarding a particular applicant appears ambiguous, follow up the letter with a telephone call to seek clarification. Please note that the hiring process has become a relatively complicated procedure fraught with potential legal pitfalls. To avoid violating state or federal laws, employers should be careful to apply a consistent approach in reviewing all applicants. Any procedure adopted should be one approved by the institution's legal counsel and human resources personnel.

Having made a strenuous effort to hire honest employees, it is critical to keep them that way. One of the best ways to minimize employee theft is to maintain high employee morale. Obvious elements of this are clear employee policies that are fairly administered; equitable wage levels; good employee-employer communication; careful grievance handling procedures; and training programs and opportunities for advancement.

The single most dangerous motivation for employee theft and vandalism is a real or imagined grievance against immediate supervisors or against the library or archive bureaucracy. Maintaining high morale, to which all responsible administrators doubtless aspire, is absolutely critical to control this motivation. If an employee is motivated by the need to convert institutional property to cash, it is at least possible that the property can be recovered. Those employees who steal as an act of vengeance frequently destroy what they have stolen.

The libraries and archives with probably the lowest theft rate are generally those whose staff members take pride in what they do and feel that they are contributing members of the library's community. These are individuals who believe that they will be treated fairly insofar as it is in the capacity of their supervisor, who understand what the institution is trying to accomplish, and who sign on to that goal. Such attitudes become critical as these individuals are involved in security-related activities.

Four job classifications of library employee require special attention insofar as security is concerned but seldom get it. Janitorial staff, security personnel, mail room staff, and casual help are on the bottom of the economic and social strata in most libraries. Usually unintegrated socially into the staff, such employees typically do the most undesirable tasks for the lowest wages and have fewer opportunities for promotion. Yet some of these very individuals have more keys than anyone else in the building. Janitors and security personnel, moreover, often can go anywhere in the institution at any time of the day or night.

It is critical that janitorial, security, and mail room staff are as carefully scrutinized when being hired as are any other employees. They also should be made to feel a part of the institution in which they work. As significant contributors to the well-being of their institutions, they should be integrated into the social activities of the library staff, and their economic welfare should be of equal concern to that of everyone else on the staff. In short, it is imperative that they feel that they are a valued part of the library team.

It is especially important to make janitorial staff and mail room staff security conscious and to enlist their cooperation in locking up, closing windows, turning off machinery, closing blinds and shades in ground floor offices, and making sure that the mail room does not become an unofficial exit and entrance for the library.

Other workers who need consideration from a security point of view are repair people or other contract laborers, an issue that is growing as more housekeeping and maintenance tasks are being contracted out. Someone in work clothes and a tool belt can often go anywhere with impunity. Workers entering a library or archive should be directed to the administrative office where a log book of pending repairs is kept. They should be required to provide positive identification. In large libraries or archives, it may be necessary to provide such individuals, as well as other casual visitors to restricted or staff-only areas, with a temporary visitor's badge. Electricians, carpenters, and the like should not be allowed to enter or work in special collections stacks without a regular staff member in constant attendance. Regular staff should have no hesitation about calling the administrative office to determine if strangers belong in normally off-limit areas. Blumberg was initially apprehended by an alert staff member in just such a way. It may be necessary to insist that cleaning and maintenance in special collections departments be done only during hours when regular staff are present.

Casual workers also need special security consideration. Most libraries supplement their workforce occasionally or regularly by the use of volunteers or, in the case of college and university libraries, student assistants. Because they are generally assigned the most tedious and routine tasks and seldom see themselves as part of the regular library staff, this group should be viewed as an important potential security risk. Library or archival volunteers also need scrutiny.

Good library and archival security, especially the elimination of motivation for insider theft, then, is very much a matter of being sensitive to one's staff and colleagues. We must be cautious in whom we hire and sensitive to their problems and needs while they are in our employ. Elimination of motivation by minimizing the opportunity to steal with impunity is also critical if theft is to be minimized.

Property Marking

To reduce theft by patrons and staff, property marking is an effective practice. All acquisitions of new printed materials should be permanently stamped as soon as is practical after being received. Although stamping with permanent ink in two places in the interior of a book is probably satisfactory, fore-edge stamping has the double value of immediate property recognition and difficulty of removal and should be considered for new books.

Stamping should routinely be the first step in processing for periodicals immediately after they are unwrapped. Security stripping, if used, should be the second step in processing incoming printed materials. The incentive for staff to steal new library materials is greatly diminished if they are property stamped and security stripped upon arrival. A policy of checking in incoming materials, particularly monographs, within a day of their arrival is also worth exploring.

The treatment of books received by the library through approval plans deserves special attention. Obviously they cannot be property stamped or otherwise marked before a collection development decision has been made about each individual title. Special precautions must therefore be taken with such volumes. They should be housed separately from other incoming library materials, preferably in a locked room or cage with restricted access. If book selection involves several staff members in the library, the approval storage area should be supervised by one or two trusted clerks who also monitor browsing by selectors in this area. If it is necessary to remove a volume for other than movement into regular processing, a record should be made of who removed the volume and when it is to be returned. Once a volume has been selected for inclusion in the collection, the clerk with approval oversight should property stamp it before it is removed for further processing.

The issue of whether to property stamp rare books and manuscripts has been much debated. Some have argued, with much merit, that a well-designed, carefully placed property mark on the obverse of the title page in a rare book is essential in all but the rarest or most extraordinary of materials. The argument that such a mark lessens the value of the book is less than persuasive. Previous owners have usually entered property marks in the volume, and such marks are an important historical record for scholars interested in the provenance of a volume. Second, the contention that a property mark lessens the financial value should not be compelling to institutions that are not in the habit of selling off their collections. If items are occasionally deaccessioned because a better edition has been acquired, any potential loss of value may be minimized by careful and tasteful stamping and, in any event, must be balanced against the insurance provided by the stamp.

In order to recover a stolen rare book, it is critical that its current ownership be clearly indicated. Appendix 1 of the ALA/ACRL/RBMS security guidelines cited in the Suggested Readings offers suggestions on appropriate methods of marking rare books, manuscripts, and other special collections.

Although it may be possible to stamp all the materials in a small but valuable collection, wholesale marking is probably beyond the resources of most major historical manuscript repositories. Fortunately, the overwhelming bulk of documents in many such repositories are historically rather than intrinsically valuable and often have little market value. Where a document is determined to be of decided intrinsic value in such repositories, it might be replaced in the collection with a photocopy and access to the original restricted. If a repository is fortunate enough to have a large collection of documents that are of great intrinsic value, it should consider creation of a use copy through microfilming or another form of mass duplication.

Obviously no argument will persuade a competent rare book curator to property mark her or his greatest treasures. Nor do such items need to be thus sullied. The great treasures in any collection should be protected by photographic facsimiles, may be specifically listed and valued in the institution's insurance policies, and are secured in the library's vaults. Unique treasures are seldom likely to be the game of the professional thief unless the end is "kidnapping" for ransom. It is the lesser-known valuables, those items whose provenance would not be instantly recognized by a specialist and that would find an easier market, for which property marking should be considered. Unfortunately, it is also such materials that make up a substantial portion of what is marketable in archives and library special collections.

Special Collections

If allowable by state law and institutional practice, a thorough, professionally conducted background screening is advisable for all candidates for special collections or archives staff positions. Candidates for employment should definitely be informed that security is an issue of great importance within the institution and that submissions in support of their application will be scrutinized with this in mind.

As has been emphasized previously, an alert staff is the most effective form of library security. Nowhere is this more important than in special collections. Although it is incumbent on libraries and archives to use the most up-to-date technology to secure such collections, the most sophisticated alarm system in the world is of secondary importance compared to a staff willing to make security one of its primary work objectives.

Such a commitment to the protection of collections means being meticulous about researcher registration, making sure that the researcher in question can produce at least two forms of identification, one of which is a government-produced photographic identification, preferably a driver's license or passport. In the reference interview, staff should query each incoming researcher and probe his or her purpose in visiting, and assess whether the researcher is knowledgeable enough about his or her subject in general terms to be a legitimate scholar.

Although the professional thief may have access to forged credentials, his atypical behavior may give him away. It takes special alertness on the part of the reading room staff to spot such behavior—a supposed scholar hurriedly leafing through collection after collection without stopping for photocopying or note taking, or constant movement in and out of the reading room. It takes a strong will on the part of the staff not to fall under the spell of a particularly charming visitor and allow her special privileges. It takes special dedication not to leave a well-known scholar alone unobserved for just a few minutes to run an errand. It takes commitment and practiced charm to insist that, no matter how distinguished or venerable a researcher may be, she cannot take her briefcase, purse, or notes into the reading room but must deposit such belongings in the convenient lockers provided, as well as use the writing materials made available by the department in the reading room. It also takes a special kind of devotion to leaf carefully through the photocopies or computer case being carried out of the reading room to make sure that no original manuscripts have accidentally found their way into the pile. Yet it is necessary. If patrons are allowed to use a self-service photocopier in the reading room, it should be equipped with colored paper to enable staff to distinguish easily between originals and photocopies. The use of colored paper by patrons is especially important if photocopying on white archival bond is used by a repository as a conservation technique for the replacement of deteriorating original documents.

No activity that reading room staff engage in has a more profound impact on the recovery of stolen items than the meticulous maintenance of access records. The ability to prove who has had access to a particular volume or box of records and when such access was granted is often a critical determinant in subsequent efforts to recover purloined books or documents. It is, as well, essential for the conviction of the miscreant responsible. This means following a rigidly formal registration method and exercising due care to make sure that no access to any archival or special collections materials is granted unless an annotation substantiating this access is made on the user's record. It also means that the institution should have a method of tracing the chronological use of a particular collection over long periods. Registration and use records are vital and must be permanently retained. Keeping a security set of registers and other finding aids off-premises is also important in maintaining a collection audit trail.

The chief administrator of special collections sets the general tone for a security-conscious department and must support staff members in enforcing reasonable security rules. Curators must take special care to design security rules that are fair and not so cumbersome as to be unenforceable. They also must be prepared for and alert to occasional lapses by even their most devoted colleagues. When the inevitable loss does occur, the curator must assume responsibility for the loss rather than shift it elsewhere until a thorough investigation is conducted.

One reaction to such a loss must be its immediate announcement despite the embarrassment it will engender. Immediate supervisors and local law enforcement officials should be notified at once. After authorization by the police and with the advice of the institution's legal counsel, other institutions in the vicinity and the relevant book and manuscript dealers should be advised of the loss in full detail. The Security Committee of the Antiquarian Booksellers Association of America should be notified at once. This group circulates "pink sheets" to its members, alerting them to missing or stolen items. Similar reports should also be sent to e-mail listservs and websites that are maintained for the immediate reporting of significant losses of books as well as to general-purpose rare book and manuscript listservs. If a thief is eventually apprehended, the institution should be wary of accepting restitution in lieu of prosecution. If such criminal activity is to be curtailed, malefactors should not get away lightly.

Many precious materials, including books with maps and prints, can still be found in the open stacks of research libraries. Systematic efforts have been made in many institutions to identify the choicest items and remove them to the rare book collection, but much of value will remain painfully vulnerable to the knowledgeable thief. Alert special collections curators will notice announcements of losses in other institutions and attempt to isolate those titles in their own collections.

Many research libraries in the United States are having to contemplate the removal of a substantial part of their collections to remote

storage because of overcrowding in their current locations. In addition
to the usual long runs of low-usage serials, it might be well for such
libraries to take the opportunity occasioned by such enforced moves to
segregate the "medium rare" books, periodicals, and serials still in their
open stacks. This is a particularly attractive concept for libraries that
have already made the easy choices about what to transfer to remote
storage because it helps to rationalize the high cost of individual volume selection. Naturally, the remote storage facility must be upgraded
from a warehouse to a climate- and pollution-controlled library facility
with the appropriate intrusion and access control systems.

Exhibitions, Insurance, and Security

Exhibitions are an important way for special collections curators and
archivists to inform the public of the value of their resources. In
libraries that are units of larger institutions, such as colleges and universities, regular exhibitions are a part of the library's responsibility
and are often seen as the way to announce significant gifts and to com-
memorate important anniversaries and events. Considering the
amount of labor involved, both in researching and mounting an
exhibition, and the importance of making a creditable appearance
in public, curators are wont to display their most interesting and valuable treasures. Individual items may be lent to other institutions for
exhibition, or entire exhibitions can move off-premises as traveling
shows.

Items being shown outside the secured precincts of the rare book
room or archive are unusually vulnerable to theft or vandalism. In addition, even if such items are covered by insurance when within the
archive or rare book department, they may not be covered when off the
premises for exhibitions or other uses, such as a classroom presentations, unless they are specifically included in a rider to the policy. Most
libraries and archives are either self-insured (that is, the institution
bears the loss) or have extremely limited policies covering major losses,
such as fire, with a substantial deductible and standardized per-item
replacement values. These policies are designed to protect general
stack collections against substantial losses from natural catastrophes.
Unless they are specifically scheduled, library materials of high monetary value are likely not to be covered by such insurance.

It is generally possible to determine through appraisals the fair
market value of rare books and art objects to use as a basis for schedul-

ing them. If an institution has but a few objects of great worth, scheduling them and paying the substantial premiums involved may be feasible. Many great collections, however, which hold hundreds or thousands of items of rarity, simply cannot afford the premiums involved in per-item scheduling. The unique nature of manuscript materials greatly complicates the determination of a fair market value, especially if the documents in question or reasonable equivalents have never appeared on sale or if they have not been individually appraised.

It is, of course, possible to get a special policy to cover the documents or books in a particular exhibition. Such a policy should cover the materials from the moment they leave the repository's vaults until they are returned. It should cover not only loss to theft but also loss by vandalism, fire, or other natural or human agencies. Such policies are likely to be expensive and require the prior appraisal of each item to be covered. Because all insurance is ultimately based on the degree of risk involved, it may be possible to reduce insurance costs by being selective about to whom and how materials are loaned. Thus a traveling exhibition loaned only to museums with adequate security and traveling on carriers that specialize in transporting art objects may cost less to insure than a similar one traveling by UPS and being shown at a library with little security.

Whether or not materials are being lent for exhibit outside the department, wise curators will be aware of the nature of their institution's insurance coverage on its collections before any loss. Larger organizations, such as major universities or museums, usually have risk management and insurance offices, part of whose responsibility is providing guidance in this area.

Insurance provides at best mere financial compensation for loss. Librarians and archivists concerned with exhibiting their institution's most significant assets in a manner that maximizes the possibility of such assets surviving would do well to heed the advice of art insurance specialist Charles Rogers, who suggests "the key to reducing the risk of loss is to improve security and identify objects by marking them."

One way to maximize security and minimize insurance costs (as well as reduce deterioration caused by display) is to show facsimiles in situations where the originals might be unduly vulnerable. Photographs, in particular, lend themselves to this technique. When originals are exhibited, evidence of property marking on the items will also deter thieves if not vandals.

An important additional safeguard for displays of original documents is to keep a visual (as well as a written) record of each item being exhibited or lent. A conservator's condition report may serve this purpose; a photocopy, a photograph, or a micrographic record will also serve. Such a file is, of course, a useful way of making sure all the items that were on display in a traveling exhibit were safely returned.

One of the times any exhibit is at its most vulnerable is during the time of its installation. Under no circumstances should one leave an open display case or a cart full of display materials unattended even for a minute. Likewise, it is important to be cautious about giving guest curators the run of one's rare book or manuscript vault in putting together a display.

Conclusion

The foregoing should be read as a generalized introduction to the complex subject of library and archival security. Nothing in this chapter is intended to be legal advice.

The manifold issues relating to the protection of one's collections against human predation are among the most emotionally charged matters with which information professionals must wrestle. They are also the ones who place archives, libraries, and the staffs who run these institutions in the most legal jeopardy. Familiarity with one's statutory responsibilities as a curator or library administrator is crucial for professional survival in our litigious society. Because the context of this essay is the protection of collections rather than that of patrons or staff, issues relating to the latter subject have only been addressed in passing. Administrators in particular, however, should also be aware of the nature of their distinct and growing legal responsibilities connected with the protection of staff and patrons while they are on library or archive premises. Library and archival administrators would also do well to familiarize themselves with statutes relating to theft and vandalism within their jurisdiction.

All interested library professionals should take pains to acquaint local law enforcement and judicial authorities with the depth and seriousness of the crisis in library and archival security. Finally, we must encourage our professional organizations to acquaint legislators with the threat to humankind's recorded memory represented by the growing epidemic of theft and vandalism within libraries and archives. All should lobby for more effective state legislation for the protection of our collections and institutions. We must also seek methods by which to minimize our own legal vulnerability as we attempt to develop and apply good and reasonable security practices.

Selected Readings

Allen, Susan M. "Theft in Libraries or Archives." *College & Research Libraries News* 51 (1990): 939–944.

American Library Association. Association of College and Research Libraries. Rare Books and Manuscripts Section. "Guidelines for the Loan of Rare and Unique Materials." *College & Research Libraries News* 54 (1993): 267–269. Also available at <http://www.ala.org/acrl/guides/loanrare. html>.

———. "Guidelines for the Security of Rare Book, Manuscript and Other Special Collections." *College & Research Libraries News* 51 (1990): 240–244. Also available at <http://www.ala.org/acrl/guides/raresecu.html>.

———. "Guidelines on the Selection of General Collection Materials for Transfer to Special Collections." 2d ed. *College & Research Libraries News* 54 (1993): 644–647. Also available at <http://www.ala.org/acrl/guides/ seltran.html>.

———. "Guidelines Regarding Thefts in Libraries." *College & Research Libraries News* 55 (1994): 641–646. Also available at <http://www.ala.org/ acrl/guides/theftinl.html>.

———. "Standards for Ethical Conduct for Rare Book, Manuscript, and Special Collection Libraries and Librarians with Guidelines for Institutional Practice in Support of Standards." 2d ed. *College & Research Libraries News* 54 (1993): 207–215. Also available at <http://www. ala.org/acrl/guides/rarethic.html>.

Banham, Russ. "Here Today, Gone Tomorrow." *Insurance Review* (October 1990): 56–60.

Brady, Eileen E. *Library/Archive/Museum Security: A Bibliography.* 5th ed. Moscow, Idaho: Catula Pinguis Pr., 1995.

Cox, Richard J. "Collectors and Archival, Manuscript, and Rare Book Security." *Focus on Security* (April 1995).

Fay, John Jay, ed. *Encyclopedia of Security Management: Techniques and Technology.* Boston: Butterworth-Heinemann, 1993.

Fennelly, Lawrence J. *Handbook of Loss Prevention and Crime Prevention.* 3d ed. Boston: Butterworth-Heinemann, 1995.

Inland Marine Underwriters Association and Society of American Archivists. *Libraries and Archives: An Overview of Risk and Loss Prevention.* New York: Inland Marine Underwriters Association, 1994. (Call 212-233-7958 to obtain a copy.)

National Employment Screening Services. *The Guide to Background Investigations.* 4th ed. Tulsa, Okla.: NESS, 1990.

Shockowitz, Tonya. "Security Issues for Archives, Rare Books and Special Collections: A Bibliographic Essay." *Current Studies in Librarianship* 19 (1995): 4–12.

Strassberg, Richard. "The Final Barrier: Security Considerations in Restricted Access Reading Rooms." *Reference Librarian*, no. 56 (1997): 95–105.

Trinkaus-Randall, Gregor. *Protecting Your Collections: A Manual of Archival Security.* Chicago: Society of American Archivists, 1995.

Turner, Anne M. *It Comes with the Territory: Handling Problem Situations in Libraries.* Jefferson, N.C.: McFarland, 1993.

Internet Sites for Reporting Losses

Archives and Archivists <ARCHIVES@cwisserver1.mcs.muohio.edu>

Ex Libris <exlibris@library.berkeley.edu>

Isolist <sallen@library.ucla.edu>

Missing or Stolen Book Alert <interloc@interloc.com>

11

■■ ■ ■■

Exhibition Policy and Preparation

■ ■ ■

ROBERTA PILETTE

Almost every library and archives does exhibitions. The exhibition area may range from a single case to rooms or areas set aside as gallery space with planned and changing exhibitions. Most professionals who have been involved in planning or installing an exhibition, whether large or small, recognize the amount of time and energy involved in putting together an attractive and successful exhibition. However, many of those same professionals may not be aware of the amount of physical stress put on the items exhibited. The physical stress comes from the change in the environment. The exhibited items are suddenly exposed to much more light and perhaps changes in temperature and relative humidity. Additionally, bound items may be held open to the same place for long periods and placed in unnatural positions. Therefore, many preservation issues must be considered in planning and mounting exhibitions.

Exhibition and Loan Policy

One of the most important preservation issues to consider is the exhibition and loan policy. Institutions large or small that are involved in exhibitions at any level should have a written exhibition policy. This policy should cover issues for both in-house exhibitions and the loan of items to other institutions for exhibition. Such a policy clarifies and corrects past practices and provides a basis for decision making. The policy needs to indicate clearly how much time is required for an item to be considered for loan or exhibition, including time for all necessary preparation work, such as reviewing items requested and gathering information. The policy must state any restrictions on exhibitions or loans because of an item's size, condition, type of media, and so on.

Whether concerning an in-house exhibition or a loan, the policy must take into consideration the individual items and the exhibition venue. A policy should clearly state who within the institution is responsible for reviewing the items requested for display and for assessing and documenting their condition, and should specify a standard, easily understood format for the condition report. The policy also needs to clearly state what is the acceptable physical condition for allowing an item to be displayed; the length of time the item will be displayed; and specifications regarding mounting, environment, and security during the exhibition.

These last-mentioned specifications are especially important and can have long-term physical effects on the items displayed. One must think of the exhibition space as having preservation requirements similar to those in which the items are normally housed. The environment in which the items will be displayed (both ambient and within the case) needs to be nondamaging. Therefore, lighting, temperature, relative humidity (RH), and pollutant controls need to be specified. The same environmental standards and concerns as expressed by Paul Banks in chapter 7 apply to materials while on exhibition. The case and mounting materials are equivalent to shelving and should not contribute to the deterioration of the displayed items. Finally, library security needs to be addressed in the loan policy as it specifically relates to items on exhibition. This specification may include the type of locks on the cases, the building alarm, and a request for guards. Close attention should be paid to security for in-house exhibition spaces also.

All the concerns related to in-house exhibition apply equally to items going out on loan. The lending institution needs to request specific information, such as a written facilities report, which allows the lender to evaluate what is happening at the borrower's gallery and case level. A written security report should also be provided. In addition, the borrowing institution should supply information about the curator, whether a catalog will be produced, and why this item is necessary to the exhibit.

Additionally, the lender needs to establish policies and procedures that cover the following:

Does the item need conservation treatment? Who will pay for the treatment?

What does the lender's insurance or the insurance of the borrower cover regarding items off-site and during transit? Who will provide the insurance?

What sorts of packing, crating, and handling are required for particular items?

What is the most practical and safe means for the transport of these particular items?

Is a courier needed? If so, who will cover the courier's expenses?

Who is handling and installing the item at the loan site?

Who is covering the overall cost of the exhibition?

The lending institution has the responsibility of gathering and reviewing all necessary information relating to the exhibition before agreeing to the loan. Having the above issues clarified in a written policy makes it much easier to evaluate each loan request and be consistent. If the prospective borrowing institution gives incomplete or unsatisfactory answers at any point in this information-gathering process, the lender has the right to say no. Having a complete checklist and requiring acknowledgment of each item, either by signature or a tick mark, before final loan approval is granted will help to ensure that every issue has been considered.

The primary concerns when considering the reasonableness of a loan request are the item's condition and the environment into which it is going to be placed. A written policy consistently adhered to can work in the potential lender's favor because it indicates concern for items under the lender's care. However, there is a caveat to all of this. If the lender places more stringent exhibition specifications on the borrowing institution than the lender can provide within its own environs, borrowers may meet the requirements because they want the item in their exhibit but will not be happy about it. This sort of overzealousness does not help the cause of preservation or the institution's reputation. When all is said and done, common sense based on good preservation information will most likely result in the best possible exhibition policy.

Loan items traveling to and from foreign countries have another layer of legal considerations. The United States has numerous detailed and complex laws that regulate the flow of material across its borders. A licensed customs broker will help thread the way through these various regulations. Customs brokers are licensed through the U.S. Treasury Department and the Federal Maritime Commission and are approved by the International Air Transport Association.

Some items will be borrowed for exhibitions that will travel to more than one site. It is important to have policies for each kind of traveling exhibition that is planned. An exhibition that will be installed in a trailer or railroad car, which functions as a moving gallery, may remain untouched in the same case, while one that will travel to a number of different sites may require that each item be packed, unpacked, and installed into a different exhibit case at each site. Each scenario has pros and cons associated with the preservation of the items on display and each has its challenges. Planes, commercial carriers, rail cars, trucks, or hand couriers may be acceptable depending on the type and value of the items and where they are going. It is not out of line to request the suspension specifications on the trailer or railroad car. In the case of an exhibition requiring numerous packings and unpackings, it is critical to know who will be supervising all the moves and the packing and unpacking, and to have facilities reports for each site. Regarding the packing and crating, there are commercial firms that will provide such services. Packing techniques can contribute to the protection or harm of an item during transit. The packing crate needs to insulate against abrupt temperature and relative humidity changes, water leaks, shocks, and vibrations. It is also important to keep instructions for packing and unpacking as clear and straightforward as possible, and materials used must be able to withstand reuse.

Exhibition Space Design—New Construction or Renovation

Although an exhibition policy is a good place to start, it will not answer all the preservation questions when talking to an architect or a designer about a newly planned exhibition space. This can be new construction or perhaps a major renovation. It is extremely important to have, at the very least, a conservator involved in all stages of the design. This may be the institution's staff conservator or a consultant. If a consultant is hired, be sure that he or she has experience in museum exhibition design. The important point is to have someone knowledgeable in preservation on the planning committee. It will be his or her responsibility to keep the architect, designers, and engineers aware of the preservation implications of decisions about lighting, heating, ventilation, cooling, case construction, and security. It is important not to rely solely on the architect, designers, or engineers to produce a preservationally sound exhibition space.

Exhibition Preparation

"Less is more" should be the motto of exhibition planning. The theme of the exhibition must be carefully developed, keeping in mind the amount of space available as well as the audience. To use every pertinent item may be overwhelming, boring, and not in the best interest of the items' long-term preservation. Even in an ideal world with unlimited funds, staff, and the perfect exhibition area, this blanket approach usually does not make sense.

However, choosing the theme and materials is only one part of planning an exhibition. The physical environment of the exhibition space must be examined and the selected items prepared for exhibiting. In an attempt to provide information regarding exhibition practices to libraries and archives, the National Information Standards Organization (NISO) has put together a committee to establish standards for library and archival exhibitions. A standard, American National Standard Z39.79-2000, *Environmental Conditions for Exhibiting Library and Archival Materials*, has been reviewed and will be available soon. This standard will be extremely useful in establishing specifications for all aspects of exhibition planning and design. It will allow preservation experts and nonexperts alike to clearly state basic specifications when discussing issues with administrators as well as with exhibition designers for such areas of concern as lighting, case construction, and individual item support.

Before embarking on compromises and facing reality regarding the physical specifications of library and archival exhibitions, it is useful to review some of the recommended guidelines for paper-based materials in libraries and archives. In William Wilson's *Environmental Guidelines for the Storage of Paper Records*, the suggested temperature and relative humidity levels for combined stack and user areas are 70°F and 30–50% ±3% relative humidity. The relative humidity level should be within this given range, taking into consideration the local climatic conditions and facility limitations. Sunlight should be avoided, and light from all other sources needs to be filtered to eliminate wavelengths below about 415 nanometers (ultraviolet light range). In *The Museum Environment*, Garry Thomson presents in the appendix a "Summary of Specifications" for exhibiting sensitive and moderately sensitive materials. He has also broken the specifications into two classes. Class 1 is for major national museums and new museum buildings. The specifications are very clearly spelled out with little room for variation. It is assumed that institutions functioning at these levels have large, important collections and are financially willing and able to adhere to the strictest specifications to preserve their holdings. Class 2 specifications are to "avoid major dangers while keeping cost and alteration to a minimum. . . . Neither ducted air conditioning nor automatic light control are assumed for Class 2."[1] Many library and archival exhibition areas fall into Class 2. These specifications offer intelligent modifications to the strict Class 1 specifications and recognize limited funding and physical restrictions. Table 1 is an adaptation of Thomson's Class 2 specifications.

This two-tiered approach recognizes the need to make compromises from the ideal. However, even trying to meet these modified

Table 1
Environmental Specifications

Light	
No direct sunlight for any type of media	
Moderately sensitive material; e.g., oil paintings	Keep lighting below 150 lux by using manually controlled blinds, or drapery.
Sensitive material; e.g., manuscripts, photos, textiles, and paper-based materials	50 lux or less; total exposure per year of 42 kilolux hours[*]
UV Radiation	Not to exceed 75 microwatts/lumen
Relative Humidity	35–50% with no sudden changes greater than 5% in either direction. Seasonal changes of greater than 5% are allowed provided they take place over one month or more.

Temperature	Reasonably constant in order to maintain relative humidity
Air Pollution	Areas and cases should be kept reasonably free of pollutants by the use of room or case devices.

* kilolux = lux × 1,000 hours; i.e., 50 lux for 70 hours (1 week of 10-hour days) = 3,500 lux hours or 3.5 kilolux hours

Adapted from Garry Thomson, *The Museum Environment*, 2d ed. (London: Butterworth, 1986).

specifications may be difficult for some institutions. The reality of budget constraints, minimal staffing, and time to plan and execute exhibitions should not and need not result in endangering library and archival materials while on display.

Getting Started

Exhibitions perhaps more than anything else are exercises in an odd mixture of practicality and invention. Anyone preparing an exhibition must consider the number, size, and location of the cases at the very beginning of the planning process. Practically speaking, few institutions will be able to design new cases for every exhibition. Therefore, it is important to consider the physical dimensions of the items to be exhibited in relationship to the size of the cases and exhibit area. Will the items fit in the cases in a preservationally sound manner? For example, a volume standing vertically in a case that is much too narrow for the book to lie horizontally will cause its open pages to slump or the text block to sag out of its cover. This is unattractive and physically damaging to the volume.

Once this most basic question of whether items will fit in the designated areas is answered, planning can continue. It is at this point that having an exhibition policy in place to address such issues as length of the exhibition, environmental concerns of the exhibit space and the individual cases, and the display methods used on individual items is essential to planning a preservationally sound exhibition.

Length of Exhibitions

To some extent, time can be the most easily controlled aspect of all exhibitions. Many libraries have "permanent" exhibitions. This often means an exhibition was installed and no one has bothered to change it, sometimes for years. Innumerable interesting and valuable books can no longer be closed without damaging their bindings simply because they were left on display open to the same page. Interesting letters are almost illegible because of fading simply because no one thought about what was displayed, where it was displayed, and how long it had been there. The general guideline is this: The maximum length of time any paper-based item should be on display is three months per year or 42 kilolux hours of light per year, whichever comes first. This is not an absolute. Learning more about materials and what contributes to their deterioration is helpful in modifying the guideline to suit the exhibition conditions in terms of light levels, temperature, relative humidity, the particular item, and institutional needs.

Damage and change in paper-based material are cumulative and irreversible. To monitor items that are frequently requested for exhibition, it is a good idea to keep an exhibition log. This can be done either with a paper file or in a simple database. The log should list the item, where it was exhibited, the length of time exhibited, and the physical conditions under which it was exhibited: general temperature, relative humidity and, most importantly, the light levels and hours of light exposure per day. Putting a manuscript on display for three months exposes it to light, pollutants, and temperature and relative humidity fluctuations. All these factors cause deterioration. If an item is exhibited for three months in an uncontrolled area, putting it in good storage for six months cannot negate the damage: The insidious thing is the subtlety of the changes. Most are not visible to the naked eye, but that does not mean the changes have not taken place. An item's exhibition history should be taken into consideration when deciding on further exhibiting. Damage to an item brought on by exhibiting must be kept to a minimum. In some instances, limiting the time an exhibition is up is the only way to minimize such damage.

Light

Lighting is perhaps the most difficult aspect of an exhibit because it affects the viewer's reaction and its damage is also cumulative and irreversible. The damage is a combination of length of exposure and intensity. Therefore, explaining to viewers why the light levels are low, why the light is on a timer, or why viewers are asked to replace a case curtain after viewing is important in gaining their cooperation and protecting the item on display. There must be enough light for items to be viewed but not enough to jeopardize the items. Reflections, glare, and uneven lighting must also be considered.

To control lighting, one must begin by identifying the problem. Light monitoring equipment must be available for use. A thorough light survey of the exhibition area and the cases is necessary. First, set up the lighting as it would be for an exhibition. Next, using a photometer, a luxmeter, or a footcandle meter as described in the chapter on environmental controls, check all visible light levels. Finally, using a UV meter, check all the UV levels. Monitoring is the only way to identify and measure problem areas. The generally specified recommendations of 75 microwatts/lumen for UV and 50–150 lux visible light for paper-based items may not be easily met in some exhibit spaces. However, striving for the ideal by lowering light levels and eliminating UV is very important. In certain situations, monitoring is not necessary to identify the problem but to confirm the degree of seriousness. Table 2 lists three common problems and possible solutions.

In the instance of sunlight falling on the case, if none of the suggested solutions is possible, only facsimiles of valuable material should be considered for display. In the other instances, if none of the suggested solutions is possible, all exhibitions should be much shorter than three months or, again, facsimiles of valuable material should be considered for display. An aid in making this decision is the Light Damage Slide Rule developed by the Canadian Conservation Institute. The slide rule calculates light damage to an item by using light intensity and time. This scale can help estimate the amount of damage done to colors (fading), but, more importantly, it shows clearly the reciprocal relationship between exposure time and light intensity. By using the slide rule, one can determine that three months at 50 lux (an ideal) is equal to approximately twenty-two days at 200 lux or ten days at 450 lux.

The Internal Case Environment

The elimination of all pollutants from exhibition cases will not be practical, necessary, or even feasible for many exhibitions, but commonsense solutions to gross pollutant problems are possible. Table 3, based

Table 2
Common Exhibition Lighting Situations

PROBLEM	EFFECTS	POSSIBLE SOLUTIONS
Sunlight on the case	• high UV and IR content • strong visible light • raises temperature; lowers RH • discolors paper containing lignin • fades sensitive media; e.g., watercolors, natural dyes, certain historic photo processes, and all modern color photos	• Move the exhibit to an area where this is not a problem. • Change the location of the case within the space so direct sunlight is not falling on it. • Install and/or use window shades or curtains. • Install protective cloths over the cases themselves, which are lifted or moved for viewing by the visitor.
Fluorescent fixtures in the case	• high UV • raises temperature; lowers RH	• Upgrade lighting to exterior incandescent or suitable halogen lamps. • Use UV filters on all lamps and make sure the case is well ventilated to allow for the escape of heat given off by fluorescent fixtures. • Remove the lamps and rely on ambient room light.
Incandescent fixtures in the case	• raises temperature; lowers RH	• Change to exterior incandescent fixtures. • Use very low wattage lamps in the case. • Put fixtures on a timer and have viewer turn on as needed. • Remove lamps and rely on ambient room light.

Table 3
Internal Case Environment

POLLUTANT/SOURCE	PROBLEM	POSSIBLE SOLUTIONS
PARTICULATES • open windows • carpets and drapes • people	• microscopic damage to fibers both physically and chemically • aesthetics	• Keep windows closed. • Mat item and put polyester film over the mat's window or encapsulate all single-sheet items. • Make sure cases close snugly and any seals are in good condition. • Limit the exhibition's length.
WOOD • plywood • particleboard • oak • pine	• urea-formaldehyde from adhesives; cross links with proteins and cellulose • organic gases	• Cover wood with plastic laminate, e.g., Formica. • Use exterior-grade woods without urea-formaldehyde adhesives. • Put down a thin, clear acrylic or polyester film sheet, which goes from edge to edge of the table. Leave table edges outside the vitrine exposed. The vapors will tend to go to the edges and outside the enclosure.
PAINT AND SEALANTS • oil modified coatings (polyurethane) • oil base or alkyd paints • polyvinyl chloride	• off-gassing of peroxides, acids, etc.	• Do *not* use
CASE LINING FABRICS • wool felt • fabrics with fire retardant • light-sensitive fabrics, i.e., silk	• sulphur containing • PVC backed and other finishes • color loss/shift; degradation of the fiber	• Use natural finished fabrics in cotton and linen. Purchase fabric from a wholesaler who will know how the fabric was processed and finished. • Wash fabrics before using.

Adapted from Jean Tétreault and Scott Williams, *Guidelines for Selecting Materials for Exhibiting, Storage and Transportation*, ver. 4.3 (Ottawa: Canadian Conservation Institute, 1993).

on Tétreault and Williams's *Guidelines for Selecting Materials for Exhibiting, Storage and Transportation*, lists common exhibit case pollutants, their sources, and possible solutions.

Air Quality—Particulates

Particulates are made up of soot, dander, paper fibers, and other minutiae commonly referred to as dust. This particulate pollution must be kept out of the cases. Well-fitting gaskets and regular maintenance can keep particulates under control. Besides being unsightly, these particulates contribute to the damage of items.

Air Quality—Gaseous

Unseen pollutants are another concern. One source of these gaseous pollutants is the exhibit case itself. The wood, glue, and fabric that are used in assembling the case can give off fumes, which react with the items displayed within the case. Many cases consist simply of a wooden table with a "glass box" or vitrine placed on top. The wood, even if sealed, may give off vapors, which are destructive to objects within the case. The sealant, fabric lining, or adhesives may be the source of the problem. Table 3 discusses some of the sources of these often unnoticed pollutants along with some possible solutions.

You can use a simple test to determine the presence of these acidic vapors: Dampen a pH strip with glycerin rather than distilled water, set the strip in the closed case for approximately ten minutes, and then read the results. This can be effective in convincing administrators that the cases need to be upgraded by improved sealing of the wood, improved backboards, and better lining fabrics. This is not a definitive test and should be used judiciously; it simply shows the presence of acidic vapors in the case. It does not identify the source, nor does it detect other kinds of damaging vapors, such as peroxides.

If a major exhibition or a significant capital expenditure on exhibit cases is planned, all materials used in case construction should be thoroughly researched. Acquire specifications on all the materials and have the materials tested if necessary *before* the cases are constructed. A local conservator may be able to help identify appropriate tests for fabric, wood, adhesives, and sealants.

Temperature and Relative Humidity

Reducing pollutants addresses only a portion of the internal environment of exhibit cases. Extremes of temperature and relative humidity, as well as wild fluctuations, have been shown to be damaging to all cellulose-based materials. Consistency or gentle changes over long periods, especially of relative humidity, have been shown to be less damaging.

Although the general exhibit area may have good environmental controls with acceptable temperature and relative humidity readings, there may still be wild temperature and relative humidity fluctuations within the cases. As indicated in table 2, internal lighting is the probable cause. To determine if there is a problem within the cases, they should be monitored. The monitoring should be done over a period of time with a hygrothermograph. Large mechanically operated hygrothermographs (roughly 6 in. × 10 in. × 12 in.) may be quite impractical for use in display cases. The electronic hygrothermographs are quite small (about 4 in. × 3 in. × 1 in.) and accurate. (Both types are discussed more fully in chapter 7.) Small thermohygrometers (1–2-inch diameter) are available and can be placed unobtrusively in a case or series of cases and read regularly throughout the day for a period of time. Keeping a record of the temperature and relative humidity readings taken in this manner can give a rough idea of any problems.

The control of relative humidity is especially critical for items on vellum and on wood. These materials are extremely sensitive to changes in relative humidity and will visibly change by shrinking or expanding. If the environment is too dry, illuminated manuscripts on vellum can shrink or cockle drastically, causing the colorants to lift off. Wood may split, causing structural problems. Any exhibit that includes these items must have relative humidity very carefully controlled. This is especially true in northern climates during the winter months, as there is a tendency, most notably in older buildings, to heat without adding moisture to the air.

If, after testing and subsequent upgrading of cases, there are still pollutant or temperature and relative humidity problems, then the use of buffers and adsorbents in a tightly sealed case should be pursued. However, a sealed case must be capable of maintaining a good environment. This calls for an exhibition conservator or exhibits designer familiar with the design and engineering requirements of such an exhibition case.

Even a generally well sealed case of one cubic meter will have approximately one complete air exchange per day. This leakage rate is based on an unsealed area equal to a 30-millimeter hole. Breaks in the seal can occur at many points and are usually a series of much smaller leaks. Because the new outside air mixes with stable, clean case air fairly quickly, the desired relative humidity or pollutant level is degraded by dilution. The buffers and adsorbents bring back into balance the slightly changed condition caused by this new air.

Several buffer materials designed to lessen the extremes in rapid relative humidity changes are available. Silica gel, a granular solid, is perhaps the most common. The Canadian Conservation Institute's technical note on silica gel (see Suggested Readings) is a succinct explanation of how to condition it. Conservation material suppliers carry silica gel in various forms—loose, packed in cylinders, or sheets. The silica gel is reusable and can be conditioned to a specific relative humidity at a given temperature; for example, 45% RH at 70°F. All buffers need to be conditioned before use, and, after a period of use, they will need to be reconditioned as they will drift toward ambient conditions in proportion to the leakage rate of the case.

Activated carbon and a variety of molecular sieves can be used to adsorb pollutants. Activated carbon, used alone, comes in a variety of forms. However, unlike silica gel, it is not reusable. The amount of surface area of activated carbon exposed to the air is critical, yet there is no formula available for determining an ideal amount of activated carbon per cubic meter of display case. The suggestion is to fill whatever area is not occupied by silica gel with activated carbon. The combination of activated carbon and zeolites used as molecular sieves is now available commercially in papers, boards, and a paintlike emulsion. Tests seem to indicate these products work well as adsorbers of gaseous pollutants, especially sulfur dioxide and nitrous oxides. Using this material to line cases or in the construction of supports may be a good way to help control these pollutants. However, in general the most effective placement of such sorbents is as close to the leakage points as possible and between the leaks and the item whenever possible. Incoming air will then wash over this sorbent, which cleans it as it moves into the case.

Buffers and adsorbers are normally placed out of sight in the base or behind the backboard of a case. To be effective, there must be a free exchange of case air between the exhibiting area of the case and the buffers. This can be accomplished by using a screen or board with a series of holes at the base or backboard. This may then be covered with fabric.

Case Design

As indicated earlier, many of the physical problems associated with exhibiting items may be with the case itself. Besides the physical and chemical issues associated with the exhibit case, there are aesthetic issues of the case and items that are exhibited in the case. There are two basic styles of cases—horizontal and vertical. The vertical case may be wall-mounted or freestanding. The horizontal case is sometimes referred to as a coffin or table case.

The proportions, dimensions, and general construction of cases vary dramatically. Each style has its advantages and disadvantages. The style of case preferred varies from exhibit to exhibit depending on the type of materials being exhibited. Often the exhibition preparer must make do with the style of case available in the institution. Very few institutions will be able to acquire new case styles to fit the needs of a particular exhibition.

Vertical cases work well for small or single-sheet items. The depth of the case will limit the size of a book that can be shown lying down or at a slight angle on a shelf. The tallest part of a vertical case may be above the eye level of viewers, especially children. Books should not be tipped open at steep angles or stood up vertically without text-block supports because of the strain on the binding. Items that are most effectively displayed vertically are those that hang in the case (matted or encapsulated) or stand on a shelf (closed book with a support or other three-dimensional objects). In vertical cases, open books can be safely and effectively displayed on lower shelves if the case is deep enough to allow for the book to lie horizontally.

Horizontal cases can be used for a wider variety of items. There is more flexibility in horizontal cases because a mix of material—three-dimensional objects, opened books, closed books, and flat paper items—can all be easily arranged in the same case. However, any exhibition made up exclusively of horizontal cases has much to overcome in attracting the interest of the casual viewer.

Display Methods

Exhibition design and installation preparation may begin once the cases are under control regarding light, temperature, RH, and air quality. To present each item in an interesting and safe way now becomes the primary concern and an aesthetic and preservation challenge.

The exhibition policy should state general guidelines for choosing items for exhibitions regarding their physical condition. If an item is critical to an exhibition and in disrepair, time and money must be allotted to treat it and bring it up to the best possible condition before display. Frequently a "must-have" becomes a "do-without" when time and money for conservation treatment are in short supply.

Bound Volumes

When reviewing books for display, there are three major points to consider in determining how the book will be displayed:

1. Its general condition

    Is the text block in one piece?

    Is the cover still attached to the text block?

    Are the hinges strong?

    Are there torn or loose pages sticking out?

2. Will it be displayed open and, if so, does it open easily?

    Is the proposed opening at the front, at the back, or near the middle?

    How far does the book open easily? Most books open easily somewhere between 90° and 130°.

3. The overall size and weight of the volume

    Does it fit in the case?

Closed Volumes   The easiest way to display a book is closed and lying horizontally. However, this can be uninformative and boring. Books with interesting covers or jackets may be laid in a case or shown standing on a shelf. If they are laid flat, nothing needs to be done. However, if they are standing on the shelf, a text-block support should be provided and the text block should be held closed with a polyester film or polyethylene strap. A book standing alone on a shelf does not have pressure on its covers to help keep the text block in its proper position within the covers; hence the need to support the text block. This is especially true of large books or books with heavy text blocks. The text-block support is a piece of alkaline board cut to fit the space at the bottom of the text block between the front and back covers of the closed book. It should be just as thick as the square of the book, the "square" being that part of the cover that extends beyond the text block.

Open Volumes   An open book should never stand on a shelf without support. When the book is open, the text block is completely unsupported and will pull and sag out of its covers. Open books should not be displayed at more than a ten-degree angle (the top of the book is raised up from the base 10°) without text-block supports. Even books that open easily and stay open in the flat position should not be displayed open to a full 180°. The amount of strain put on the sewing and the spine could cause the book to develop a preferential opening—that is, to always open to the same pages or to develop a gap in the text block at the exhibited opening even when the covers are closed. To prevent this, books displayed open but lying on a flat surface require support of some form under their covers. Small stacks of alkaline board or board folded into tentlike triangles can provide adequate support. Columbia University Libraries' videotape *Shedding Light on the Case* (see the Suggested Readings) describes simple, inexpensive exhibition methods.

Commercially available book cradles adjust to fit a wide variety of books and openings. A cradle can also be custom-made for a particular book at a particular opening. However, a cradle made for one particular book almost never fits another book. Be prepared to discard or disassemble all custom cradles at the end of an exhibition. These cradles can be made from acrylic sheets (such as Plexiglas), 5-mil polyester film, or a variety of alkaline boards. Making cradles from board or film requires a good board cutter, and acrylic sheet requires an acrylic sheet cutter and a heater to mold it. The alkaline board also requires a means of creasing.

A difficult decision is whether to use a full book cradle or a simple support, such as the tentlike triangles mentioned earlier. Common sense and experience are the only specific guides. Books come in far too many sizes, shapes, weights, and ease and degree of openability for hard and fast rules. In general, an open book needs a cradle that fully supports both covers when the book

> is shown at any angle; that is, the top or head of the book is higher above the case base than the bottom or tail of the book (some case bases are angled and the book may simply lie on the base)
>
> has a limp-cover binding
>
> has a fragile binding
>
> has a fragile attachment between text block and cover
>
> has an extremely heavy text block
>
> is a large format; that is, oversize quarto, folio, or elephant folio

Books with foldouts present a particular problem. Removing a foldout for exhibition is *not* an acceptable solution except in the *most extenuating* of circumstances and only after a thorough discussion with the curator and a professional conservator. To display the foldout in situ, the book should receive a support appropriate to its opening and then the opened foldout receives its own support. The support should follow the undulations of the foldout. The foldout should not be flattened excessively as it will need to be folded back into the book.

Single-Sheet Items

Certainly manuscripts, cards, drawings, and any of a number of two-dimensional items found in archives and libraries are usually more straightforward to exhibit than bound volumes. If the flat item is reasonably stable and in fair condition, a number of simple and safe options are available.

Laying the item on a shelf or in a case requires simply an alkaline board cut to the size and shape of the item. This provides support, separation of the case lining from the item, and an opaque ground preventing the case lining's color from showing through or the light passing through the item if it is laid on a glass shelf. It is a good idea to use photo corners or polyethylene or polyester film straps to hold the item to the support.

Polyester film in sheet form can be a quick, inexpensive way to protect an item. Full encapsulation of an item before being displayed flat or hanging is an excellent and crucial means of protecting it. This is especially true if the item is fragile or will be called for frequently after being displayed. However, friable media, such as pastels, charcoal, and graphite drawings, should never be put under polyester film because the static electricity of the film pulls loose particles off the paper.

Items to be hung may need more protection than lightweight polyester film. Matting is an attractive and effective alternative. A simple mat consists of two alkaline boards with a window cut in the top board. The item is placed on one board and the board with the window is situated over the item so it can be viewed through the window opening. Several preservation matting guidelines are available, which show the basic window mat, and a variety of ways to hold the item in place. The hinging of an item using Japanese tissue and starch paste can be tricky. Some papers, especially architectural papers and linens, can be very sensitive to moisture and should be done by someone experienced with such papers. If the mat is only temporary, there are other ways of holding the item in place—for example, using custom-made photo corners or polyester film straps for supports.

Attaching items that are matted or encapsulated to the back wall of a case can be problematic. If the backboard will accept pushpins, the mat or encapsulation can be safely pinned to the back. Pins should *never* be stuck in an *original* item. Always pin through the polyester film or use the pins to hold the mat to the backboard. Stainless steel L-pins can be most useful in holding matted items to a case's back wall.

If the backing fabric has enough nap or tooth to allow the hook side of a hook-and-loop fastener (Velcro) to grab and hold, it may be easier to simply hang the item using a self-adhesive hook side of such a fastener. Put the hook on the back of the polyester film or the mat and simply press the item in place. The self-adhesive hook fastener should *never* be stuck directly on an *original* item.

Framing is a more expensive means of display, but can offer more protection from temperature and relative humidity fluctuations than a simple mat. Framed items also need not be displayed in a case. When framing an item, consideration should be given to all aspects of the package. All paper-based items should be matted before framing. Following the preservation matting practices is the necessary first step. The rabbet of the frame must be deep enough to accept the minimum package made up of glazing, two thicknesses of mat board with the item, and a backing support board. By adding silica gel panels and an outer layer of polyester film, and sealing the edges with a chemically stable "framing" tape, RH can be controlled within this sealed package. The recent production of mat board containing a core of activated carbon and molecular sieves, which acts as a pollutant sponge, can give additional protection.

Attaching a framed item to a wall or back of a display case can be done with picture hangers available through framing suppliers. There are security hangers that require following specific motions and using certain tools. Some museums and libraries attach brackets to wooden frames and secure the framed piece in place with screws. The value of the piece, where it is to be hung, the policies of the institution, the type of security system in place, and the size of the item should be considered in deciding how it will be hung.

Conclusion

Exhibitions clearly serve an institutional purpose in terms of outreach and education, but administrators and staff should never lose sight of the need to protect and preserve library and archival materials at all stages of exhibition preparation and implementation. Careful attention to professionally acceptable exhibition policies, techniques, and requirements will permit valuable or irreplaceable materials to be displayed without compromising their long-term survival.

Note

1. Garry Thomson, *The Museum Environment*, 2d ed. (London: Butterworth, 1986), p. 268.

Suggested Readings

American Library Association. Association of College and Research Libraries. Rare Books and Manuscripts Section. Committee for Developing Guidelines for Borrowing Special Collections Materials for Exhibition (Ad Hoc). *Guidelines for Borrowing Special Collections Materials for Exhibition.* Chicago: ACRL, 1990.

Buck, Rebecca A., and Jean Allmann Gilmore, eds. *The New Museum Registration Methods.* 4th ed. Washington, D.C.: American Association of Museums, 1998.

Canadian Conservation Institute. "Encapsulation." CCI Note 11/10. Ottawa: Canadian Conservation Institute, 1995.

———. *A Light Damage Slide Rule.* Ottawa: Canadian Conservation Institute, 1994.

Columbia University Libraries. *Shedding Light on the Case.* Videotape. New York: Columbia University, 1990.

Farr, Gail E. *Archives and Manuscripts: Exhibits.* Chicago: Society of American Archivists, 1980.

Foster, Chris, Annette Manick, and Roy Perkinson. *Matting and Framing Works of Art on Paper.* Washington, D.C.: Foundation of the American Institute for Conservation of Historic and Artistic Works, 1994.

Greenfield, Jane. *Books: Their Care and Repair.* New York: H. W. Wilson, 1983.

Klein, Larry. *Exhibits: Planning and Design.* New York: Madison Square Pr., 1986.

Lafontaine, Raymond H. *Silica Gel.* CCI Technical Bulletin, no. 10. Ottawa: Canadian Conservation Institute, 1984.

Lull, William P., and Paul Banks. *Conservation Environment Guidelines for Libraries and Archives.* Ottawa: Canadian Council of Archives, 1995.

Marcon, Paul J., and Thomas J. K. Strang. *Circular Slide Rule for Cushion Design.* Ottawa: Canadian Conservation Institute, 1990.

——. *PadCAD Computer Program for Cushion Design.* Ottawa: Canadian Conservation Institute, 1999.

Martin, Susan B. "Polyester Film Book Supports." *Abbey Newsletter* 14 (June 1990): 55.

Mecklenburg, Marion F., ed. *Art in Transit, Studies in the Transport of Paintings.* Washington, D.C.: National Gallery of Art, 1991.

Mowery, John Franklin. "Packing Books for Travel." *Guild of Book Workers Journal* 23, nos. 1–2 (1984–1985): 58–68.

National Information Standards Organization. *Environmental Conditions for Exhibiting Library and Archival Materials.* Bethesda, Md.: NISO, in press. ANSI Z39.79-2000

National Park Service. *Museum Exhibit Lighting: An Interdisciplinary Approach: Conservation, Design and Technology.* Washington, D.C.: American Institute for Conservation of Historic and Artistic Works, 1997.

Nicholson, Catherine. "What Exhibits Can Do to Your Collection." *Restaurator: International Journal for the Preservation of Library and Archival Material* 13 (1992): 95–113.

Reeve, James K. *The Art of Showing Art.* Tulsa, Okla.: HCE Publications and Council Oak Books, 1986.

Stolow, Nathan. *Conservation and Exhibitions: Packing, Transport, Storage and Environmental Considerations.* London: Butterworth, 1987.

Tétreault, Jean, and Scott Williams. *Guidelines for Selecting Materials for Exhibiting, Storage and Transportation,* ver. 4.3. Ottawa: Canadian Conservation Institute, 1993.

Wilson, William K. *Environmental Guidelines for the Storage of Paper Records: A Technical Report Sponsored by the National Information Standards Organization.* Bethesda, Md.: NISO, 1995.

Witteborg, Lothar P. *Good Show! A Practical Guide for Temporary Exhibitions.* Washington, D.C.: Smithsonian Institution, 1981.

12

Selection for Preservation

CAROLYN HARRIS

Librarians and archivists must make the critical determination of which materials will be important in the future. Difficult decisions must be made to ensure that deteriorated library and archival materials receive the most appropriate preservation options based on the intellectual content, physical aspects, and condition of each item within the context of the mission and policies of the holding institution.

Reduction of chemical and physical deterioration, as discussed elsewhere in this book, is a crucial preservation activity because it affects all materials in the collection under the care of the library or archives. However, each item in the library or archives continues to deteriorate at an individual rate based on its physical and chemical qualities and on its use. Physical deterioration is breakdown of the structure of the item so it no longer functions adequately. For a bound volume, this includes problems relating to paper, leaf attachment, and binding primarily caused by the use of the item. Chemical deterioration is most often seen as embrittlement of paper because of hydrolysis and oxidation—chemical processes affected by the materials used in the original manufacture and by the environment in which the paper has been housed. Procedures must be implemented to identify the materials that are deteriorated either physically or chemically, and to make a selection decision to preserve each item.

Decisions to add materials to library and archival collections are made daily. These decisions relate to current user needs. In academic libraries, this may be for instruction or research; in a public library, to respond to the community's information needs. The decision may also relate to developing a collection to support the study of a specific subject area. Although simple mending or even library rebinding of deteriorated volumes may appropriately be undertaken without significant review, for seriously deteriorated items a second or reselection decision must be made. Does this item or collection still make the contribution to scholarship assumed when it was purchased or accepted into the collection?

It is very difficult to determine what materials will be needed in the future. Scholarship responds to intellectual discourse and disciplinary trends over time. Materials little used today may be used in innovative ways by future scholars. For example, a scientific monograph of today becomes the fodder of the historian of science tomorrow; vanity press items, bad poetry, romance novels, and popular magazines become documentation for social history; textbooks document educational practice. However, decisions have to be made. No one institution will have the funds to preserve everything in its collections; some materials will be of little importance or will be preserved elsewhere; other materials will no longer meet the mission of the institution.

Three assumptions are made in selecting what to preserve:

No one institution can afford to preserve everything in its collection. Cooperative agreements will ensure that more items are preserved, but the resources do not exist to preserve everything.

To accomplish the preservation of those materials that should be preserved, priorities must be set among collections, priorities that must be based on the quality of the collections and the vulnerability of materials to loss. Local institutions must define their strengths and concentrate their preservation resources on those strengths. Nationally, and increasingly internationally, priorities must be set among the collections of a subject area so resources are spent as efficiently as possible.

Not every item needs to be preserved. Perhaps a representative sample of a class of materials will be enough to serve the needs of scholars in the future. Perhaps some materials will never be called for. Librarians and archivists, with the assistance of scholars when appropriate, are called on to make decisions as to what should be preserved.

Ultimately, the decision to preserve library materials must be made on an item-by-item basis. Each item deteriorates at an individual rate depending on its physical composition and its use. However, the large scale of the preservation problem usually requires that priorities for preservation action be based on considering entire collections. But collections as a whole are made up of individual items. Policies and procedures for treating the individual items that make up these collections will be based on physical condition of the item rather than on quality of the work. Priorities among these collections must be set on a local and a national, or increasingly an international, level.

This chapter is concerned with selection on a general level: how decisions are made as to which items and collections should be preserved, according to what criteria, and what the preservation options are. Physical treatment, reformatting, and other preservation options require a more complex set of selection decisions. Those are dealt with in other chapters.

Identification

Identification is the process of observing that an item is deteriorated and forwarding that item for routine treatment or bibliographic review. Identification is most often a by-product of other library processes. This approach often identifies as many deteriorated materials as the preservation program can manage. It also results in the identification of materials currently used that, because of this use, have a priority for preservation treatment. Special projects will identify materials through separate independent processes.

Deterioration of bindings is usually obvious, although problems with paper strength and leaf attachment may require a more careful review of the item. When a deteriorated volume of a multivolume or serial work is identified, the entire set should be reviewed and decisions made in relation to the condition and relevance of the complete title.

Identification is done through at least one of the following seven ways:

Condition and Use   Identification of deteriorated materials is most often made when materials are used. As volumes are returned at the circulation desk, staff members review them and forward deteriorated materials for a selection decision. Volumes with damaged bindings, detached pages, or flaking embrittled paper are easily identified. Users of the library—faculty, scholars, students—will often notice deteriorated volumes and bring them to the attention of library staff. As these users become more aware of preservation concerns, they are more likely to do so. The circulation staff must be aware of the procedures for handling deteriorated volumes and show appropriate concern when problems are brought to their attention.

Stack maintenance personnel, especially those responsible for shelving and order of the materials, should also be on the lookout for deteriorated materials that may be used internally but not necessarily checked out. Part of the orientation and training of these staff members should be the understanding of the process of deterioration and the identification of preservation problems.

Condition and Library Processing   Staff members in other areas of the library or archives also may encounter deteriorated materials. The acquisitions and gifts and exchange staffs will see materials as they come into the collection; cataloging staff may see materials that have come for first time cataloging or for recataloging. The volumes they have identified should also be set aside for a selection decision. In archives, much preservation work is done during the appraisal and processing activities, including the identification of specific items that need additional treatment. One of the responsibilities of curatorial staff and library selectors is to manage the existing collection. As they review the collections, they will identify materials that need preservation attention.

Condition at Shelf   Many special projects require a review of the materials at the shelf. Items may be identified for preservation during shelf reading, bar coding, or security taping projects. A project for conversion of cataloging records into machine-readable form (recon project) may also be an appropriate time to review materials at the shelf. Preservation projects may be implemented to identify deteriorated materials in specific portions of the collections. Special collections materials often require review by the curator and a conservator to identify special problems.

Collection and Condition   Often collections as a whole are identified for preservation attention, as is discussed later in this chapter. In this case, the library staff members review each item within that collection to identify deteriorated materials.

Scholarly Review   Faculty, researchers, or scholars individually, as a group, or through a project administered through a professional organization may identify deteriorated individual titles of permanent research value that should be preserved.

Vulnerability to Loss or Deterioration   Some materials may be identified for preservation because they are more likely to deteriorate. Examples of this are newspapers or foreign publications printed on ephemeral paper, or materials that are to go on exhibition.

Value or Uniqueness   Some materials identified for preservation attention because of their importance will be given high priority for preservation. This includes materials of high monetary value or ones that are unique and therefore vulnerable to loss.

Identification Work Flow

Responsibility for identification of deteriorated items should be assigned to all library staff who come into contact with its collections. When an item is identified, a circulation record should be made to facilitate finding the item if a user should request it. A form may be designed to travel with the book indicating who identified it, which collection it came from, and what treatment might be desired. The form can also be used later to designate the selection decision, the searching process, and cataloging information.

Materials identified as deteriorated may be placed on a special shelf or book truck in the circulation unit or other section where they are found. Those that can be repaired in-house or commercially rebound may be sent directly for treatment without review by subject specialists. When the untreatable materials reach a critical mass, the selectors are asked to review them for withdrawal, storage, or preservation reselection decisions. An alternative work flow is to send these materials as they are found to a unit of the preservation department, which will make the initial triage decisions and do the preservation searching. Then the materials are forwarded to the selector for a decision.

Decision Making

After deteriorated materials have been identified, decisions must be made about whether they will be retained and treated. The decisions should be made by the selector, bibliographer, subject specialist, or curator responsible for the development and maintenance of the collection. In some cases an overarching collection development policy will eliminate the need for individual item decisions, but those policies should be made by the collection development staff with the advice and assistance of preservation staff. With clearly articulated policies, support staff will be able to make most of the decisions. Only those requiring reselection decisions or that are not obvious need be referred to the bibliographer.

A library's preservation policy should derive from its collection development policy. For example, materials in an undergraduate collection may be treated to remain on the shelf as long as possible, and withdrawn or replaced when they become untreatable. Libraries may preserve materials in some subject areas but not in others. Materials in special collections may be retained in original format whatever the cost. A public library may preserve local history materials, but not older business materials or fiction. The policies should be made in the context of the mission of the institution. Many libraries will not preserve such materials as offprints, textbooks, or later editions, reprints, or collected works that include no significant new material.

Many preservation programs have a policy that any materials that can be treated through an in-house repair facility or a library binder are immediately forwarded to those units. These materials will usually be relatively new and the paper still flexible. Because these materials have problems indicating they have been used and because the treatment is relatively inexpensive, a policy may be made that they are to be treated without the relatively costly decision-making process.

However, for materials in which the paper has become embrittled and those materials with artifactual value, a reselection decision must be made. The bibliographer, selector, or curator is responsible for determining which materials are still relevant to the collection or to future scholars and should be treated. These options, retaining and preserving in original format or reformatting, involve expensive processes. Therefore it is important to make informed decisions.

Other library options, including deaccessioning (or weeding), transfer to off-site storage areas, and transfer from general collections to special collections, require analogous decision making. This is recognized in recent literature in the field that discusses these processes in combination. The Collection Management and Development Section of the Association for Library Collections and Technical Services has published a *Guide to Review of Library Collections: Preservation, Storage, and Withdrawal,* and the Rare Books and Manuscripts Section of the Association of College and Research Libraries of the American Library

Association has published guidelines for transfers from general to special collections. Weeding in general collections, deaccessioning in special collections, appraisal of collections for addition to an archive, and preservation decisions also require decisions review by those knowledgeable about the collection and its use.

The role of the faculty in academic libraries must be considered. Most faculty members do not have the time or interest to be involved in individual item-level preservation decisions. The selector will have to determine when it is appropriate to ask for advice. Formulation of policy statements should include faculty involvement and understanding of the consequences of the policies. The selector and the preservation staff may take the opportunity of such policy formulation to discuss with faculty the need for preservation and the available options.

As part of the review process for preservation, the selector or bibliographer must have information about the item in order to make an informed decision. This involves bibliographic searching of local bibliographic files and regional or national bibliographic utilities to determine

> the relation of the item to the collection. Are there other copies, other editions, other materials by the same author? Based on policy decisions, materials that one would not necessarily expect to find in that library or that are not integral to the collection may not be preserved.

> whether other accessible copies exist through cooperative arrangements, in the geographic area, or through interlibrary loan. If copies are readily available and it is reasonable to expect they will remain available, the library may decide to rely on other institutions for access.

> whether the item has been preserved elsewhere. If another library has preserved the item and provides access to it, the institution may not want to duplicate effort and costs. A decision must be made for the local institution to replace its copy or to depend on the other institution for access.

> whether replacements are available commercially. If another copy, reprint, facsimile, or microform is available, the library will not want to duplicate effort, but may want to acquire the replacement for local users.

This information will help the selector in deciding which materials do not need to be preserved in the local collection because they exist in other institutions or have already been preserved. The selector needs only to decide whether the item should be replaced locally or put back on the shelf and allowed to die a peaceful death. However, if this search does not eliminate the item from consideration, the selector must make a decision.

Criteria for Decision Making at the Item Level

Criteria for item-level decisions are best expressed as a series of questions to be asked about the material:

Does the Item Have Artifactual Value? Library and archival materials have two aspects: visual content and physical content; each item has a text or illustrations that exist on a substrate. The text or other visual content is usually of prime importance for preservation. It is considered by many scholars, librarians, and archivists to be the content of the item. However, scholars who study printing, publishing, papermaking, and binding history consider those aspects of any item of primary importance—constituting in effect their text. The look and feel of the carrier of the text is also of importance to social historians; it adds to the understanding of the use of the text.

Artifactual, intrinsic, or iconic value is defined as having an attribute that makes the item important for its physical characteristics. Attributes that indicate that the physical item should be preserved may be age or date of printing; important or unusual bindings, paper, or printing; or illustrations. The exhibition value, provenance or association, or aesthetic qualities of the item should also be considered. Any item that may need to be authenticated in the future must be retained in original format for further study.

The issue of artifactual value has been debated fiercely. Some scholars, such as G. Thomas Tanselle, feel that every item has value as an artifact. Archivists and librarians realize that there will never be resources to preserve every physical entity. Brittle materials cannot be rejuvenated and thus it may be imperative that the text be preserved before the physical object is completely lost. In some fields and in some libraries, preserving every item may be an appropriate policy. For example, the Harry Ransom Humanities Research Center at the University of Texas has collected every copy of the first printing of *Ulysses* that could be found in order to study the process of publishing James Joyce's work.

The National Archives and Records Administration, the Library of Congress, and other libraries and archives have written policies on the retention of materials in original format. A collection development policy should include this information for every appropriate subject.

Preservation is concerned with both the permanence of the information and of the medium that carries and conveys that information. If an item is determined to have sufficient artifactual value, the original item should be preserved. This may require conservation treatment to stabilize the item and restore it to a useful state, or a protective enclosure to reduce further deterioration.

Is the Item Important to the Study of Its Field? Does it contain primary work, or important secondary work? Is it indexed or abstracted, or listed in important bibliographies of the field? Is it important to the publishing record of its field, for example, a first edition? This is a very subjective area of the decision, based on the selector's knowledge of the field and its history.

It can be argued that each subject area relates differently to its literature and that preservation decisions must take into account these differing approaches. Scientists use the literature of science differently than classicists or historians use their primary and secondary sources. Social scientists may only be interested in original data. However, predicting use based on the researchers in one subject does not take into account the interdisciplinary nature of archival and library materials; a different discipline or one we cannot now imagine may have use for these materials even after their primary function is obsolete.

Is the Item Bibliographically Complete? The most complete copy should be preserved; one missing pages, issues, or volumes should be left to others to preserve unless it is the most complete copy available. If feasible, a copy should be made complete before preservation by borrowing the missing parts through interlibrary loan. This is especially important for multivolume and serial titles. Other libraries may make decisions based on the fact that one institution has preserved a copy; if that one copy is incomplete, users will not be assured of access to the whole.

Will Its Preservation in Microformat Save Considerable Space without Limiting Access Unduly? Back volumes of scientific journals may be put on microfilm because they are consulted rarely and take up much space. Although this pertains primarily to the decision to microform an item, it can be an important criterion for the decision.

Has This Item Been Heavily Used? Or will it be used in the future? This is a difficult criterion because there is little indication that current or past use indicates future use. Current use, however, may be the best indication of future use. If the item has been used frequently, especially recently, it should be preserved. If no one has used it in its time in the collection, it may not be as important.

Are There Any Constraints Caused by Copyright Laws? Although collections are empowered to replace deteriorated materials for the collection, copyright must be considered for those materials not in the public domain when photocopy or microfilm reformatting is done.

Is This Item in Danger of Being Lost? Some materials that are used heavily or are in a very fragile format may be given preservation treatment before they deteriorate further in order to prevent future loss.

Does This Item Have Permanent Research Value? This concept is very difficult to define and is quite subjective. It can be seen as a combination of all the other criteria. If the preceding criteria indicate that the item should be preserved, then that item has permanent research value.

Once the decision has been made to preserve an item, it is important that the best option be chosen. Figure 1 lists many of these options

---

Figure 1
Options for Treatment of Individual Titles

- Planned Deterioration
  Will survive use
  Not important enough to treat
  Preserved elsewhere

- Withdraw, Deaccession
  Out of scope for collection
  Other copies, editions in
    collection
  Available elsewhere, not neces-
    sarily locally

- Repair
  Only minor damage
  Facilities available
  Would not withstand machine
    binding
  Retain original binding

- Rebind Commercially
  Major damage
  Heavy use
  Not artifactual

(continued)

Figure 1 *(continued)*

- Protective Enclosure
  Can't be repaired
  One deteriorated volume of a
    multivolume set
  Rare or valuable in original
    format
  Little use

- Replace
  Can't be repaired
  Replacement available
  Local copy necessary

- Reformat/Preservation
    Photocopy
  Can't be repaired
  Heavy use (reserve, reference)
  Paper copy necessary

- Reformat/Preservation Microfilm
  Brittle
  No artifactual value, if original
    will be damaged by filming
  Use copy to protect vulnerable
    original

- Reformat/Digital Copy
  Access primary goal

- Transfer to Limited
    Access/Storage Collection
  Vulnerable to use
  Valuable or rare
  Limited use

- Conservation Treatment
  Warrants cost of conservation
    treatment
  Artifactual value
  Rare or valuable

along with criteria for each option. The decision not to preserve may lead to withdrawing the item or replacing it on the shelf until it is too deteriorated to use. This is called planned deterioration or benign neglect. Planned deterioration, however, should be the result of conscious decision, not simple oversight. For example, newspapers or other materials available elsewhere on microfilm may be kept so that the user has access to them as long as they are usable.

Selection and Decision Making at the Collection Level

Many libraries may decide that only materials that are circulated are to be preserved. However, it is important to future scholarship that significant collections of materials relating to specific subject areas remain accessible regardless of current use patterns. Library staff identifies important or "great" collections for preservation attention. Identifying collections as a priority for preservation attention may result in better storage conditions or controlled access in addition to treatment or reformatting. The collection development and management staff working with the preservation staff should identify these collections based on criteria that indicate their quality in relation to other collections in the subject area.

The Yale University Library has completed a study to determine its most important collections. A committee identified 140 coherent subject groupings and special named collections in a priority order for preservation attention. Their approach was to keep the integrity of the broader intellectual value of whole subject areas regardless of use patterns and "to identify groups of materials that should be preserved and within those groups items that need preservation."[1] The criteria used were size, strength, makeup, academic priorities, value to scholarship, and preservation needs.

A few coordinated attempts have been made at defining the great collections on a national level, such as the Research Libraries Group (RLG) Great Collections Microfilming Project. But in each case, it has been the work of the local institution to determine which of its collections are important to the scholarship of the specific subject and therefore are a national priority. Scholarly groups have worked through the Commission on Preservation and Access (now part of the Council on Library and Information Resources) to assist in defining the great collections in their subject fields.

Collections already in a library's special collections department may be relatively easy to identify as important and thus worthy of consideration for preservation priority. However, many institutions have large subject collections built over time, in some cases many such collections, which represent subject strengths. These collections should be identified for establishing their preservation priority. Such collections may be significant because they meet local academic or community research priorities or because they meet national needs. They may have met current needs at some point, but those needs may have changed. The quality of these collections may be determined through the use of several decision criteria.

Size of Collection   Quantity does not always indicate quality, but collection size gives some indication of strength. *The National Shelflist Count*, published in 1986 by the Resources and Technical Services Division of the American Library Association, compares the size of collections based on subject. A collection that ranks high in numbers of items in relation to other collections in that subject should be considered for preservation attention.

Strength Indicated by Conspectus Level   The Association of Research Libraries North American Collections Inventory Project, based on the development of the Research Libraries Group Conspectus (now the responsibility of Washington Library Network, which has merged with the Online Computer Library Center, OCLC), is an online inventory of research library collections. The conspectus indicates levels of collecting by subject. The local institution indicates whether it has collected retrospectively or collects currently to what level within subject areas defined by the Library of Congress classification. Although the conspectus is admittedly a subjective document and is not yet complete, and not every library has participated in developing their conspectus values, it can be useful for determining collection strengths in relation to other collections within the same subject areas. The levels are from 0 (out of scope) to 3 (instructional), 4 (research level), and 5 (comprehensive). The conspectus indicates both absolute levels in relation to the universe of publications in the subject area and a comparison with other collections in that subject. A collection that ranks at least at 4, or research level, should be examined for treatment given its research value and priority as a subject area collection. Level 5 (comprehensive) indicates the presence of special materials, and as such, suggests a priority for preservation activities.

Many libraries will contain one or two level 4 or above collections. Major research libraries, however, may contain a hundred or more level 4 collections, making the conspectus values less useful for determining preservation priorities.

Past, Current, or Projected Future Use of Collection   High current use indicates local interest and priority. Use through interlibrary loan or visiting scholars indicates national priority. The strongest collections should logically receive heavy use from either local or national constituencies. Although difficult to project, discernable trends in scholarship may indicate future use. Collections with use from local or national constituencies should be given priority for preservation.

History or Provenance of Collection   Collections may have strength because they were built under special circumstances. A significant gift or endowment in one area, or strong faculty, alumni, curator, or donor interest, may have resulted in strong collections. In some cases a deed of gift may entail a legal obligation to retain and preserve a collection.

Publications or Bibliographies Based on the Collection   Are there well-known bibliographies or publications that are based on the collection, or has information about the collection been published? This suggests that the collection may be important in the future because of enhanced access.

Quality and Extent of Bibliographic Control   Is the collection under bibliographic control, completely cataloged in a national database? Increased access makes this collection more important for future scholars. If the collection does not have adequate bibliographic control, the cost of preservation activities may be considerably higher if they entail more extensive conversion of records or original cataloging.

Available Funding   Preservation of entire collections is an expensive proposition. It is prudent to give priority to collections that have a priority for internal funding or will attract outside government or private funding. Although this is political in nature, it is a pragmatic consideration in setting priorities among collections.

Media of the Materials in the Collection   Are the majority of the items in a collection of an ephemeral medium that dictates that they need to be preserved sooner than other collections? For example, newspaper or pamphlet collections, gazettes, and telephone books may be more at risk than less fragile collections. Color, cellulose nitrate– and cellulose acetate–based photographic media and glass plate negatives are at risk and should be considered a priority, as should all magnetic media.

The Cooperative Responsibilities of the Institution   Has the institution made any commitments to the preservation of materials in a specific collection through local, state, regional, or national cooperative programs? Past commitments may indicate strong collections.

Faculty Review of Collections   Are faculty, scholarly professional organizations, or other groups of scholars interested in preserving this collection? Has this collection been identified as possessing certain or specific strengths that other collections in the subject area do not have? The Modern Language Association, the American Philological Association, the Renaissance Society, medievalists, and art historians have become involved in determining what should be preserved in their fields.

Condition and Vulnerability of the Materials in the Collection
Does the collection have a considerable number of materials that have deteriorated? The collections with the most preservation problems

should be given priority for treatment. Is the collection vulnerable to loss in the near future?

Materials Preserved Elsewhere   Are there other libraries that have taken responsibility for materials in this subject area? Should this collection be added to their materials? Or should this collection not be highest priority because it duplicates other libraries' or archives' materials? It is often difficult to find out if the materials have been preserved elsewhere. The scope notes of the RLG Conspectus include information about preservation activities; the National Endowment for the Humanities Division of Preservation and Access lists at its website <http://www.neh.gov> its most recent awards, with multiyear award lists available upon request from the office; and the Association of Research Libraries is planning to keep a database of projects. Often it is not until a sample of records in a national database has been searched that it is discovered that another institution has treated a considerable number of materials in that subject area.

However, the decision to ignore a collection's preservation needs because another institution has done a project in that subject area must be considered very carefully. The overlap of collections is widely variable, and one institution's collection of the same subject area may comprise very different individual titles.

Subject of Collection   In some subject areas, the need for preservation is greater because of the patterns of a discipline's relation to its literature. Literary scholars need access to all editions of works; historians need original source documents; and social scientists may need machine-readable data as much as recent monographic literature. This combines some of the preceding criteria: Priority can reasonably be given to collections that include materials from developing countries or printed during wartime on low-quality paper, materials primarily from the brittle-paper period (1850 to 1950), or original source materials in historical subjects, such as the published records of social service organizations.

Using these criteria, important collections can be identified by collection development and management staff. It is very difficult to decide which subject collections should be given priority. Faculty or selector interest in preservation, funding opportunities, the possibility of entering into cooperative projects, or identification of collections of strength that are no longer of primary importance to current users provide other means of setting priorities.

Preservation Strategies at the Collection Level

Once a collection has been given priority for preservation, the institution has to decide how to treat the individual items within that collection. Several strategies have been identified for attacking the preservation problems of a collection that has been selected for preservation attention.

Clean Sweep/Vacuum Cleaner Approach

Variously described as a clean sweep or vacuum cleaner approach, this strategy involves treatment of all items in the collection. If microfilming is the appropriate treatment for that collection, all volumes may be microfilmed, anticipating their embrittlement. This strategy may be appropriate if there is an access or publication aspect to the preservation of the collection and if one of the goals of the project is to provide off-site access to a formalized body of material. Because of the preference for original formats, wholesale microfilming of collections that may not be in crisis condition is warranted in only a very few cases. Such treatment may be preferred if the microfilming will not destroy the original format, and if space is available for the volumes to be replaced on the shelf for local use.

Condition at Shelf

A collection is made up of individual items. Criteria described earlier for individual items should be used for making a preservation decision for each item based on the physical condition and artifactual value of that item. Condition and artifactual value become the only issues in deciding which treatment is appropriate if a broad policy decision has already been made that every item in the collection is worthy of preservation. The appropriate preservation treatment for each item is still crucial.

Scholarly Review

Researchers, scholars, and faculty may be involved in preservation selection within collections. The collection may be deemed important, but each item may still be subject to faculty review for importance to scholarship. A faculty committee may develop a list of the most important titles in the field or review materials as they are identified. An example is the American Philological Association project to microfiche the important literature in classics printed between 1850 and 1918.

Costs

Although ideally the cost of treatment should not dictate the treatment, practically it must be an important consideration. The treatment should not cost more than the item is worth. An item may be put into a protective enclosure to slow deterioration even though the appropriate option would be full conservation treatment, which would be more costly than the item merits. Reformatting is more costly than minor or routine physical treatment. Another consideration must be the cost of making individual item decisions. These decisions can take considerable time. Policy decisions that obviate the need for individual decisions help to keep costs to a minimum.

Conclusion

The decision to preserve materials on a collection or individual level is a difficult, time-consuming, and expensive endeavor. A process must be developed to identify materials that are deteriorated. Each institution must determine policies to guide the decision-making process, so that decisions can be made as rationally and routinely as possible. Policies must relate to the mission of the institution. The strengths of the collections and the most important materials in the individual collections must be identified as well as the materials most vulnerable to loss. Political considerations, such as costs, funding, and local interest in the collections, must be taken into account. The most appropriate and cost-effective preservation option must be chosen for each item. The other chapters in this book discuss in detail the process of deciding which preservation option is most appropriate for which type of materials and the policies and procedures relating to each option.

Note

1. Gay Walker, "Advanced Preservation Planning at Yale," *Microform Review* 18, no. 1 (1989): 20–28.

Suggested Readings

American Library Association. Resources and Technical Services Division. *Titles Classified by the LC Classification: National Shelflist Count.* Chicago: ALA, 1986.

Association for Library Collections and Technical Services. Collection Management and Development Committee. *Guide to Review of Library Collections.* Collection Management and Development Guides, no. 5. Chicago: ALA, 1991.

Atkinson, Ross. "Preservation and Collection Development: Toward a Political Synthesis." *Journal of Academic Librarianship* 16, no. 2 (1990): 98–103.

———. "Selection for Preservation: A Materialistic Approach." *Library Resources & Technical Services* 30 (1986): 341–353.

Bagnall, Roger, and Carolyn Harris. "Involving Scholars in Preservation Decisions: The Case of the Classicists." *Journal of Academic Librarianship* 13 (1986): 140–146.

Bonk, Sharon, and Sara Williams. "Stock Revision, Retention and Relegation in U.S. Academic Libraries." In *Collection Management in Academic Libraries,* edited by C. Jenkins and M. Morley, 213–234. Aldershot, England: Gower, 1991.

Brown, Charlotte, and Janet Gertz. "Selection for Preservation: Applications for College Libraries." In *Building on the First Century,* edited by J. C. Fennell, 288–294. Chicago: Association of College and Research Libraries, ALA, 1989.

Byrnes, Margaret. "Preservation and Collection Management: Some Common Concerns." *Collection Building* 9, nos. 3, 4 (1988): 39–45.

Child, Margaret. "Deciding What to Save." *Abbey Newsletter* 6, no. 4 supplement (1982): 1–2.

———. "Further Thoughts on Selection for Preservation: A Materialistic Approach." *Library Resources & Technical Services* 30 (1966): 354–362.

———. "Selection for Microfilming." *American Archivist* 53 (1990): 250–255.

Cox, Richard J. "Selecting Historical Records for Microfilming: Some Suggested Procedures for Repositories." *Library and Archival Security* 9, no. 2 (1989): 21–41.

"Guidelines on the Selection of General Collection Materials for Transfer to Special Collections." *College & Research Libraries News* 48 (1987): 471–474.

Harvard University Library. *Preserving Harvard's Retrospective Collections.* Cambridge, Mass.: Harvard University Library, 1991.

Hazen, Dan C. "Collection Development, Collection Management and Preservation." *Library Resources & Technical Services* 26 (1982): 3–11.

———. "Preservation in Poverty and Plenty: Policy Issues for the 1990's." *Journal of Academic Librarianship* 15 (1990): 344–351.

McCrady, Ellen. "Selection for Preservation: A Survey of Approaches." *Abbey Newsletter* 6, no. 4 supplement (1982): 1, 3–4.

O'Toole, James. *On the Preservation of Books and Documents in Original Form.* Washington, D.C.: Commission on Preservation and Access, 1989.

Research Libraries Group. Preservation Committee. "The Book as Object." In *RLG Preservation Manual*, 81–84. Mountain View, Calif.: RLG, 1986.

Richards, Daniel T., and Lucretia W. McClure. "Selection for Preservation: Considerations for Health Sciences." *Bulletin of the Medical Library Association* 77, no. 3 (1989): 284–292.

Riecken, Henry. "Selection for Preservation of Research Materials." *ACLS Newsletter* 2, no. 3 (1990): 10–12.

"Selection of Materials for Microfilming." In *Preservation Microfilming: A Guide for Librarians and Archivists*, edited by Nancy Gwinn, 26–60. Chicago: American Library Association, 1987.

Tanselle, G. Thomas. *Libraries, Museums, and Reading.* Sol. M. Malkin Lecture in Bibliography. New York: Book Arts Pr., 1991.

Tomer, Christinger. "Selecting Library Materials for Preservation." *Library and Archival Security* 7, no. 1 (1985): 1–6.

United States. National Archives and Records Service. *Intrinsic Value in Archival Materials.* Staff Information Paper 21. Washington, D.C.: NARS, 1982.

Williams, Lisa B. "Selecting Rare Books for Physical Conservation: Guidelines for Decision-Making." *College & Research Libraries* 47 (1985): 153–159.

13

The Conservation of General Collections

JAN MERRILL-OLDHAM
and NANCY CARLSON SCHROCK

The majority of materials acquired by academic and public libraries are processed, housed, and serviced as "general collections." Contrasted with special collections, general collections are typically shelved in open stacks accessible to patrons (although in some libraries materials are retrieved on demand from closed stacks). Made up largely of books, journals, and microforms covering a broad range of subjects, general collections are the largest and fastest-growing component of most libraries' holdings. As a rule, materials are more important for the information they contain than as artifacts; that is, they are not rare or unique, but this varies from institution to institution. The general collections in larger research libraries are more likely to include materials that have become valuable over time but that have not been identified for transfer to special collections.

Most materials in general collections postdate 1800, although again, in the older and larger institutions, significant holdings from the eighteenth and earlier centuries are likely to be discovered among modern imprints. Books can usually be borrowed by the library's primary clientele (local residents or university students, for example), and by others through interlibrary loan; journals can be used freely within the library but cannot be borrowed. Circulation policies are by no means uniform, however. In some libraries, journals are allowed to circulate after a period of high demand; in others, no materials circulate.

Although handling and age take their toll on all library holdings, general collections are particularly vulnerable. Materials are not valued as objects, their use is unsupervised, photocopying is usually unrestricted, and circulation can be heavy. At any point there are likely to be some materials for which demand is intense—new fiction in a public library, for example, or books on reserve for popular undergraduate courses. The steady growth of online catalogs, the retrospective conversion of card catalogs to machine-readable form, and the proliferation of electronic reference sources have stimulated greater use of some categories of materials than ever before. When items become damaged, the need to repair them quickly can result in treatments that are expedient rather than durable and nondestructive.

Interesting examples of efforts to bind, rebind, and repair worn and damaged materials can be found in most libraries. Such evidence, viewed collectively, reveals how approaches to the care of collections have changed over time. Much has been said about the extensive damage done to rare and valuable books and papers (both before and after their value was recognized) in the name of restoration, and about the emergence of modern conservation theory and practice. Historical approaches to the repair of materials in general collections have been similarly uninformed, and the implementation of appropriate alternatives slower to emerge.

From Mending to Collections Conservation

Before the twentieth century, most of the methods and materials used for routine book and paper repair were relatively benign—paste and paper for page tears, leather and cloth for damaged bindings. A repair manual published in 1924 by a vendor of library supplies drew inspiration from traditional bookbinding methods and materials. It described the use of imitation leather for recasing and rebacking, gummed parchment paper, water-soluble paste, replacement endpapers, and "a special cream tinted Japanese tissue."[1]

This traditional approach was gradually replaced by methods requiring less skill and time to execute. In 1931, the first "Scotch"-brand cellophane tape appeared, as did other rubber-based pressure-sensitive tapes; acrylic tapes (such as "Scotch Magic Mending Tape") emerged in 1961. These new products were adopted for library use, and various specialty products emerged. Tapes for repairing bookbindings were supplied in a rainbow of colors so that repairs could be made to match original book covers. In some libraries, tens of thousands of volumes were temporarily restored to usefulness with mending tapes, rubber cement, and white glue. Pamphlet binders also appeared on the market, their spines made from flimsy cloth and their boards from mechanical wood pulp. Such binders have been used for decades by libraries large and small.

The introduction of new, unstable repair materials unfortunately coincided with new trends in book manufacturing, including increasing reliance on hot-melt adhesive binding ("perfect binding") in place of sewn books; the use of paper instead of cloth to cover the cases of hardbound books, and the production of paperback editions in addition to or in place of hardbound books. All were less durable than the casebound book developed during the nineteenth century.

Also significantly, the mid-twentieth century saw the closing of many of the in-house binderies that had been established in large libraries. The loss of jobs and training opportunities in hand bookbinding meant that fewer people had book repair skills, especially advanced skills. Coupled with this trend, dramatic increases in library acquisitions, steady increases in library use, and inadequate budgets for commercial rebinding left libraries with little recourse except to make generous use of tape and glue as an alternative to full rebinding.

By the 1970s, the nature and extent of the damage done to books by these expedient methods was quite evident. Tapes used to repair bookbindings age in various ways. Some oxidize and drop off, leaving a crusty residue and the book without structural support. Others develop gummy ridges around their edges, which collect dust and grit, and transfer to the surfaces of shelving and other books. Many of the tapes used for paper repair cause sticky, translucent brown stains; become hard and stiff, causing paper to fracture; or oxidize and fail. Household glues and pastes also degrade, causing stains, growing hard and brittle with age, or losing their adhesive properties.

In general, inexpert repairing of books accelerates their deterioration. They crack apart when opened, pages break away from bindings, and bindings break away from texts. Pamphlets glued, stapled, or sewn into acidic binders also sustain damage. The binders become brittle and crumbly, weakening and staining their contents and sometimes breaking away, leaving texts damaged or unprotected. Staples cause rust stains and paper ruptures, and adhesives stiffen and discolor pamphlet covers and texts.

Growing concern during the 1970s and 1980s about the brittlebook problem focused unprecedented attention on the physical condition of library collections, deficiencies in modern paper and book manufacturing, and the need to recast existing collections maintenance programs. A 36,000-volume condition survey conducted by the Yale University Libraries' Preservation Department from 1979 to 1982 remains the largest and most thorough of its kind to date.[2] The Yale study confirmed worst-case estimates of embrittlement in U.S. libraries. Overall, 37.1 percent of the books sampled had brittle paper and 82.6 percent had paper with a pH below 5.4, indicating a level of acidity that is likely to cause rapid embrittlement. The need for repair was equally startling. Data suggested that approximately 235,000 volumes in Yale's main research library alone required mending or rebinding. Interestingly, inexpertly repaired books were recorded as "mutilated." Overall, findings support the results of most of the smaller surveys conducted in research libraries before and since.

A flurry of publications during the 1980s provided guidance for libraries committed to improving and expanding their repair programs for general collections. Jane Greenfield, Hedi Kyle, and Carolyn Morrow described and illustrated techniques that reflected the understanding of book structure, materials, and conservation principles promulgated by rare book conservators. During the 1980s, several research libraries upgraded repair procedures following the earlier lead of several innovative conservators, including Willman Spawn at the American Philosophical Society Library, Jane Greenfield at Yale, and Paul Banks at the Newberry Library.

Fortunately, recognition of the need for better book repair techniques did not emerge as an isolated consideration. During this period, the term *collections conservation* began to be used by librarians to describe the programmatic application of conservation principles to general research materials—which are invaluable in the aggregate, but do not warrant the item-by-item documentation and optimum treatment given to special collections. In 1990, the Collections Conservation Task Force of the Research Libraries Group (RLG) Preservation Committee described the principles underlying the concept of collections conservation in a memo to members of the full committee:

> Collections conservation: A preservation management strategy for the physical treatment and protective housing of endangered research materials that allocates treatment resources for maximum benefit to the collection. Collections conservation is one component of a comprehensive program, and is based on the following principles:

- Resources are focused on materials with highest preservation priority
- The useful life of materials in their original format is maximized, thus enhancing access
- The scale of the collections conservation program is linked to the scale of the problems in the collections; emphasis may shift as needs change
- The cost effectiveness of treatments is maximized by batching work; using permanent, durable materials; and employing sound methods
- Special collections materials are included as appropriate to the collections approach
- Other preservation options are considered when feasible, acceptable, and more cost effective than conservation treatment."[3]

Components of a Collections Conservation Program

The goal of a collections conservation program is to improve and stabilize the physical condition of library collections. This can involve a broad range of activities, their scope dependent upon the training, skills, and experience of the program manager; whether the program exists within the context of a comprehensive preservation effort; and the availability of resources. A full complement of responsibilities includes:

Establishment of a communications network within the library or system of libraries, which enables collaborative development of policies, work flows, and mechanisms for decision making

Development of specifications for a range of conservation treatments appropriate for general collections; and, in the absence of a rare book or paper conservator, for noninterventive refurbishing and rehousing of special collections

Management of a repair workshop or conservation laboratory, including evaluation of materials to determine the types of treatment or protective housing they require; treatment and housing of materials; standards setting and quality control; staff training and supervision; work flow management; and selection and maintenance of supplies, tools, and equipment

In the absence of a rare book or paper conservator, management of contracts for the treatment of special collections

Direct management of, or involvement in the management of, the library's commercial binding program, preservation photocopying program, and/or mass deacidification program—including the management of contracts for external services

Preservation needs assessment, including designing and conducting condition surveys

Environmental monitoring and participation in the development of environmental specifications for building renovation and construction projects

Disaster preparedness and recovery, and response to mold and insect infestation

Large institutions were the first to acknowledge this concept of collections conservation programs in a formal way. In 1985, the University of California, Berkeley, hired a "conservator for general collections," and in the following year the University of Connecticut hired its first collections conservator.

Collections Conservation Personnel

A collections conservation program requires personnel to develop and manage the program and to treat materials. A conservator can perform both functions and participate in library decision making and policy-setting; a technician's expertise is limited to treatment and to the supervision of workshop operations.

The Collections Conservator

Conservators are highly trained, skilled professionals who know the history of paper and book production, the chemistry of materials, and environmental science. This intellectual background is coupled with extensive bench training. In recent years the value, for the conservator, of a broad background in librarianship has been recognized, and many have earned a master's degree in library science. The University of Texas at Austin offers a formal master's degree program that combines bench training in conservation with academic courses in library science and conservation theory. Some practitioners have earned an M.L.S. independent from, and before or after, extensive training, apprenticeships, and practice in conservation.

An enduring definition of the collections conservator, as distinguished from the special collections conservator, was articulated at a meeting of the Association of Research Libraries (ARL) in 1988: a professional conservator who "manages a high-volume production-oriented operation, and develops strategies for conserving large collections of general research materials in their original format."[4] It is important to note that the collections conservator may or may not be qualified to treat special collections, and that this factor will be a significant determinant in establishing the nature and scope of a library's collections conservation program.

The Conservation Technician

Conservation technicians support the work of collections conservators in larger libraries, and may be the only staff engaged in book and paper repair in smaller libraries. With proper training a technician can acquire the skills needed to select and execute sound treatments, but may or may not be qualified to pull problematic items from the work flow (materials that do not deserve the investment of time and funds required for repair, for example, or that are too valuable to repair using routine procedures). Typically, the technician lacks the breadth of training or educational background needed to develop policy and to participate in broader collections management activities within the library.

Ideally, technicians should study basic bookbinding under a skilled binder, and receive additional training in the more specialized procedures required for collections conservation. In reality, training is often gained through trial and error on the job and through short workshops. Both approaches have limitations. The former is only as good as the instructions and evidence left by the predecessor and the instincts of the technician, and provides no ready means to learn new techniques. The latter can provide a general introduction to treatment procedures but cannot prepare technicians to apply them appropriately, or to handle the complex demands associated with treatment of the wide range of materials found in library collections.

Extended training programs for technicians are more effective, particularly where there is time for one-on-one instruction and critique. In the past such opportunities were few. Pioneering institutions included Johns Hopkins University, which began offering book repair workshops in 1981, and Southern Illinois University, which offered training beginning in 1982. Both programs, now concluded, were partly grant supported. Among more recent opportunities, the University of California, Berkeley, with funding from NEH, has offered training for technicians from the libraries of all campuses of the UC system, and Cornell University has trained staff from (mostly smaller) libraries in New York, with support from New York State. Both the California and Cornell programs included six weeks of intermittent instruction combined with practice in the home institution. In 1992, the University of California, Berkeley, Library convened a conference titled "Training the Trainers" (also NEH sponsored) to stimulate the development of additional training opportunities for conservation technicians. This effort has spawned a number of regional training activities.

Although not specifically directed toward the needs of libraries, short courses in box making and bookbinding offered by crafts schools and private practitioners are a valuable means of improving hand skills and increasing students' understanding of book structure. Because such instruction may or may not be directly relevant to library conservation, techniques must be evaluated by a supervisor before they are incorporated into library practice. There are also opportunities for more extensive training, such as the two-year bookbinding program offered by the North Bennet Street School in Boston, which includes training in book repair and conservation rebinding. Training opportunities are tracked by the Guild of Book Workers in a periodically updated publication.

Although the need for professional development for conservators is acknowledged in most institutions, ongoing training for technicians working in isolation is equally important and not always recognized. An investment in continuing education for technicians is returned to the library many times over if the result is more competently treated collections. Training for librarians who are responsible for collections maintenance, and who have a technician on staff but no conservator, is also critical. Supervising librarians must become familiar with collections conservation theory and practice in order to develop guidelines for making treatment decisions appropriate to a collection's value and prevailing patterns of use. They must also be able to judge the quality of the treatments being performed and to monitor output. The American Library Association and state and regional library associations sponsor relevant programs.

Student Assistants and Volunteers

Often the efforts of collections conservators and technicians are supplemented by student assistants and volunteers. It is crucial that untrained, temporary employees work under the direct supervision of trained personnel. In libraries where materials are, on the whole, permanently retained, and where there is no conservator or technician on staff, boxing and commercial library binding are probably better responses to wear and damage than in-house treatment. In cases where a technician assumes responsibility for training and overseeing the work of students and volunteers, library managers must keep in mind that the term *supervisor* is appropriately used to reflect such increases in job responsibility, and that the term *conservator* connotes advanced training and education.

Professional Development

The Guild of Book Workers has provided bookbinders and book conservators with their first opportunities to share ideas and skills. The guild initiated annual standards meetings in 1980. Each year since then, four conservators, binders, or book artists have demonstrated techniques that represent high standards of practice. Though not specifically targeted at book repair, standards meetings and the informal conversations that surround them have resulted in the formulation of techniques and principles that have been adopted by libraries. In 1984 the American Library Association and the Library of Congress cosponsored a one-week seminar, "Library Preservation: Fundamental Techniques," that included hands-on instruction in basic conservation treatment procedures (surface cleaning, paper repair, pamphlet binding, construction of protective enclosures, and basic book repair), lectures, and formal and informal discussion.[5] The program was significant because it brought together several instructors and a large group of participants from different types of libraries nationwide for an extended period.

Yet another event that helped to focus national attention on collections conservation trends and issues was a meeting of the Physical Quality of Library Materials Discussion Group at the 1991 Midwinter meeting of the American Library Association, at which practitioners displayed models and discussed varying approaches to treatment and problem solving. This meeting was followed by a similar, expanded program for the newly formed Library Collections Conservation

Discussion Group (LCCDG) at the annual conference of the American Institute for Conservation (AIC) in 1992. Training instructions and other materials shared among attendees were published as an ARL SPEC Kit, and LCCDG now meets regularly in conjunction with AIC. Resource materials shared among collections conservators at the 1992 Berkeley conference "Training the Trainers" (referred to earlier in this chapter) have also been published. The publication of policies and procedures from various institutions; continued communication at state, regional, and national meetings; serial publications, such as the *Abbey Newsletter* and *The Book and Paper Group Annual;* and electronic resources, such as the Conservation Distribution List and Conservation OnLine continue to stimulate the development of standards of practice, to expand treatment options, and to shape and legitimize the role of the collections conservator within the broader professional landscape.

The Nature of Collections Conservation Treatments

Although collections conservators share with rare book and paper conservators a commitment to the long-term preservation of materials in their original format, the greater accessibility and lower artifactual value of general collections have resulted in the emergence of approaches that depart from those used for special collections. As Carolyn Morrow noted in a 1991 paper, the two practices are very different, although they share some of the same equipment and employ staff with seemingly similar skills: "Much like a cafeteria [differs from] . . . a fine restaurant, both may be high-quality, use good ingredients, employ excellent cooks, and use many of the same tools, but the clientele, mission, and presentation of the product differ markedly."[6]

As in all fields of conservation, collections conservation staff use durable, chemically stable materials, and undertake treatments that are appropriate to their level of expertise and that can be executed properly with available equipment. Refurbishing and rehousing projects may involve procedures identical to those employed by special collections conservators. The principles of minimal intervention, single standard of treatment, and item-level documentation that underlie the treatment of artifacts, however, are not applied in treating general collections. Instead, maximizing the life and usability of the text at reasonable cost and within a reasonable time is the primary concern. This matrix of goals favors strategies that achieve functionality, longevity, and high production levels rather than preservation of the integrity of the artifact. Endpapers and even original bindings may be sacrificed if it is anticipated that an item will be heavily used and photocopied.

In place of the item-level documentation prepared for materials in special collections, documentation for general collections conservation consists of generalized treatment specifications. A specification typically includes a statement of scope indicating the circumstances under which a treatment is applicable, a description (sometimes illustrated) of techniques and materials, and estimates of the time and costs involved. The procedures for which specifications have been developed focus on cloth case bindings, paperbacks, pamphlets, and, in more advanced programs, certain types of leather bindings. Also specified are preventive and protective measures, such as pamphlet binding, box making, and the construction of pockets for accompanying materials, such as maps and disks.

Fundamental to collections conservation treatments are the principles of batch processing, cost-effectiveness, and highly organized work flow. Items are sorted, grouped, and processed based on the type of treatment required, so that they can be moved through the workshop efficiently without sacrificing good craftsmanship. Although quality control is essential, the treatment of general collections is nonetheless characterized by compromise in a way that the treatment of special collections is not. It is far more important to return a heavily used modern dictionary to the shelves as quickly as possible, for example, than it is to ensure that paper repairs are perfectly executed and nearly invisible. Furthermore, where usability and durability are key objectives in treating the dictionary, these qualities might well be forgone when treating a rare book that will be consulted infrequently and under supervision, and that would lose value if altered.

Treatment Options

The range of procedures that are performed within a collections conservation program is directly dependent on the nature and scope of available resources. For the purposes of this chapter, treatment procedures have been grouped into six categories to suggest the types of problems and issues that are addressed by a comprehensive program.

Preparation for Library Use

Except for a relatively few titles that specifically target the library market (some reference books, for example), publishers' bindings, pamphlets, scholarly journals, and popular magazines are not designed to withstand repeated reading and copying over a long period. They must be made sturdier before circulation, where possible, and repaired as soon as damage is noted. Early intervention is cost-effective because preventive treatments are easier to perform than complicated repairs, and they require less time, fewer materials, and less skill. Most treatments that fall into the "preparation" category can be performed by student workers and library volunteers with proper instruction.

Pamphlet Binding   Pamphlets are sewn or stapled into binders made from alkaline, buffered board with sturdy cloth spines, or are bound between alkaline boards using some means of mechanical attachment (usually staples, linen thread, or plastic combs). Board covers and pamphlet binders are available commercially or are made in-house. If staples are used, they are stainless steel or some other nonrusting metal.

Tip-ins   Loose errata sheets that sometimes accompany books and journals are tipped in by applying a thin line of adhesive along the binding edge of the sheet. Indexes to journals sometimes arrive after issues have been bound, and are tipped or hinged in provided they are not too thick. (The introduction of numerous pages often requires rebinding.)

Pockets   Loose plates, maps, computer diskettes, and other media accompanying books must be secured in pockets before circulation. Pockets are made from cloth, Tyvek, or alkaline paper, and are constructed so that they provide adequate support without inhibiting the insertion and removal of materials. For loose materials that will circulate without books, pockets are built into pamphlet binders.

Paperback Reinforcement   If paperbacks do not merit commercial binding, or if budgets can't support binding, covers are reinforced using some combination of alkaline boards, sturdy cloths, and plastic laminates. Appropriate reinforcement procedures do not involve the application of tape to book pages.

Other   Preparation for shelving also includes tightening the hinges of newly acquired books (see book repair), slitting uncut pages, repairing torn pages (see paper repair), and constructing wrappers and boxes (see construction of protective enclosures).

Preparation for Commercial Library Binding

Treating a volume in-house before it is sent out for commercial library binding can sometimes improve significantly the library binder's product. In appropriate situations, pages are repaired using Japanese paper and starch paste (because library binders use pressure-sensitive tape in routine practice). Covers are pulled away from sewn text blocks, and the binding margins of first and last pages are repaired with Japanese paper to improve the results of commercial recasing (that is, attaching new endpapers and a new case but leaving the text block intact). Sewing structures are repaired so that sewn volumes can be recased rather than milled along the spine and adhesive bound. Where sewing is unsalvageable but signatures must be retained (as with certain music or atlases, for example), the volume is disbound and signatures are repaired so that the commercial library binder can resew the volume.

Book Repair

Unlike preparation for shelving, book repair is remedial. It corrects damage that has occurred through poor manufacture, use, abuse, or aging. Repair materials are chosen for their permanence, durability, and physical and aesthetic compatibility. Papers are alkaline, adhesives are stable, and cloths are strong. Where weak cloths must be used to achieve color matches or for some other reason, they are lined with fabric or paper before use.

Hinge Tightening   Case-bound books usually break down first in the hinges, along which the covers flex. The case becomes loose, inviting more serious damage. Because of deficiencies in the methods and materials used in modern book manufacturing, this weakening is sometimes evident in new books, and often occurs in books once they have circulated. To remedy the problem, glue is applied along the insides of the hinges, between the endpaper and the inside of the case, and the book is dried under pressure. Hinge tightening strengthens the binding considerably and helps to ensure that a book can withstand repeated use.

Tip-ins   When one or more pages are missing from a book or journal, a copy of the volume is borrowed from another library through interlibrary loan and photocopies of missing pages are made. When volumes can't be borrowed (which is usually the case with journals), photocopies of missing pages are ordered. Acquired copies that are acidic, single-sided, or not registered front to back are recopied. The resulting facsimile pages are trimmed to size and tipped or hinged in provided there are only a few. The reincorporation of numerous pages often necessitates rebinding. Loose pages can also be tipped in, but they often indicate that the paper or binding is failing and that more drastic measures are required.

Paper Repair   Tears and splits in pages and paper covers are often repaired with long-fibered Japanese paper and starch paste. Tissue coated with a heat-activated adhesive is used for papers sensitive to moisture, such as coated papers. "Archival" pressure-sensitive tapes may be suitable for materials that will eventually be weeded, but office-type tapes are avoided because of the damage they cause over time.

Structural Repair for Standard-size Case-bound Books and Paperbacks   Although no two books are exactly alike, case binding construction is fairly consistent and treatments can therefore be grouped into categories. Where the text block is intact, treatments are usually easier to batch and execute. Repair of volumes with damaged text blocks typically requires more skill, time, and sensitivity to particularities of the item in hand. Typical treatments include replacing original endpapers; reconstructing the spine of the binding; repairing the boards; removing the case, repairing it, and reattaching it to the text block; and removing the case, cleaning the spine of the text block, repairing sewing, attaching new endpapers, relining the spine, and recasing the text block in its original case or in a newly constructed case. When the text block is so damaged that it requires complete disbinding, repair, and resewing, and the paper is flexible, commercial binding is usually the option of choice. The same is true when an adhesive-bound text block breaks apart.

There are many variations on these basic treatments and approaches to executing them, but greater standardization of terminology and methodology is emerging as collections conservators meet regularly and publish. Whether a procedure is relatively simple or difficult to execute depends on many factors. It is one thing to recase a 1993 publication printed on strong alkaline paper and sewn with sturdy nylon thread, and another to treat a fragile nineteenth-century volume with embrittling paper and a fragile sewing structure.

Structural Repair for Other Types of Bindings   The further collections conservation staff proceed beyond the treatment of pamphlets, standard-size case-bound books, and paperbacks, the more they must know about book structure and the more skilled they must be. In libraries where there is a collections conservator on staff, more complicated treatments are likely to be performed for general collections, including the repair of books that are sewn on cords; oversize volumes that require split-board constructions and more complex spine treatments; books with older, fragile, machine-stamped bindings; and books with leather bindings. Again, whether a procedure is incorporated into a collections conservation program depends on the level of available conservation expertise.

Construction of Protective Enclosures

Books, loose plates, photographs, individual or groups of pamphlets, and many types of nonpaper media are housed in wrappers, phase boxes, double-tray boxes, and other protective enclosures. Enclosures serve multiple functions. They protect valuable materials, new and old, that merit special protection from dust, light, and mechanical damage; deteriorating materials that can neither be repaired nor discarded; and groups of items that must remain together on the shelf. Structures range from simple paper wrappers that can be made by relatively unskilled staff, to complicated boxes made of board and cloth that hinge at the spine, have inner wrappers, and must fit precisely. General principles guide the construction of all types of enclosures: Board, paper, and other materials are permanent and durable; the enclosure is of a size and weight that poses no damage to its contents; and the contents can be removed and replaced easily such that the enclosure itself is not a source of wear and tear.

Paper Treatment

Library holdings that include a significant percentage of older, acidic books and large collections of flat paper (manuscripts, maps, posters) present special problems for conservation staff. Conservation work that requires complex paper treatment is performed only by conservators or by experienced technicians under the supervision of a conservator, in facilities with adequate equipment, including a large sink, water filtration system, and fume hood. A brittle book that is not a suitable candidate for microfilming or photocopying might be deacidified, each page encapsulated in polyester film, and the encapsulated pages post bound (at which point, the item is likely to be transferred to a special collection for safekeeping). A manuscript collection might be flattened, staples and paper clips removed, and major tears mended. Pressure-sensitive tape might be removed from a twentieth-century music score, or from an interesting machine-stamped cloth binding. Time-consuming—and thus expensive—treatments such as these are not performed without discussing them with bibliographers and curators, but the discussions are less involved than they would be with very valuable or unique objects, and little if any documentation is developed. Such procedures as stain removal, treatment of parchment or vellum, or treatment of works of art on paper fall outside the scope of a collections conservation program.

Treatment of Special Collections

In the absence of a conservator for special collections, collections conservation staff may do some work with special collections in collaboration with curatorial staff. Such activities as constructing book jackets, wrappers, and boxes; rehousing collections of photographs and manuscripts; and assisting with exhibit preparation are appropriate.

The publications listed in Suggested Readings at the end of this chapter provide detailed descriptions of the techniques, equipment, and materials used in general collections conservation programs, and discuss the factors that inform decision making and treatment in established facilities.

The Relationship of In-house Treatment to Commercial Binding and Reformatting

The ability of a library to procure commercial binding services has a profound influence on the nature and scope of its conservation activities. The smaller the library, the narrower in-house capabilities are likely to be, and the broader the range of problems for which commercial binding is used. The smaller the binding budget, the more important early intervention becomes. In libraries in which little or no money has been allocated for commercial binding and where conservation capabilities are modest, withdrawal is often the only available response to extensive damage. Where both a conservation and a commercial library binding program exist, guidelines are established regarding the types of materials that will be treated in-house and the types that will be sent out for library binding. Decisions are based on such factors as the ease and speed with which a treatment can be performed in-house, the relative cost of in-house versus commercial treatment, the relative importance of rapid turnaround time, the age and condition of the text block, the relative merits of retaining the original binding, the size and skills of the conservation staff, and the size of the accumulated backlog of books needing repair.

The ability of a library to deal with brittle materials also influences conservation decision making. In a library that supports a comprehensive preservation program, the collections conservator, collaborating with a collection development librarian, can decide to repair and return a semibrittle book to the shelf or to replace or reproduce it in some way. In a library where options for reproducing brittle materials are not in place, returning them to the shelf as is, or withdrawing them, are likely alternatives.

Implementing a Collections Conservation Program

All libraries require rudimentary collections maintenance programs. Whether more sophisticated and extensive efforts are needed and undertaken depends upon the nature and condition of the collections, the amount of use they receive, available resources, and the institution's ability to identify new resources to support conservation activities. Some general principles apply to general collections conservation programs, however, regardless of the size and nature of the parent library.

To be effective, treatments must be applied systematically to defined categories of material within a coherent context. The creation of a context involves assessing the needs of the collections, determining what resources are available within or could be commanded by the institution for conservation, developing a long-range plan to meet needs, and implementing the plan under appropriate leadership.

A successful collections conservation program is integrated into overall library operations. The implications of purchasing hardbound copies of books versus paperbacks are clear to acquisitions librarians. Circulation staff members identify damaged items and route them for treatment. Shelvers understand the relationship between shelving practices and the longevity of materials, and operate from a commitment to assist with preservation of the collections. Interlibrary loan staff recognize materials that are too fragile to be put through the rigors of interlibrary exchange without treatment, protective housing, or at least inclusion of a written alert to borrowing readers. Collections managers are able to identify brittle paper, and understand how the condition of materials factors into decision making with regard to weeding, replacement, and reformatting. End-processing decisions, such as where to place bar codes and book pockets, what kinds of labels to use, and what types of paper to use for bookplates and how to apply them, are influenced (or made) by collections conservation staff.

Mature collections conservation programs in research libraries may handle a large volume of material annually. In fiscal year 1992–1993, of the 114 ARL member libraries responding to the ARL Preservation Statistics Questionnaire, 47 (41 percent) reported totals of over 10,000 books, pamphlets, and paper items treated, and protective enclosures constructed in-house.[7] To achieve such production levels, workshop space must be designed to facilitate a logical, efficient work flow. Work surfaces must be sufficient, and there must be adequate space for large pieces of equipment (board shears, for instance). Workstations stocked with tools and precut supplies increase efficiency, as do well-organized supply racks and cupboards. Libraries without access to conservators will find examples of workstations in the collections conservation manuals and can visit libraries that have repair facilities. Workstations for laboratories where a broad range of treatments is undertaken should be designed by conservators. In all cases, the effectiveness of the work space is critical for maximizing output.

Regardless of the size and scope of a collections conservation program, standards of practice are established and documented so that treatment decisions are consistent and can be made easily. In-house manuals are written or, more likely, are adapted from published sources.

To increase efficiency and make best use of staff skills, library materials are sorted and batched so that similar procedures can be undertaken on several volumes at once. This reduces per-item treatment time and increases production levels. When simple tasks, such as binding new pamphlets, tightening hinges, and tipping in errata sheets, are grouped, student workers and volunteers, who may be able to execute only a few types of procedures, can be employed to maximum advantage. Good management of routine tasks can free technicians and conservators to focus on more complex work. Depending on local circumstances, the head of the collections conservation program may spend a considerable amount of time on training, supervision, and program management.

Organizational Issues

The effectiveness of a collections conservation effort is highly dependent on the way in which mechanisms for policy-setting, decision making, and work flow are developed, and on the relationship of the program to other preservation activities and to the organization overall. Approaches to the establishment of a workable program will differ markedly across institutions based on the size, collecting patterns, and mission of the library.

Organization and Staffing

In large research libraries, preservation activities are usually clustered together within a discrete department. The department is administered by a preservation librarian who has overall responsibility for policy-setting; work flow, budget, and personnel management; and integration of the department's efforts with other library programs and with programs at other institutions. The conservation unit is one of several within the department and is headed by a special collections conservator or by a collections conservator. If both are on staff, one will likely report to the other depending on relative technical and management experience. In the largest libraries, there may be both a special and a general collections conservation unit, the heads of each reporting directly to the department head. The collections conservator manages day-to-day collections conservation operations; works with managers and staff throughout the organization to set priorities and make treatment decisions; and collaborates with the department head to establish conservation policy and goals, develop special projects, and plan for growth, change, and project implementation. The work of the collections conservator may be supported by additional conservators (rarely), technicians (likely), and, in academic settings, student assistants. Staffing models for research libraries holding over 2 million volumes are presented in *Preservation Program Models: A Study Project and Report.*[8]

In smaller academic and public libraries the preservation program is likely to focus exclusively on general collections, and there is less likely to be full-time staff. There may be a manager who has other responsibilities (collection development or serials management, for example) and a collections conservator or technician who also has responsibility for bindery or shelf preparation or both. The conservator or technician is often assisted by support staff and, in academic libraries, by student assistants. Although few libraries outside the research library community currently employ collections conservators, this may change as recognition of their value to an institution grows and as training opportunities increase.

In libraries that cannot make a major commitment to collections conservation, either because resources have not yet been identified or because the collections do not merit an extensive program, preservation activities will probably be administered part-time by a librarian with other responsibilities, and treatment performed by a technician assisted by students or volunteers. Small public libraries are least likely to employ a technician, but can nonetheless mount a successful treatment program provided that involved staff at all levels acquire perspective and training through appropriate means. Treatments may be performed part-time by staff, or a trained staff member may train and supervise volunteers.

Priorities

Fundamental to the mission of a collections conservation program is treatment of materials that are in demand. Barclay Ogden has expressed the principle well: "[Consideration of both] condition and use is the best strategy for selection. . . . [It] assumes that funds and facilities are likely to remain in too-short supply in the foreseeable future to undertake preservation with any goal other than solving today's problems first; . . . achieve[s] the lowest rate of expenditure . . . and . . . channel[s] funding to areas of immediate need."[9] Although use is an imperfect predictor of demand, it is generally a meaningful indicator. Reference and collection development librarians (curators, subject bibliographers, selectors, generalists with selection responsibilities) are also instrumental in identifying materials that are at risk. In larger libraries the collections conservator interacts regularly with staff who build collections and monitor their use. Where treatment is performed exclusively by technicians or students and volunteers or both, the supervising librarian may select and evaluate items for treatment.

A second general principle driving priorities is that the sooner materials are identified for treatment, the more easily and quickly they can be repaired, as discussed earlier in this chapter. Treatment in a small public library, for example, might focus largely on tightening the hinges of books that have just begun to loosen in their cases. Timely intervention can reduce significantly the number of materials that ultimately become damaged beyond the ability of staff to repair them. In a conservation program that reflects this principle and the principle of use as an indicator of demand, the condition of materials is reviewed both at the point of receipt and before they are reshelved, and problems are addressed as promptly as possible.

Conclusion

The overarching goal of a collections conservation program is to support and further the mission of the library at large. In practical terms, this means solving problems proactively and reacting to articulated needs. Where conservation is seen as a resource-absorbing frill, preservation priorities are probably inconsistent with those of the organization as a whole. Where administrators, managers, and staff understand the importance of conservation treatment and seek advice and services, it is likely that the collections conservation program is well conceived and effectively managed.

Notes

1. Gaylord Brothers, *The "Toronto Method" of Book Repairing* (Syracuse, N.Y.: Gaylord, 1924).

2. Gay R. Walker, Jane Greenfield, John Fox, and Jeffrey S. Simonoff, "The Yale Survey: A Large-Scale Study of Book Deterioration in the Yale University Library," *College & Research Libraries* 46 (1985): 111–132.

3. Research Libraries Group, Collections Conservation Task Force, memo to the RLG Preservation Committee regarding "Enclosed Questionnaire," September 4, 1990.

4. Carolyn Morrow, "Staffing the Preservation Program," in *Preservation: A Research Library Priority for the 1990s: Minutes of the 111th Membership Meeting of the Association of Research Libraries* (Washington, D.C.: ARL, 1988), 29; and Jan Merrill-Oldham, ed., *Meeting the Preservation Challenge* (Washington, D.C.: ARL, 1988), 29.

5. *Library Preservation: Fundamental Techniques—A Series of Six Training Videotapes Illustrating Simple Conservation and Repair Procedures for Library Materials* (Washington, D.C.: National Preservation Program Office, Library of Congress, July 1987).

6. Carolyn Morrow, "Conservation's Programmatic Concerns: In-House and Contracting Out" (paper presented at the Rare Books and Manuscripts Preconference [to the 1991 annual conference of the American Library Association], "Keeping the Facts in the Artifacts," Chapel Hill, N.C., 25–28 June, 1991).

7. Jutta Reed-Scott and Nicola Daval, comps., *ARL Preservation Statistics 1992–93: A Compilation of Statistics from the Members of the Association of Research Libraries* (Washington, D.C.: ARL, 1994), 20–25.

8. Jan Merrill-Oldham, Carolyn Clark Morrow, and Mark Roosa, *Preservation Program Models: A Study Project and Report* (Washington, D.C.: ARL, 1991), 38–41.

9. Barclay W. Ogden, "Preservation Selection and Treatment Options," in *Preservation: A Research Library Priority for the 1990s: Minutes of the 111th Membership Meeting of the Association of Research Libraries* (Washington, D.C.: ARL, 1988), 41; and Merrill-Oldham, *Meeting the Preservation Challenge*, 41.

Suggested Readings

Abbey Newsletter: Bookbinding and Conservation. Austin, Tex.: Abbey Publications, 1975– .

The Book and Paper Group Annual. Washington, D.C.: Book and Paper Group, American Institute for Conservation of Historic and Artistic Works, 1982–. Annual.

Conservation DistList, a discussion list moderated by Walter Henry of the Stanford University Libraries Preservation Department (subscribe through <consdist-request@lindy.stanford.edu>) and Conservation OnLine (CoOL), a full-text database of preservation information related to library, archive, and museum collections (available at <http://palimpsest.stanford.edu>).

Etherington, Don. "Selected Repair of Joints and Bindings." *Guild of Book Workers Journal* 30, no. 1 (spring 1992): 24–28.

Grandinette, Maria, and Randy Silverman. "The Library Collections Conservation Discussion Group: Taking a Comprehensive Look at Book Repair." *Library Resources & Technical Services* 38 (1994): 281–287.

Greenfield, Jane. *Books: Their Care and Repair.* Bronx, N.Y.: H. W. Wilson, 1983.

Guild of Book Workers. *A Geographical Listing of Study Opportunities.* New York: The Guild. Revised periodically.

Jones, Maralyn, comp. *Collection Conservation Treatment: A Resource Manual for Program Development and Conservation Technician Training.* Berkeley: University of California Library Conservation Department, 1993.

Kyle, Hedi. *Library Materials Preservation Manual: Practical Methods for Preserving Books, Pamphlets and Other Printed Materials.* Bronxville, N.Y.: Nicholas Smith, 1983.

Morrow, Carolyn Clark, and Carole Dyal. *Conservation Treatment Procedures: A Manual of Step-by-Step Procedures for the Maintenance and Repair of Library Materials.* 2d ed. Littleton, Colo.: Libraries Unlimited, 1986.

Silverman, Randy, and Maria Grandinette, comps. *The Changing Role of Book Repair in ARL Libraries.* ARL SPEC Kit 190. Washington, D.C.: Association of Research Libraries, 1993.

14

Commercial Library Binding

■ ■ ■

JOHN F. DEAN

In fiscal year 1996–1997, the 115 reporting member libraries of the Association of Research Libraries recorded that, of the $38 million spent on preservation (excluding staff salaries and wages), more than 67 percent ($26 million) was expended on contract binding and contract conservation. The remainder was spent on contract photocopy (1.7 percent), contract microfilm (15 percent), various other contract costs (3.3 percent), supplies (9.3 percent), and equipment (3.6 percent). Considering that contract binding and contract conservation costs are usually supported from within the libraries' regular budgets, as opposed to the grant funding often used for reformatting, it is clear that contract binding and conservation consumes a significant portion of the libraries' overall preservation expenditures. Contract or commercial library binding appears to be the only preservation expenditure for many libraries, particularly smaller ones. Expenditures on library binding have probably declined as a percentage of total preservation budgets over the past several years because of the increase in library preservation programs and the need to support their operations, but the reliance placed on contract binders is still significant.

It is likely that the traditional collection management view of library binding as a means of organizing periodical issues and strengthening book covers is still influential, but there is an increasing realization among librarians that binders can play an important role in the preservation and conservation effort. However, as the complexity and variety of treatment options increase and the capabilities of binders grow, the burden of informed decision making falls more heavily on librarians. It is evident that librarians must have a clearer understanding of the issues involved in binding structure and conservation as a means of identifying library binding needs.

Librarians should become familiar with binding structures, especially leaf attachment techniques, and develop some basic knowledge of the historical development of book construction. As many binding decisions must be made on older materials, especially items in need of rebinding, a thorough understanding of the techniques used in their binding will help to determine appropriate instructions to the binder.

The Library Program

In many libraries, the binding program is firmly established in a technical services unit, usually serials. As most binding funds seem to be expended mainly on periodical binding, the organizational location seems logical, particularly if the unit is concerned solely with the operational aspects of the program.

However, the binding program is too often viewed simply as a processing function, with little or no connection, philosophical or technical, to the broad concerns of collection management and preservation. Preservation awareness among librarians seems, in many cases, to be somewhat abstract and theoretical and does not seem to have directly affected the way many traditional library functions operate. The binding programs in many libraries are thus driven primarily by concerns of short-term practicability and tradition rather than by considered preservation judgment. The approach is often uncritical and unsystematic; binding decisions are made purely on the basis of precedents and the uncertain judgment of nonadministrative library personnel, and the results are painfully evident in the collections of all our libraries. Vast numbers of books, which may never be used, are bound in an unnecessarily destructive and high-cost fashion designed for high use. Many serials, for example, are determined to be "high use" and bound accordingly because of heavy initial demand, although during the period of the most intensive use they are not protected by any binding. In these cases, use has often diminished significantly by the time binding occurs. Books to be sent to the binder for rebinding are often not properly examined by the binding clerk, and the binder is left to make many of the crucial decisions. This approach to the binding program is, in essence, an abdication of responsibility by the librarian as it is not fiscally or conservationally sound stewardship. Although it is not practical or desirable for the librarian to examine every item sent for binding, it is appropriate for the librarian to develop a considered binding program designed to link established categories of materials with forms of binding appropriate to the collection and patterns of use.

Managerial Issues

The way in which decisions are made depends largely on the administrative and managerial structure of the library. If the library has an identifiable preservation program, the person responsible for conservation and preservation operations, planning, and education should develop the binding program. If the library does not have a preservation program, the need to examine the binding procedures provides an opportunity to develop one. Several publications describe the framework and characteristics of a preservation program, of which binding and its in-house alternatives are essential components. A coherent and effective program can be established by any size library. The preservation program itself must be similarly integrated with the library's collection development program. Although most libraries have similar binding requirements, it is important that a binding program be designed to respond to the specific needs of particular collections. This can only be achieved by developing a sound working knowledge of binding principles and by studying the effects of binding programs past.

In any examination of periodical binding, for example, it is important to consider patterns of use *after* binding. Where use records are kept for bound periodicals, they often indicate that levels of use are extremely low for all disciplines. If this proves to be the case, the approach to binding specifications for these materials should be concerned with the stability of materials and structure over time (that is, that the bindings be stable and the binding structure not sag or otherwise deteriorate merely by standing on the shelf) and their flexibility (that is, the ease of opening). The managerial responsibility to monitor the effects of past binding practices and relate the conclusions to current specifications clearly suggests that the binding program be developed outside the routine technical services operations. A successful program must be designed around the following considerations.

First, the extent to which the library is able to mount and support in-house binding and repair operations must be established. Most in-house operations consist of a preparations section, concerned with the pre-shelf processing of current materials, such as pamphlets and paperbacks; and a repair unit, concerned mainly with the repair of circulating books. A preparations unit capable of processing all new paperbacks and pamphlets has much to commend it if the work can be performed quickly, soundly, and inexpensively. Paperbacks may be minimally bound to protect them at the shelf and during moderate use, while reserving commercial case binding for those items requiring remedial treatment after extensive circulation.

Second, the relevance and cost-effectiveness of the binding specifications must be clear and the contract or agreement with the binder must be unambiguous. The specifications drawn up by the librarian are based on a combination of factors involving studies of patterns of use, familiarity with binding structures, the capabilities of the binders, their willingness to cooperate in addressing particular needs, and the realities of budget constraints. Specifications should detail the types and descriptions of bindings that the library requires. Although the current *Library Binding Institute Standard* can provide a helpful base for the specifications, it should not necessarily restrict the librarian if the library's needs are not addressed. Sample contracts appear in the *Guide to the Library Binding Institute Standard for Library Binding*. (A new ANSI/NISO/LBI standard for library binding incorporates the results of a number of various materials and methods testing projects.)

Discussing specifications with a number of binders can help to ensure that the main thrust of the library's needs is not compromised. Contracts generally incorporate the specifications, but also describe service obligations (for example, turnaround time, provision of preparation systems, liability) and the division of responsibilities. For example, the current *Library Binding Institute Standard* and *Guide* describe "Custom Periodical Collation," in which the binder assumes responsibility for extensive collation, including checking issues for completeness, position of tables of contents, and so on and "Standard Periodical Collation," in which the binder merely ascertains that all issues are present and in correct order. The latter choice is much preferred, as full collation in the library before shipment can remedy oddities quickly and effectively. If the library is already fully collating periodicals before shipment, it is important that this be reflected in the contract, as "custom collation" is expensive and should not be paid for if not needed.

The contract need not be complex and legalistic unless this is a particular requirement of, for example, a state-supported library. A detailed letter of understanding or agreement, signed by the librarian and binder, will often provide the necessary safeguards to both parties and ensure that there are few ambiguities. As with many other outside contractual arrangements, a great deal can be learned from a visit to the binderies under consideration and from discussing concerns with librarians in other libraries.

Third, a productive and mutually beneficial relationship with a binder is dependent upon an efficient and informed library binding preparation operation. Although logically binding preparation should be a function of the preservation department, this is not strictly necessary, providing that the specifications and contract have been constructed in the light of the library's preservation program. Although primarily a clerical function, binding preparation requires a good basic knowledge of library operations, organizational and work-flow skills, strong interpersonal and transactional abilities, and a thorough understanding of binding principles.

The preparation of periodicals involves accurate record keeping to ensure uniformity of style and makeup, and sensible scheduling to balance binding consignments throughout the year. Although consistency is important in periodical binding, it should not prevent the critical examination of instructions every time a periodical is bound. Preparation systems have been greatly improved, largely because of increased automation in binderies and the spin-off benefits to libraries. Improvements include software that links a library's binding database to the binder's database, and binder-supplied multiple binding slips. Clearly, it is tempting to avoid altering binding formats once the instructions have been encoded, but binding programs should be dynamic and under constant review.

Books prepared for rebinding cover a wide range of styles, conditions, and ages, and some knowledge of book structure is essential if unnecessary damage is to be avoided. It is particularly important that the preparer be able to identify the original leaf attachment method and determine whether it can be saved. As with all materials sent for binding, the preparer should check for folded maps and charts, close-to-the-edge printing, centerfold items, and all other hazards likely to be damaged by trimming, and clearly state the instruction "do not trim" to the binder.

When bound volumes are returned to the library, the preparer should carefully inspect them to ensure that the general specifications and specific instructions have been followed. In terms of appearance, the books should be free from adhesive spotting on the covers and edges, boards should be square and even, turn-ins should be level and uniform, buckram should be tight against the board edges and neat at the corners, lettering straight and centered, end sheets smooth and uncreased, joints even and well set. In terms of structure, the leaf attachment should be sound and consistent, the opening flexible and even, backbone linings should be exactly as specified and adhere firmly and evenly, the back lining cloth should extend evenly onto each end sheet, end sheets should function smoothly without separation from the text block but without wide attachment, and board thickness should be proportionate to the book.

The occasional defective volume should be returned to the binder for remedial action. If defects appear on a number of volumes, the binder should be asked to discuss them and to propose a solution. Reputable binders are anxious to hear about any dissatisfaction with their work and are eager to resolve any problems.

Finally, decision making should be done book by book within the context of the collection and patterns of use, and not merely determined entirely by precedents. A set of decision-making guidelines should be drafted to ensure that a consistent approach is taken and to reduce subjectivity. Figure 1 shows a possible approach to establishing guidelines.

Figure 1

Decision-making Guidelines: Commercial Library Binding and In-house Alternatives

TYPE OF BOOK	IN-HOUSE OPTIONS	COMMERCIAL BINDING OPTIONS
Ordinary paperback, thicker than 1/4", adhesive bound	• Stiffen	• Double-fan adhesive, case bind
Ordinary paperback, thicker than 1/4", sewn through the fold	• Stiffen	• Save sewing, case bind • Double-fan adhesive, case bind
Ordinary paperback, less than 1/4"	• Pamphlet case	• Double-fan adhesive, case bind
Spiral-wire or plastic comb binding	• Remove wire/ plastic, sew or fan-adhesive bind, cloth strip up backbone, stiffen	• Double-fan adhesive, case bind

(continued)

Figure 1 *(continued)*

TYPE OF BOOK	IN-HOUSE OPTIONS	COMMERCIAL BINDING OPTIONS
Periodical with normal mix of paper, leaves glued or stapled, margins normal or small, low or moderate use. For permanent retention		• Double-fan adhesive, quarter buckram (if aesthetic sensibilities are offended by quarter buckram, case binding flush at tail may be used)
Periodical with heavy coated stock, leaves glued or stapled, margins small, low to moderate use. For permanent retention		• Roughen leaves at back edge, double-fan adhesive, quarter buckram
Periodical with heavy coated stock, leaves glued or stapled, margins wide, high use. Not for permanent retention		• Oversew, quarter buckram • Roughen leaves at back edge, double-fan adhesive, quarter buckram
Periodicals in single-issue sections (e.g., *Time*)		• Hand or machine sew through fold according to thickness of issue, quarter buckram
Periodicals in sewn multiple sections		• Hand or machine sew through fold, quarter buckram • Double-fan adhesive, quarter buckram
Periodicals with complete single issues (e.g., annual reports with complete pagination)	• Stiffen individual issues	• Bind when accumulated as appropriate
Rebind. Previously stiffened paperback damaged by heavy use		• Double-fan adhesive, case bind
Rebind. Publisher's binding, sewing intact	• Repair	• Recase
Rebind. Publisher's binding, sewing broken or previously adhesive bound		• Sew through fold, case bind (likely to be expensive) • Double-fan adhesive, case bind

Historical Development

Modern binding design fails to consider the storage function because the use of squares (projections of the cover beyond the edges of the text block) is ultimately destructive to the binding. Our mental image of the way a book should appear (round back; squares at head, tail, and fore edge) is based on a model that was largely inappropriate by the end of the sixteenth century. Nevertheless, librarians have enthusiastically addressed issues related to binding in an attempt to formalize efforts to remedy some of the ills of modern binding structure.

In 1905 the American Library Association (ALA) formed a bookbinding committee, and in 1911 published a set of specifications by Arthur Low Bailey for the guidance of librarians. Expansions of the early ALA specifications were published in 1923 and 1928 as the result of recommendations by the Committee on Bookbinding and the Library Group of the Employing Bookbinders of America. Many of these specifications were heavily influenced by the inventive Cedric Chivers, who had patented a semimechanized form of oversewing in 1904, and committee member Elmo Reavis, one of the perfecters of the oversewing machine between 1920 and 1923, and later the first president of the Library Binding Institute (LBI). From the 1970s until the eighth edition of the LBI standard in 1986, oversewing was repeatedly recommended without reservation. The new standard recognizes the need to choose from a variety of leaf attachment methods to meet the needs of different volumes, different use patterns, and different institutional contexts.

The standards espoused by Douglas Cockerell and the [Royal] Society of Arts in England at the turn of the twentieth century assumed that all text blocks would be sewn onto five flexible cords (that is, not sawn-in), and books "of little interest or value" sewn on three unbleached linen tapes. Even the cheapest binding, the fourth of Cockerell's categories, had split-board construction (in which the cover board is split to accommodate tapes or other slips, providing a stronger attachment between text and cover) and was covered in buckram. The chief differences between modern commercial library binding construction and the methods common at the beginning of the twentieth century when Cockerell drafted his standards are that the skill levels of individual binders have declined but labor costs have increased significantly, and that through-the-fold sewing is generally not practicable for most monographs because of the high preparation costs and not possible for most periodicals because they are often made up of single leaves. Split-board construction has given way to casing; thus, almost all bindings produced by library binders in the United States have the outer covering made separate from the text block. The main objectives of binding remain the same, however: strength appropriate to levels and types of use; flexibility, to enable unrestrained access to the book; reversibility, to enable rebinding should this be necessary in the future; stability, so that the binding continues to provide long-term protection to the book; and permanence and durability so that as far as practicable the binding materials and structures should not degrade readily.

Library Binding Methods

Preparation

An essential first step in binding is collation. The text block should be checked by the binder page by page to ensure that it is complete. Plates, maps, and so on must be checked against the list or table of contents. During collation, the binder should be alert for tears or missing leaf portions, which should be marked for later correction. Any leaves or portions of the text block that are missing should be reported to the librarian before any work is performed.

Leaf Attachment Methods

Whether a periodical or a monograph, the basic methods of leaf attachment available from most binders remain the same:

   1.   Through-the-Fold Sewing by Hand. This method may be used only if a text block has sections or gatherings with folds. In the case of rebinding, the text block must be carefully "pulled" or taken apart to remove the original sewing and to preserve the section folds as much as possible. Invariably, a considerable amount of time must be spent on restoring damaged folds with narrow strips of tissue and paste before actual sewing can begin. Periodicals consisting of single-section issues generally do not require this extensive preparation.

   The most common sewing methods employed by library binders are onto cords or onto tapes. The cord method as practiced by commercial binders invariably involves sawing grooves across the section folds at each cord position, sinking the cords into the grooves, passing the thread in a single line across the cords, and gluing the frayed ends of the cord down onto the end sheets. Although this method of hand sewing can be performed much quicker than any other, it is weak because the thread does not encircle the cords and can easily break along the entire section length; moreover, the sawn-in grooves allow glue to flood into the inner margin, making the opening stiff and inflexible.

If a text block is sewn onto tapes, the tapes lie flat across the section folds with the only piercing of the folds made by the sewing needle. (It is important to note that some binders will actually saw a shallow groove on each side of the tapes to speed the sewing process, a practice that is to be deplored.) There should generally be no fewer than three tapes, unless the text block is very small (less than seven inches); if the text block is large and heavy, the number of tapes should increase.

As this method of preparation and sewing is quite labor-intensive, the cost is likely to be high relative to other methods. For text blocks that have folds to begin with, it is most suitable for text blocks with narrow margins, for valuable or heavily used books, or for periodicals that must open flat or that must have a reversible structure.

2. Through-the-Fold Sewing by Machine. Many of the preceding comments apply equally to machine sewing. This method may be used if the text block has folded sections and does not require extensive fold repair. The most common machine in America, the Smyth National, generally sews without tapes or slips, although tapes can be "sewn through" if requested. (Because the Smyth National is used so extensively, machine sewing is frequently referred to as "national sewing".)

Although machine sewing is not as durable as good-quality hand sewing onto tapes, it is preferred to recessed cord sewing, as the thread is not continuous but is a series of individual thread "staples," and a break does not loosen the entire section. As with hand sewing, it is important that the backbone be double lined with a woven material and paper liner. (The *backbone* is the back edge of the text block along which the leaves or sections are fastened together; the *spine* is that portion of the cover that fits over the backbone; and the *back* is simply the last page of the text block.)

Machine sewing is most suitable for text blocks that must open flat (musical scores, for example) and that do not require extensive preparation or have thick section folds. In many cases, the cost can be quite modest, providing that the preparation is not too time-consuming.

3. Oversewing. This method, and those that follow, require single leaves. In the past, even volumes with folded sections were turned into single leaves in order to oversew them, but this method is now more often used on text blocks that are increasingly issued in single-leaf form. Machine oversewing is extremely strong with virtually unbreakable sewing.

Preparation for oversewing (in common with other single-leaf attachment methods) begins with the "planing" or "milling" of the back edge of the text block to remove old glue and turn it into single leaves. Groups of leaves corresponding to sections are placed on the machine where needles pass at an angle through holes prepunched at frequent intervals in the back edges of the leaves, creating a series of lock stitches at each gathering and at the back.

Oversewing is suitable for materials that will be subjected to heavy short-term use and that have a gutter margin of no less than $5/8$ inch and flexible paper. This method results in a relatively inflexible backbone and consumes more margin than any other method under discussion. The perforating effect of the holes punched five to an inch causes paper to break easily as it loses flexibility over time, and oversewn volumes are virtually impossible to rebind. Unfortunately, indiscriminate use of the method has irretrievably damaged many fine collections.

4. Side Sewing. This method is not a real alternative to the other methods as it can be used only for thinner text blocks, generally those less than $1/2$ inch. It consists of (usually) machine stitching through the entire body of the text block in a manner somewhat similar to domestic machine sewing.

When great strength is required, as in high-use children's books, side sewing is appropriate providing that the inner margin is adequate (not less than $3/4$ inch). Because the method has a perforating effect, it should not be used for materials of permanent value, as the paper will easily break along the sewing line if the paper begins to lose flexibility.

5. Adhesive. Over the years, bindings dependent upon adhesive only as a leaf attachment method have developed an uncertain reputation. Much of the prejudice against adhesive leaf attachment is based on the poor performance of publishers' bindings held together by "perfect" binding techniques. In perfect binding, the adhesive is applied directly to the edge of the text block in a method designed to hinge each leaf separately to a film of adhesive. Although the edge is sometimes roughened or perforated, the adhesive does not generally penetrate onto the leaf surface. Perfect binding lends itself particularly to high-speed edition binding. Although some library binders still use perfect binding techniques for (particularly) the low-cost binding of paperbacks, double-fan adhesive binding is now the standard and preferred method for most binding.

In the double-fan method, the adhesive is applied to the backs of the leaves, which are first fanned over in one direction and then in the other, so that a narrow line of adhesive is laid on the actual surface of each leaf, effectively adhering it to adjacent leaves. The method may be applied by hand or machine, but in both cases, the back is fanned in two directions (double) in order to ensure complete coverage. As with all forms of adhesive binding, the type of adhesive used is crucial; in this case, the required adhesive is an internally plasticized (copolymer) polyvinyl acetate, which is chemically stable with long-term flexibility retention.

Another important factor is the receptivity of the paper fibers, and a general concern is that heavily coated paper stock, such as that used for high-finish color printing, uses coating to such an extent that the adhesive does not actually hold the fibers but simply bonds to the coating. Sanding the back edge of text blocks to more fully expose the fibers significantly improves the adhesion of the emulsion. Notching, a method of grooving the back edge to extend the surface, is also used as a partial answer to the coated-stock problem.

Binding Structure

Case Binding   The structure most favored by library binders, irrespective of the method of leaf attachment or whether serial or monograph, large or small, is case binding, in which the cover ("case") is fabricated separately from the text block.

After preparation (collation, leaf attachment, attachment of end sheets) and before casing, the text block is usually trimmed on a paper cutter at the fore edge, head, and tail. This trimming, for volumes that need complete reassembly, is acceptable provided that the margin is adequate and the trim is not excessive. Unfortunately, as most binders use standard "squares" (that is, that portion of the cover board that protrudes beyond the text-block edge) of $1/8$ inch, text blocks tend to be trimmed to fit the precut boards. This sometimes results in excessive trimming to bring a text-block "down to the mark." It is important that librarians clearly indicate their concern if text blocks are continually cropped or to communicate their preference for "no trim" if margins are close to the edge. This can also be problematic if periodical issues vary in size, as binders will trim to make their heights and widths as uniform as possible.

After trimming, the text block is generally rounded and backed. *Rounding* is the shaping of the backbone into a curve in order to more evenly distribute the swelling or extra thickness caused by the section folds and sewing structure. *Backing* is the forming of shoulders by bending the sections outward from the center to help support the text block in its case. For most text blocks, rounding and backing are performed as one operation in a rounder-backer machine.

After rounding and backing, the backbone is lined with a piece of stretch cotton cloth that covers to just short of the head and tail and extends onto the front and back end sheets by approximately one inch. If the text block is thick or heavy, the backbone is double lined with stretch cloth or with a second liner of paper.

While the text block is being processed (forwarded), the title and other lettering are applied to the covering material (usually an acrylic-coated cotton or cotton and polyester blend buckram), the boards and inlay (spine lining strip) are assembled, and the case made. Generally, cases are made to a set pattern, with the boards $1/4$ inch taller than the text block ($1/8$-inch square at head, tail, and fore edge) and set back from the inlay about $1/4$ inch. The corners are generally "library style," in which the buckram is folded over to form an uncut corner, and the head and tail caps are reinforced with cord or rolled paper. The case is then stamped in gold or, more usually, white foil. Most binders use automatic stamping presses with alphabet wheels directed by computers. Lettering information is encoded into a database for repeat titles, such as periodicals, and carried on disks maintained and exchanged by the library or in a central database accessed remotely by the library. In both cases, the form and length of the title are essentially determined directly by library staff; thus, premium charges for "extra" title lengths can be substantially reduced by careful control at the point of entry.

The final stage of binding is casing in, whereby the text block and case are united, the end sheets glued, and the whole thoroughly pressed.

Most library binders perform this form of binding efficiently and conscientiously, and the results are creditable. There are, however, some inherent problems with the basic design that relate, as noted, to the need to present a final product that fulfills our expectations in terms of appearance rather than performance.

Rounding and backing are frequently misapplied and, when used on heavy text blocks with cases that have large squares, fulfill no useful function. The weight of the text block causes the bottom edge to sag onto the shelf between the squares, and the rounded shape is lost. In addition, adhesive-bound text blocks should not be rounded and backed as there is no swelling from fold mending or sewing thread to distribute; moreover, there is evidence that the rounding of a double-fan adhesive text block actually disrupts the bond and weakens the leaf attachment. It is important to round most sewn text blocks to consolidate swelling and to counteract the tendency of a backbone to become concave by repeated use. To retain the round and to provide a stable structure, it is most important that the case be flush at the tail to eliminate sagging, and that the backbone be consistently double lined with cloth and paper. Adhesive binding should generally not be rounded but should have the backbone solidly lined, and the text block should always be flush at the tail.

Quarter-Buckram Although the Library Binding Institute treats it as a "nonstandard" method, quarter-buckram can be an effective structure for adhesive-bound periodicals. In this structure, the binding is not a case, but is actually built onto the text block. After the text block has been adhesive bound and the backbone lined with stretch cloth, a pair of boards is glued directly to the end sheets at approximately $1/4$ to $1/2$ inch from the back edge. The boards are precut to standard sizes and are laid flush with a common edge. The prestamped buckram, cut to the height of the text block and to extend roughly two inches onto the front and back boards, is glued and laid directly onto the lined backbone and set firmly into the joints. When dry, the text block is lightly trimmed at fore edge, head, and tail. This square structure is unashamedly utilitarian but highly stable. The flush shape prevents any kind of structural distortion even if the text block is shelved on its fore edge, and the cover-lined backbone retains its shape after repeated uses. Because there is no rounding and backing to distort the flexing mechanism, the text block is very flexible. Some library binders now offer this binding as a standard product under various names, such as econobind and LUMSPEC binding. (The LUMSPEC was designed to provide librarians with a low-cost storage binding and is described in "Minimum Specifications for Binding Lesser Used Materials." See the Suggested Readings at the end of this chapter.) Some binders now offer a hybrid flush binding with a flat backbone that is flush at the tail, but the structure is still based on the buckram case, and the cover material does not reinforce the adhesive leaf attachment.

Recasing This method of binding is designed to preserve the original leaf attachment (usually through-the-fold sewing) and to remedy minor tears and paper damage, while replacing the damaged or worn original outer binding. Some library binders have been recasing books for many years, but lack of standard procedures and, in some cases, insensitivity to the original structure have led to inappropriate structures and librarian disillusionment. Most commonly, binders have damaged text blocks by using inappropriate techniques. Heavy boards and buckram more suited to standard periodical binding have been used on small books with incongruous results. A number of binders, however, can now perform recasing with some degree of skill and sensitivity, especially if the following procedures are used.

The appropriate candidates for recasing are text blocks that have sound or only slightly weak paper and sewing, and that need to have the original binding replaced with a new cloth case. In many cases, these text blocks will be of lasting value; thus, the methods and materials should be selected for their reversibility and nondamaging nature.

After collation, the remnants of the original binding are removed, and any end sheets, bookplates, or other elements to be saved are put aside. Any tears or missing leaf portions are repaired using Japanese tissue with a moist adhesive, such as starch paste or methyl cellulose, or using a chemically stable, heat-activated mending material.

Old linings and adhesive are then removed from the backbone, an operation that requires care to avoid irreparable damage to the sewing or the backs of the sections. If the first and last sections are loose, they may be lightly overcast through a single end-sheet flyleaf. Although a number of end-sheet styles may be used, the most practical are simple single-folio end sheets with a tissue hinge, or double folio. A sturdy method for double-folio end sheets is to glue three tapes across the backbone in simulation of a tape-sewn volume and sew the end sheets onto the tapes, catching the existing thread at the kettle stitches.

The backbone is glued and the text block is rounded and backed if needed. Because of the tenuous nature of some original sewing structures, it is most important that the binder perform this operation with some care, which invariably precludes the use of a rounder-backer machine. Linings appropriate to the size and weight of the text block are applied to the backbone.

Boards of appropriate thickness are cut to size and covered. The cover materials should always be woven and appropriate to the thickness of the text block. Thus, thin text blocks should be covered in a cloth rather than the heavy buckram typical of library bindings.

Lettering may be done onto the cover material or finished case, usually the former, and, when the case is glued down to the end sheets, the book is pressed. At this point, any original bookplates and other materials saved from the original binding are enclosed or mounted in the new structure.

Although there are many variations on this style that respond to innumerable problems, the binding is quite basic and will provide a conservationally sound, flexible, reversible binding for a large category of material.

Special Services

A few library binders provide a broad range of conservation and preservation services, either directly or through affiliation with conservation operations. In many ways, this is a logical development as most library binders at one time had special sections set aside for nonstandard bindings, map mounting, and restoration (the latter tending to cater to the family Bible trade).

Today, a number of binders offer solvent deacidification and welded polyester encapsulation for routine flat-paper items (maps, charts, posters, and so on), and at least two can provide much more sophisticated flat-paper treatment for a broad range of problems. Several binders can provide routine stable photocopy replacements for brittle books. Some binders continue to express interest in providing a more comprehensive range of services, including paper strengthening, the production of microforms, and the use of digital imaging for text reproduction.

The development and verification of an effective and low-cost mass deacidification system continues to be elusive. Of the many systems that have been tried, only the Wei T'o solvent system by Richard Smith and the Bookkeeper III system by Preservation Technologies seem to be viable. The Library of Congress uses the Bookkeeper III system, but the unit cost is high and careful selection of treatment candidates is necessary. Many binders have evinced interest in linking an appropriate process with their other services, and the Bookkeeper III system does have the potential for on-site operation. There is much to commend this view: Binders have the established customer networks, efficient transportation systems, materials handling expertise, effective record-keeping systems, and genuine commitment to serving and retaining clients. At this point, it is difficult to predict the actual sales potential of mass deacidification until costs become more affordable for libraries; moreover, capital investment for installation is likely to be substantial, and, without the cushion of grant support, a binder would be taking a serious gamble on the likelihood of recovering it.

Conclusion

It is evident that the current level of expenditures by libraries on commercial library binding indicates the importance of binding as a preservation activity and a legitimate area for considered resource management. Unfortunately, this importance is not reflected in the managerial structure of most libraries, and decisions affecting the long-term stability of the collections and many thousands of dollars are still made by clerical staff with little knowledge of the needs of the user and only a perfunctory acquaintance with binding structure. It is ironic that many library administrators regard preservation as a fiscal black hole while apparently content to allow their only dedicated preservation funds to dribble away in uncontrolled binding programs.

In most cases, a sensible combination of sound in-house preparation and repair programs, and a well-organized and constantly monitored library binding program, can actually reduce costs rather than increasing them, reserving the savings for further development of the preservation program. Many libraries have substantially improved their programs, fully integrating them with an overall collection development approach to preservation that has been both cost-effective and satisfying for the staff involved. Although much remains to be done to bring all libraries and binders into a more productive and critical relationship, the signal efforts of ALA, LBI, and individual librarians, binders, and conservators over the past few years have stimulated broad discussion and analysis of the role of commercial library binding. This can only be beneficial to programs and collections.

Suggested Readings

American Library Association. Library Technology Project. *Development of Performance Standards for Library Binding: Phase I.* Chicago: ALA, 1961.

Dean, John F. "The Binding and Preparation of Periodicals: Alternative Structures and Procedures." *Serials Review* 6 (July–September 1980): 87–90.

———. "The Preservation of Serials." In *Advances in Serials Management 3*, 233–263. Greenwich, Conn.: JAI Press, 1989.

Library Binding Institute. *The New Library Scene.* Edina, Minn.: LBI, 1981– . Quarterly.

"Minimum Specifications for Binding Lesser Used Materials." *ALA Bulletin* 52 (June 1958): 51–53.

National Information Standards Organization. *Library Binding and Library Prebound Books.* NISO Z39.78-2000. Bethesda, Md.: NISO, in press.

Parisi, Paul A., and Jan Merrill-Oldham, eds. *Guide to the Library Binding Institute Standard for Library Binding.* Chicago: American Library Association, 1990.

———. *Library Binding Institute Standard for Library Binding.* 8th ed. Rochester, N.Y.: Library Binding Institute, 1986.

15

Preservation Microfilming and Photocopying

■ ■ ■

EILEEN F. USOVICZ
and BARBARA LILLEY

The replacement of deteriorating volumes or documents with micro-forms or photocopies—generally called *reformatting*—is an important component of most larger preservation operations. Much of the paper manufactured in the period between approximately 1850 and 1950 tends to become too brittle to be usable. As science does not have a way of making brittle paper flexible and the physical reinforcement of brit-tle paper is not usually feasible, libraries have chosen in many cases to convert the original brittle paper–based text into either microfilm or another paper-based bound volume through photocopying. In archives, preservation replacement may be driven either by fragile or deteriorating original documents or by the need for expanded access. The photocopy is the format that most readers would choose for ease of use and portability, but microfilm has the advantage that relatively inexpensive duplicates can be made once initial filming is done. Preservation microfilming, in which a master film is carefully pre-served, also provides security against loss, but preservation photocopy-ing usually does not. Each method of preservation replacement has technical, policy, and staffing considerations.

Preservation Microfilming

Preservation microfilming is the process of recording on photographic film the text and illustrations of library and archival materials. When manufactured, processed, and stored in accordance with appropriate standards, silver gelatin microfilm on polyester base, the only film type appropriate for use in preservation microfilming, has a life expectancy of approximately five hundred years.

The term *preservation microfilming* refers to more than the life expectancy of the film, however. Preservation microfilming requires the production of microfilm images of high technical and bibliographic quality. Some commercial applications of microfilm may require that the film produced be retained for only a few years before it is discarded, or that only one generation of film be produced. The production of microfilm of the highest possible quality may not be practical, affordable, or even reasonable in such nonpreservation applications.

Preservation microfilm, however, is intended to serve as a medium for the permanent recording of records. Three generations of microfilm are typically produced in preservation microfilming projects: a master, a print master, and a service copy. The master is intended to serve as the permanent storage copy; the print master, produced from the master, is the film generation from which multiple service copies may be printed; and the service copy is the film made available for routine use. Because some loss of quality may be expected from one film generation to the next, the master film must be of a higher level of quality than might be necessary if only one film generation is to be produced. High quality also facilitates the scanning of microfilm into digital format. The level of quality required of preservation microfilm ensures not only that the film produced is suited for its present use, but for future uses as well.

It has been said that preservation microfilming is more "art than science." In fact, microfilming can be approached with much more science than it often is. Producing film of the highest possible quality is not as simple as contracting with a microfilm service bureau, which may or may not appreciate the difference between preservation microfilming and other microfilm applications, nor is it as simple as hiring staff with minimal training to operate a camera and a film processor. Understanding the stages of the production process and the impact that each stage has upon the others, then taking steps to limit the variables at each stage, make it possible to consistently produce high-quality microfilm images. Preservation microfilming approached in this fashion becomes "more science than art."

Preservation Microfilming Guidelines and Standards

Microfilm is a mature technology for which standards have long existed. Preservation microfilming for libraries and archives, however, represents a small fraction of the worldwide micrographics industry, an industry predominantly concerned with nonpreservation applications of microfilm. The goals of preservation microfilming, therefore, are not the primary concern of standards-making bodies, such as the American National Standards Institute (ANSI) and the International Organization for Standardization (ISO). In the absence of standards that specifically addressed preservation microfilming for libraries and archives, some organizations, notably the Library of Congress and the National Library of Medicine, attempted in the 1960s and 1970s to adapt commercial filming practices to the microfilming of library and archival materials. The Research Libraries Group's microfilming guidelines of the 1990s represent the most recent and extensive effort to adapt general microfilming standards and practices specifically to preservation microfilming of library and archival materials.

Although they are not formal standards, the RLG guidelines for preservation microfilming published in the *RLG Preservation Microfilming Handbook* (1992) and the *RLG Archives Microfilming Manual* (1994) have been widely accepted as de facto standards for preservation microfilming within the United States and, increasingly, in the international community.[1]

ANSI standards, such as MS23 *Standard Recommended Practice— Production, Inspection, and Quality Assurance of First Generation Silver Microforms of Documents* (1998), are excellent sources of information on microfilm equipment, film, production practices, and quality factors. (See the Suggested Readings at the end of this chapter.) MS23 leaves it to the producer of the film to determine what level of quality is required in each application because this standard is intended to provide information to producers of microfilm for all purposes. The RLG publications previously mentioned, however, specify levels of quality acceptable for the preservation microfilming of library and archival materials, and provide a great deal of other information specific to library and archival materials that is not found in standards publications.

The Preservation Microfilming Project

Before the filming process begins, several important steps must be taken to ensure preservation-quality microfilm. The first step is to understand how to manage a preservation microfilming project. Such projects are well established and are well documented in the literature. The RLG manuals referred to earlier, along with the second edition of *Preservation Microfilming: A Guide for Librarians and Archivists* (see Suggested Readings), cover preservation microfilming in much greater detail than this chapter can, and are intended for anyone planning preservation microfilming projects. In addition to step-by-step directions, they provide samples of documents mentioned in this chapter, such as requests for proposals and vendor contracts.

Most institutions do not have an in-house microfilm laboratory, and unless they are planning to continue with large-volume filming, it is not cost-effective to set up an in-house lab. Most institutions find it much more cost-effective and trouble-free to contract out for microfilming services.

Because most projects are for filming a defined collection with a definite beginning and end, the second step will be to estimate the size of the project by estimating the number of exposures and reels of film that will be created. This is accomplished by sampling the collection to estimate the average number of pages per volume and the number of volumes to be microfilmed or, for manuscript and archival collections, the number of exposures per linear foot. This information is essential when working with microfilm vendors—it is the only way they can provide an accurate estimate of the cost for their services.

Contracts

Once the total amount of microfilming to be done has been established, the process of contracting for the work begins. This will involve several steps:

- Identifying microfilm vendors that do preservation-quality work
- Sending requests for proposals (RFPs) to the vendors
- Evaluating the proposals
    Checking references of the vendor
    Comparing costs

Comparing services

Visiting the vendors' facilities if at all possible

- Negotiating the contract

Many institutions, especially government ones, including state colleges and universities, have guidelines or staff to assist with contracting procedures. These should be consulted even before writing an RFP. In some cases, specific bidding and contract procedures may be required by law.

Work Plan

A detailed work plan is essential to conducting a successful project. Because many microfilming projects are grant-funded, it is necessary to establish the number of staff and amount of time needed as well as equipment and space requirements before beginning the project (and usually before submitting the grant proposal to a funder). A work plan must include levels of staffing and each person's responsibilities, a timeline, and step-by-step procedures.

Bibliographic Review

To avoid duplication of filming, every title that is to be filmed should first be searched in the national bibliographical databases RLIN and OCLC. Reprint sources should also be consulted to find out if the title is available as a reprint. This information is then given to the bibliographer or curator who will decide if the title is to be microfilmed.

Queuing/Prospective Cataloging

Once it has been determined that a title is to be microfilmed, a MARC record is created or amended to show the institution's intent to film the title. This allows other institutions to avoid the cost of duplicate filming of the title in the meantime.

Preparation

Properly preparing materials for filming will ensure that only complete volumes or collections are filmed and that they are filmed in the correct order. Preparation consists of two steps.

Collation   Each work is examined page by page to ensure that it is complete. If pages or volumes are missing, damaged, or unreadable, replacements are ordered through interlibrary loan.

Targets   "Eye legible" signs, or targets, that can be read by the naked eye without the use of a microfilm reader are photographed along with the text. They include bibliographic and directional indications that are always placed at the beginning and end of each reel, and sometimes include notes on the physical condition of the volume or document. Targets help users understand where items are on a reel and what they are seeing (or not seeing in the case of missing or illegible pages). Often an institution will make these targets itself. If not, many microfilm vendors offer this as a service. If an institution wishes to have its vendor produce the targets, the service must be included in the contract.

Shipping

If, as is usually the case, actual filming is to be done by an outside service bureau, the prepared volumes are shipped to the vendor for filming. Some vendors offer a pickup service while others require customers to use a common carrier. Again, this should be spelled out in the contract. Insurance on the materials while in transit and at the vendor's facility, and who is responsible for it, should also be covered in the contract.

Institutional Staff Involvement

Whether the institution has a separate preservation department or the project is being managed by a curator or other staff person, it will involve more than just the project manager. Microfilming projects affect all departments in a library or archive. Bibliographers, curators, or archivists will be asked to help with selecting materials for microfilming; cataloging staff will be involved with queuing and cataloging the microfilm; circulation staff will assist with charging out materials to the project; reference staff will have to know what materials will be unavailable to users and for how long; and the mail room may be involved with sending and receiving shipments. It is important that all parties are involved from the very beginning, not just after funding has been received for the project. Their input is vital to winning support for the project and ultimately for its success.

Film

Silver gelatin microfilm is the only film type suitable as a camera master film. The film emulsion consists of silver halide crystals suspended in gelatin. When struck by light, the silver halide crystals form nuclei, which create a latent image on the film. The image becomes visible when the film is developed.

Silver gelatin microfilm is available on both polyester and acetate bases. Polyester film base is stronger and more stable than acetate film base and, therefore, is the only film base material suitable for preservation microfilm. Acetate film base, in addition to being easily torn, is subject to "vinegar syndrome." As the acetate base material deteriorates, it produces acetic acid, resulting in a vinegar-like odor. Other signs of acetate deterioration are warping and embrittlement of the film base.

Microfilm is available in three standard widths: 16 mm, 35 mm, and 105 mm. Typically available on reels are 16 mm and 35 mm; 105-mm film is available on reels or as cut sheets of 105 × 148 mm. Although other film sizes have been used in some preservation microfilming projects, 35-mm film is preferred because it permits the use of lower reduction ratios, typically ranging from 8X to 14X, than are possible when filming on 16-mm microfilm or 105-mm microfiche, which typically require the use of reduction ratios of 24X and above.

Lower reduction ratios result in larger images, and larger images necessarily allow better image quality. A finite number of silver grains in the film are available to define text and images on that film. When lower reduction ratios are used, more silver grains are utilized in defining the larger characters of text on the film. When filming at higher reduction ratios, fewer silver grains are available to define the smaller characters.

Another consideration in choosing larger 35-mm film is that less information may be lost if the film is scratched or damaged than would be the case with the smaller images that result from the higher reduction ratios used in 16-mm microfilm or 105-mm microfiche.

Cameras

Planetary Cameras

Planetary cameras, in which both the document and the film are stationary during exposure, are the cameras most commonly used in preservation microfilming. Most such cameras are capable of using

16-mm or 35-mm film. Disbound items are filmed by placing them on the camera's copy board; bound materials may be filmed in a book cradle placed on top of the copy board.

Until recently, the Kodak MRD II microfilm camera was virtually the only camera used for preservation microfilming in libraries and archives and is still widely used. This camera is equipped with manual controls as well as analog exposure and voltage meters that provide for gross control of the camera's functions, although it may be outfitted with a digital voltage meter and an automatic exposure device. The exposure on the MRD is controlled by varying the illumination level by means of a rheostat while the shutter time and aperture settings remain fixed.

Kodak stopped manufacturing the MRD II in the early 1990s. Although used MRD IIs remain available, a new generation of 35-mm microfilm cameras has recently been developed. The Hermann and Kraemer (H&K), the Elke, and the Gratek are among the newest microfilm cameras designed for the library and archives market. These cameras have microprocessor-controlled functions that allow a finer level of exposure and focusing control than is possible with the Kodak MRD II. Finer optics generally permit these new cameras to exceed the resolution achieved by the typical Kodak MRD II. Some of the new cameras are equipped with pneumatic or electronically operated book cradles for the filming of bound materials.

It has generally been our experience that fully automatic exposure units are not entirely successful when employed in preservation microfilming projects because the sensitivity range of these units tends to be limited. This is not a problem when high-contrast materials are filmed, when there is not much variation in paper colors and textures, or when a nonpreservation microfilming application does not require the production of images of consistent densities. Most preservation microfilming projects involve a wide range of paper colors and textures as well as low-contrast materials. Automatic exposure units are typically unable to appropriately expose such varied materials so that the required film density is achieved. If fully automatic exposure devices are used, it will likely be necessary to shift to a manual exposure mode for items that fall outside the known range of these exposure units.

Fiche Cameras

Although step-and-repeat or fiche cameras are used primarily in commercial applications, some preservation microfilming projects have been filmed on them. The step-and-repeat camera is a type of planetary camera. Both the film and the document are stationary at the time that the exposure is taken. The exposure may be manually varied or the camera may be equipped with an automatic exposure device. Step-and-repeat cameras generally use reduction ratios of 24X and above. The camera's film unit moves after each exposure to create a grid pattern on 105 × 148-mm film. Some fiche cameras, however, are designed to fill an entire 148 × 105-mm fiche with one large image. These are called A6, or full-frame, fiche cameras.

Rotary Cameras

Rotary, or flow, cameras are not generally used for preservation micro-filming. Rotary cameras use 16-mm film and typically film at reduction ratios of 24X and above. Only unbound materials can be filmed on a rotary camera, as the documents to be filmed are fed into the camera and then moved through it on belts. Brittle materials can become jammed and damaged in the rotary camera's document transport mech-anism. Skewing of pages may also occur. Both the film and the docu-ment are moving as the exposure is taken in a rotary camera, which may result in lower resolution than would occur if both the film and the document were stationary during the exposure. The exposures are not manually changed for each document filmed on a rotary camera. A standard exposure is typically selected for all items to be filmed, or the camera may be equipped with an automatic exposure device.

Setting up a microfilm camera involves much more than simply finding a space and plugging it in. A series of tests and adjustments must be performed before filming may commence. These tests for light balance, resolution, calibration, and exposure should be conducted in the proper sequence to ensure accurate results.

Film Processing

Processors

Silver gelatin film processors are available as either tabletop or larger deep tank models. The film processor consists of several tanks or chambers in which the film is developed, fixed, washed, and dried. Tabletop processors typically develop one reel of film at a time and are appropriate for low-volume microfilming facilities. Tabletop processors operate at higher temperatures and slower speeds than deep tank processors in order to compensate for their smaller solution tanks. Deep tank processors are designed to develop several reels (spliced together) at the same time.

Deep tank processors are used in medium- to high-volume operations and require a greater level of technical expertise to operate than most tabletop processors. Deep tank processors are preferred over tabletop models because the larger tank capacity and greater dwell time permit processing at lower temperatures, which generally results in more consistent film densities.

Although deep tank processors may be technically superior and more versatile than tabletop processors, this does not mean that tabletop processors cannot process preservation-quality microfilm if properly operated and properly plumbed. Indeed, a tabletop film processor is the best choice for a low-volume microfilming operation that cannot justify the cost of a deep tank processor.

Processing Control

Film processing control is essential in a preservation microfilming lab and establishes the basis upon which filming and processing may proceed. Processing control is established and monitored through the use of microfilm control strips. Control strips are lengths of camera film that have been exposed on a sensitometer, a device that exposes strips of film in the same way every time, producing a scale with steps of varying densities, or degrees of opacity, on the film. The control strips are developed and density readings are taken on the steps. Film processing should result in the same density readings, plus or minus a narrow margin, on the control strip each day. If the expected control strip density is not achieved within the allowable tolerance, exposure tests and production film should not be developed. Action must be taken to identify the source of the film processing irregularity and correct it. More control strips are processed until the desired density result is achieved. Only at this point should exposure tests or production work be developed. It is also prudent to examine the processed control strips for scratches at the beginning of each day before any production work is developed.

Control strips must be processed before any production work is processed as well as periodically throughout each workday to make certain that processing conditions have not changed. The results of the control strip should be recorded and plotted on a graph.

Polysulfide Treatment

A polysulfide treatment to protect silver images from oxidation has been developed by the Image Permanence Institute. Silver film is subject to oxidation from a number of environmental sources. The result of oxidation is the appearance of mirroring on the surface of the film or small red spots, referred to as redox blemishes or measles. These spots can obliterate the information on film. Once damaged by redox blemishes, information cannot be restored. Proper polysulfiding effectively inoculates silver film from the threat of oxidation by converting a percentage of the silver in the film into silver sulfide, a more stable form of silver.

A polysulfide solution may be added to a tank of the processor. Polysulfide treatment may be performed at the same time that the film is processed, or it may be done as a postprocessing treatment. After polysulfiding, a film sample should be evaluated for proper treatment according to ANSI/NAPM IT9.15: *Imaging Materials—Methods for the Evaluation of the Effectiveness of Chemical Conversion of Silver Images against Oxidation.*

Quality Control

Microfilm Inspection

Quality checks for appropriate resolution and density are performed before frame-by-frame inspections for missing pages or other bibliographic irregularities, because poor resolution or unacceptable density may cause rejection of all or major portions of a reel of film.

Resolution

Resolution is the ability of the microfilming system to record detail. The *microfilming system* consists of all that goes into the production of the finished film: film stock, camera optics, exposure, and film processing. The resolving capability of the microfilming system is referred to as *systems resolution* and is expressed as line pairs per millimeter (lppm).

Resolution is measured by filming a standard resolution test chart conforming to ANSI/ISO 3334-1991: *Micrographics—ISO Resolution Test Chart No. 2—Description and Use* and examining the image of the test chart under a microscope. The resolution test chart consists of a series of progressively smaller pairs of line patterns. Above each pair is a number. The higher the number, the smaller the pair of line patterns beneath it; hence, the finer the resolution. On this standard resolution target are twenty-six pairs of line patterns which are numbered from 1.0 to 18.

The number of line pairs per millimeter resolved is determined by multiplying the reduction ratio by the number above the smallest set of line patterns on the resolution test chart resolved when the film is examined under a microscope. For example, if the reduction ratio at which the test chart was filmed is 12X and it is possible to resolve the line pairs beneath the 10.0 number on the filmed image, the resolution achieved is 120 lppm.

Discussions of "line pairs per millimeter" can be misleading and really only become meaningful if one knows not just how many line pairs per millimeter were achieved, but at what reduction ratio the resolution test chart was filmed. One might think that if film produced by camera A achieves 192 line pairs per millimeter and film produced by camera B achieves 120 line pairs per millimeter, camera A has achieved a higher level of resolution than camera B, but this is not necessarily the case. If camera A filmed at a reduction ratio of 48X, the 4.0 pattern on the resolution test chart was resolved in order to achieve 192 lppm. If camera B filmed at a reduction ratio of 12X, the 10.0 pattern on the resolution test chart was resolved in order to achieve 120 lppm. In this example, it is possible to resolve eight smaller pairs of line patterns on the resolution test chart on the film produced by camera B than on the film produced by camera A.

Quality Index

Quality Index (QI) is a method of evaluating resolution that attempts to relate the height of the smallest printed lowercase *e* in the original material to the line pattern resolution on the filmed image in order to predict the legibility of text over the desired number of film generations. Quality Index has three levels: high, medium, and marginal quality.

The Quality Index method of evaluating resolution has limitations, however, because it depends on filming materials containing the printed lowercase *e*. The QI method thus cannot be used to evaluate the resolution of film of handwritten materials, materials containing non-Western text, or illustrations.

Information about resolution and the Quality Index method may be found in ANSI/AIIM MS23: *Standard Recommended Practice— Production, Inspection, and Quality Assurance of First Generation Silver Microforms of Documents* (1998) as well as in the RLG handbooks.

Density

Density refers to the opacity of the film and is expressed as a logarithm of the amount of light striking the film and the amount of light passing through the film. On master negative film, the maximum density (Dmax), or background density, is the dark part of the image, and the minimum density (Dmin), or base plus fog, is the clear part of the film on which there is no image.

Film density is measured with a transmission densitometer. The densitometer should be calibrated against known standards each time that it is turned on (at least once per day) to ensure the accuracy of the density readings.

Recommended master negative film background densities for various types of documents are published in both the RLG Guidelines and ANSI/AIIM standards. It is important that the background density of the film be appropriate for the characteristics of the original material to ensure the legibility of the filmed images over the desired number of film generations as well as to facilitate any future scanning of the film. Because all images on a reel of film are likely to be duplicated at the same film duplicator exposure setting, the less density variation on a reel the better.

Consistent, appropriate film density can be a more significant issue when filming low-contrast documents, such as those found in library and archival collections, than when filming high-contrast documents. Although high-contrast documents are likely to be adequately reproduced whether the film's density is 0.80 or 1.30, low-contrast documents may be legible at a film density of 0.80 but illegible at a film density of 1.30. Although text of some low-contrast documents may be legible on the master negative even when the background density is higher than is recommended for that type of material, the same text may not be legible on duplicates of the film because there is a loss of resolution and an increase in contrast with each film generation. When filming low-contrast documents, it is generally true that lower film densities are better than higher.

Methylene Blue Test

Thiosulfate is the agent in the microfilm fixer that removes the unexposed silver halide crystals during processing. It is important that a methylene blue test for residual thiosulfate, a test that measures the effectiveness of the film wash process, be performed on a blank piece of processed film within two weeks of the date on which the film was processed. Excessive levels of residual thiosulfate can result in deterioration of the film.

Light Box and Reader Inspection

The master film should be wound over a light box and inspected for scratches, blurring, fogging, water spots, chemical stains, and other flaws. A duplicate film (or sometimes the master negative) is placed on a reader and examined frame by frame. The inspector ensures that all pages or documents have been filmed and that all the targets are correct. The inspector also notes any scratches, blurred images, and other imperfections.

Some filming operations produce a duplicate film from the master and inspect the duplicate for completeness on a reader, rather than risk scratching the master film during a reader inspection. Other filming facilities, however, inspect master negatives on a reader because they find it too costly to discard the duplicate films made for this inspection when errors that require refilming are identified. Any error that requires that a correction be spliced into the master (one missed page, for example) results in the rejection of the duplicate that was made for purposes of inspection because duplicate films may contain no splices. The microfilm reader should be properly maintained as well as cleaned and tested for scratching on a daily basis in order to lessen the possibility that film of any generation will be scratched. Whatever generation of film is inspected, it should never be rewound on the reader. Rather, the film should be rewound using a pair of rewinds.

Microfilm readers are probably the least well maintained of all micrographic equipment. Some might say that there is no such thing as a nonscratching reader and therefore master films should never be inspected on a reader. It could also be said that there is no such thing as a nonscratching camera, a nonscratching film processor, or a nonscratching microscope. Certainly the manufacturers of microfilm readers do not design them with the intent that they will scratch the film. Rigorous cleaning and attentive maintenance usually make the difference between equipment that consistently scratches and equipment that does not. Each microfilming operation must weigh the risks and benefits of inspecting a master film or a duplicate film on a reader and then make the proper choice for its particular circumstance.

Splices

Ultrasonic splices are formed by internal friction as vibration and pressure are applied to film simultaneously. Ultrasonic splicers are used to splice polyester base film. Because ultrasonic splices are strong and employ no adhesives that can be damaging to film, they are the only splices appropriate for use in preservation microfilm.

Duplication

Duplicating Film

Duplicating film is available in silver, diazo, and vesicular. Duplicating films may be either sign-maintaining (negative to negative or positive to positive) or sign-reversing (negative to positive or positive to negative). Sign-maintaining film is called Direct Duplicating Film. Sign-reversing film is called Print Film.

Silver gelatin duplicating film is available as sign-maintaining or sign-reversing film. Diazo film is a dye-based, sign-maintaining duplicating film. Developed diazo films may appear black, blue, blue-black, or purple. The image on vesicular film is formed by bubbles in the polyester base. The background of vesicular film may appear light blue or green, beige, or gray. Vesicular film is a sign-reversing film.

While silver film is the only type that can be used for camera masters, the best choice of film for duplicates depends on cost, use factors, and to a lesser extent the image quality of the orginal being duplicated. Although diazo and vesicular films have shorter life expectancies than properly processed and stored silver, both are more resistant to scratching, as well as being cheaper to produce than silver, making them the most common choices for service copies. Since image contrast is increased in diazo and vesicular duplicates, silver film may be preferable for duplicating low-contrast or poor quality originals, however.

Duplicators

Most microfilm duplicators are contact printers. Diazo and vesicular duplicators both print and develop the duplicate film. Silver film duplicators only print the duplicate. The silver gelatin duplicate must then be processed just as the camera film is. Duplicators are available in low-speed tabletop models appropriate for low-volume operations, or in high-speed models for medium- to high-volume duplicating operations.

Tests to ensure that excessive resolution loss does not occur during duplication, and exposure tests to ensure that the resultant duplicate density falls within the required density range, should be performed before production duplication takes place. Brief duplicator tests for resolution and appropriate density should be conducted on a regular basis.

Duplicate Inspection

At least one resolution test chart on each duplicate film should be examined under a microscope to ensure that there has not been an unacceptable loss of resolution during duplication. Some loss of resolution occurs from one film generation to the next, but this loss should not be greater than 10 percent, or one resolution pattern.

Density readings are taken on the clear leader and the interframe spacing of negative duplicates, and on the black leader and interframe spacing of positive duplicates. Duplicate density guidelines can be found in the RLG microfilming publications as well as in ANSI MS43: *Standard Recommended Practice—Operational Procedures—Inspection and Quality Control of Duplicate Microforms of Documents and from COM* (1998).

Duplicate microfilms should be inspected over a light box to ensure that there are no scratches, stains, blurring, or other physical flaws.

Preservation Microfilm Production Issues

The following are issues that are often overlooked but that should be considered when planning a preservation microfilming facility or evaluating an existing facility.

On-site Filming and
Off-site Processing

On-site filming and off-site processing is a risky combination because the filmer is not able to exercise processing control. All the control procedures in place at the camera may be wasted effort without good processing control. Although any photofinisher may produce vacation photos of acceptable quality, much less latitude is possible when processing microfilm of textual materials, especially low-contrast materials. Before film is sent off-site for processing, the filmer will have to ensure that the processing agent maintains fine enough processing control to meet the goals of preservation microfilm, and this means more than just being able to pass a methylene blue test. The goal of preservation microfilming—to produce images of the highest possible quality—requires that film processing results be repeatable and predictable and fall within a narrower density range than may be permissible in nonpreservation microfilming applications.

Off-site processing can also result in delays in the development of calibration tests, exposure tests, and tests to confirm that camera repairs have been successful. These delays may result in long periods of camera downtime. An entire week's production may be sent to the processing facility at one time. The risk in batch processing is that a camera may malfunction, yet the filmer may be unaware and continue to film. The malfunction would not be discovered until all the film had been processed. This can result in a good deal of refilming that would not have been necessary had the film been developed and inspected on a daily basis.

Laboratory Staff Skills

Successfully filming library and archival materials in accordance with preservation standards and guidelines requires a more skilled staff than may be necessary in other microfilming operations. Fully automatic camera exposure controls are generally not able to produce films within the required density range because the materials in many archival and library collections vary greatly in paper and ink colors and quality. Manual exposure systems require operator judgment, and this judgment takes time and experience to acquire. Camera operators must also develop a sensitivity to the careful handling of brittle or valuable materials as well as an appreciation for the aesthetics of filming. Staff responsible for film processing must fully understand film processing control procedures and carry them out faithfully to ensure the overall success of the filming operation. Finally, film inspectors must exercise reasonable judgment in assessing film quality and determining when retakes are necessary.

Preservation Photocopying

There are times when reformatting onto microfilm is not appropriate. Reference materials, such as indexes and dictionaries, finding aids, music scores, and some clipping files, are best used in hard-copy format. Users do not want to load a roll of microfilm to look up the meaning of a word or the location of a document. In these situations, preservation photocopying is an appropriate option. It provides readers with a usable copy of a brittle out-of-print title. It does not, however, provide a master negative that serves as a backup in case the hard copy is lost or destroyed. For this reason, some institutions will also microfilm titles that they photocopy. Preservation photocopying should not be used in place of microfilming solely because of resistance on the part of readers to microfilm.

Although no standards cover every aspect of preservation photocopying, the guidelines from the American Library Association's Reproduction of Library Materials Section include an excellent description of preservation photocopies and cite related standards. Important considerations are the use of permanent and durable paper, and adequate adhesion of toner to the paper.

As with preservation microfilming, vendors are available that provide this service. A number of university preservation divisions have written contracts listing their specifications for preservation photocopying and would be willing to share this information. It would be wise to become familiar with these specifications before either choosing a vendor or considering an in-house operation.

Although it is possible to do preservation photocopying in-house, there are staffing and equipment considerations. To produce preservation-quality photocopies, the copy machine must be maintained at its highest operating level and ideally should not be used for general copying. Staff need to be trained to produce two-sided copies with the pages in registration to each other and to pay high attention to detail in a repetitive work situation. Even a good in-house operation will have limitations as materials to be photocopied may be oversized or include color illustrations. In these cases, it is definitely worth exploring the services and costs of a vendor. If materials are copied in-house, they will need to be sent to be bound as a separate operation; if a vendor is used, binding will probably be included as part of the transaction.

For those institutions interested in photocopying as a preservation option, it may be worth investigating the cooperative preservation photocopying program at the University of Kansas–Lawrence. This program, called BRITTLE, allows institutions to post on a listserv on the Internet a title they would like to have preservation photocopied. Other institutions participating in the program that hold the title may opt either to also have a photocopy made to replace their brittle copy, or choose to do nothing while noting that another institution has had a preservation photocopy made. The institution whose copy is to be photocopied coordinates the work through the University of Kansas Preservation Division, which has the contract for the work with a vendor. This program is open to large or small institutions regardless of how many titles they anticipate doing per year.[2]

Conclusion

The choice of microfilm or photocopy for preservation replacement of deteriorating books and documents involves a number of considerations. Among these are the nature of the material (reference work, individual document or series, and so on), whether the replacement is stand-alone or part of a project, and whether the replacement is to contribute to the national—indeed, even international—preservation effort. On the latter point, preservation photocopies benefit almost exclusively the local institution, while preservation microfilming, by providing a master film from which relatively inexpensive copies can be purchased by other institutions, contributes to the global preservation effort.

Regardless of whether microfilming or photocopying is used in preserving a text, it is important to be sure that the production staff, equipment, and service technicians produce the highest possible quality film or photocopy. Equipment, whether a camera and processor or a photocopy machine, must be properly set up and maintained so that each functions at the highest possible level. Good initial training must be provided for staff, and continuing educational opportunities should be made available. It is expected that all standards established for library and archives preservation will be met regardless whether the product is film or photocopy and whether the product is produced by an outside vendor or in-house operation.

Notes

1. Nancy E. Elkington, ed., *RLG Archives Microfilming Manual* (Mountain View, Calif.: Research Libraries Group, 1994); and Nancy E. Elkington, ed., *RLG Preservation Microfilming Handbook* (Mountain View, Calif.: Research Libraries Group, 1992).

2. To subscribe to BRITTLE, send an e-mail message to <listproc@ukans.edu>. Leave the subject line blank and in the body of the message type: Subscribe BRITTLE Firstname Lastname

Suggested Readings

American Library Association. Association for Library Collections and Technical Services. Reproduction of Library Materials Section. Copying Committee. Subcommittee on Preservation Photocopying Guidelines. "Guidelines for Preservation Photocopying." *Library Resources & Technical Services* 38 (1994): 288–292.

Fox, Lisa, ed. *Preservation Microfilming: A Guide for Librarians and Archivists.* 2d ed. Chicago: American Library Association, 1995.

Harris, Carolyn, Carol Mandel, and Robert Wolven. "A Cost Model for Preservation: The Columbia University Libraries' Approach." *Library Resources & Technical Services* 35 (1991): 33–54.

Formal Standards

American National Standards Institute. *Imaging Materials—Methods for the Evaluation of the Effectiveness of Chemical Conversion of Silver Images against Oxidation.* ANSI/NAPM IT9.15-1997.

———. *Micrographics—ISO Resolution Test Chart No. 2—Description and Use.* ANSI/ISO 3334-1991; ANSI/AIIM MS51-1991.

———. *Standard Recommended Practice—Operational Procedures—Inspection and Quality Control of Duplicate Microforms of Documents and from COM.* ANSI MS43-1998.

———. *Standard Recommended Practice—Production, Inspection, and Quality Assurance of First Generation Silver Microforms of Documents.* ANSI/AIIM MS23-1998.

16

Special Collections Conservation

ELEANORE STEWART

The conservation of special collections materials cannot be understood in isolation. What are special collections? Who uses them and for what purposes? And, most importantly, what characteristics should conservators preserve to ensure the continuing utility of these materials for scholars of today and the future?

Special Collections

The definition of special collections varies by institution but generally they can be defined as collections of materials in their original form. Principally, but not always, such materials are older, difficult to acquire, and, accordingly, of greater rarity and value than those items found in general collections. In many cases, the materials found in special collections do not start out being "rare"; they can be collections of ephemera or extremely complete subject collections whose value only becomes apparent over time.

Traditionally, special collections contain large numbers of materials of bibliographic interest: significant editions; works of exceptional aesthetic value; notable associational worth or provenance; and exemplars of binding, printing, or illustration history. But special collections are much more than aggregations of bibliographic superlatives. The collections, often unique, of authors' or scholars' personal papers and books, significant manuscripts, photographs, film, and even of sound recordings or data tapes provide resources for scholarly research. They can be used endlessly, answering new questions or the same questions asked in different ways, as academic interests and ideologies change over time.

What frequently unites the users of primary source materials—academics, students, genealogists, authors, journalists—is their need to view the physical evidence present in these materials, that is, their artifactual value. Although special collections materials are important for their intellectual content—the ideas they contain—they are also objects of material culture in which information is carried by the form of the object itself. Paper, typography, manuscript ink, bindings, owners' marks, and bookplates all provide valuable clues to the discerning scholar. Evidence relating to the author's or publisher's intent, the accuracy of a text, or the history of a book's production, distribution, and ownership can be found in them. From these individual stories, the larger picture of the transmission of ideas through society is developed.

Preserving Artifactual Value

Reproductions can never replace the original. Beyond the fundamental truth of this statement, reproductions have significant shortcomings that affect their value as objects of scholarly scrutiny. They are limited first by the loss of tonal values and surface qualities inherent in the copying process—essential information for scholars of images. Additionally, a reproduction can introduce misleading features, such as show-through from the back of the page that resembles a notation or causes the misinterpretation of a word. Finally, an incomplete or inaccurate original may have been used for the reproduction. In the case of printed books, even if the original was accurate and complete, it is only one example of the edition and cannot represent the edition as a whole. Reproductions of artifacts do have value in easing the use of the originals. For some scholars, they may be all that is needed; for others, they confirm the need to view the original.

The original is also useful for the evidence it can provide through scientific analysis. Developments in analytic equipment and microscopy have allowed the contribution of significant physical evidence to the field of bibliographic research. This analytically derived evidence can also be used to help papermakers, leather manufacturers, and conservators understand why materials from certain eras have lasted while others have deteriorated. This information can be used to produce long-lasting repair materials so that conservation treatments need not be undertaken as frequently as they are today. This potential for analysis of an object is never exhausted; each successive generation of analytic equipment is more sophisticated than the last and renders previously analyzed subjects capable of revealing new information. In short, beyond capturing textual information, facsimiles and microfilm can never replace the original.

Scholars of the Book

In addition to the preceding artifactual values, books as objects are used by a small, but growing group of scholars. Many factors influence what appears on the pages of a printed book: the author's intentions, the publisher's intentions, the human and mechanical processes of book production, and the economic and social forces of book distribution. The interplay of these issues is critical for many types of scholars: students of intellectual history who base their theories about culture on the books and ideas current during various periods, textual scholars pursuing the version of the work as an author intended it, or historians of the technical processes involved in manufacturing a book. All these scholars are dependent on the physical evidence present in historical works.

The role of the descriptive bibliographer is to accurately describe, through a complex set of conventions, the individual forms encountered, attempting to reconstruct the "ideal" copy of a text as the printer or publisher intended to present it to the world. She or he then describes the variants of this ideal that are encountered and determines their sequence of production, defining editions, impressions, issues, and states of a given work. The resulting descriptive bibliography allows for the identification, and often the location, of the texts that are the objects of study for scholars; it is the groundwork for all subsequent bibliographic or scholarly analysis.

Textual bibliography attempts to explain through physical analysis the production process of a particular book and to understand which differences result from the publisher's or printer's activities and which from the author's. To understand the sequence of textual variants and their relationships to one another, the bibliographer must have a firm grounding both in descriptive bibliography and in printing and publishing history. The ultimate goal is to produce a text as near as is possible or practical to the author's intentions.

A third form of bibliography is the field of historical bibliography, the study of the history of book production: printing, binding, and publishing. Source material includes the information available in government archives and in the relatively rare collections of printers' and publishers' records, but much of it is gathered from internal evidence from the books themselves, by identifying type and printers' ornaments or binders' tools.

Conservation and Conservators

What Is Conservation?

Although the precise definition is elusive and endlessly arguable, generally speaking, conservation involves a rigorous respect for the integrity of the object and an appreciation of its role as an object of material culture. There is a commitment to prolonging the life of the object through preventive action and through the use of stable materials and appropriate techniques of treatment. Conservation implies a limitation of intervention in treatment and of aesthetic reintegration (touching up or resupplying aesthetic detail). Finally, conservation treatment must be accompanied by documentation of the condition of the object upon receipt as well as the recording of procedures and materials used in treatment.

Conservators of Special Collections Materials

Professional conservators are highly trained and skilled practitioners. They know the history of the various methods used to produce books, manuscripts, and photographs, and they understand the chemical nature and deterioration processes of these materials as well as the limits and risks of the treatments used to address them. Conservators combine this technical background with manual skills and apply them to the practice of responsible conservation treatment. They are distinguished from conservation technicians by their level of experience, education, and manual skill, and from restorers by their adherence to a set of standards of practice that are discussed in detail later in this chapter.

Initially, the field of conservation was heavily weighted toward the conservation of paintings, art on paper, and antiquities, but the rise in value and importance of historical materials since the 1960s has promoted the development of other specialties, including photographs, books, and manuscripts and archival materials.

Conservators are trained either through apprenticeships or through graduate-level degree programs. Apprenticeships may be formal or informal and with one or a number of institutionally or privately practicing conservators. Because an apprentice's training is often controlled by the working pressures of the training location and by the types of materials present in the conservation laboratory for treatment, it can take many years to be exposed to the variety of treatments a well-rounded level of experience requires. This daily work must also be supported by rigorous extracurricular reading and course work to provide the theoretical underpinnings necessary to support full professional status.

"Program"-trained conservators generally reverse these characteristics: They are well educated in the theory of conservation treatment in their chosen field and exposed briefly to a wide variety of treatment problems, but they lack, and must acquire, the sound judgment that ensues from the experiences gained in a long exposure to the unpredictability of treating a variety of historical materials. Conservation programs typically have certain academic and work-experience prerequisites, and require at least two years of course work and a final year of internship. Three years of "bench work" following graduation is generally considered a minimum to attain a professional level of practice.

Conservation Science

Related to the practice of conservation is the field of conservation science. Some explanation of this discipline is useful to an understanding of how the theoretical gains of the research laboratory are ported into the world of applied practice and may help to explain the sorts of answers conservators are likely to give, answers often thought to be frustratingly long and inconclusive by librarians or archivists who have posed what they consider a simple question.

Conservation research is carried out at private research institutes, such as the Getty Conservation Institute, at national institutions, such as the Library of Congress, and by individual scientists in conservation training programs or laboratories throughout the world. Their research agendas are often driven by institutional problems or priorities, many of which relate only indirectly to the problems and questions that arise in the context of preserving library and archival materials. In addition, there are far more questions than the small cadre of conservation scientists can hope to answer. There have been some recent efforts to organize communication links and to forge research agendas relevant to both conservation scientists and institutional conservators. Efforts by the Preservation and Access Program of the Council on Library and Information Resources and the Getty Conservation Institute are notable in this area and are leading to research projects focusing on conservation issues of direct relevance to libraries and archives.

Another problem in conservation research is that of experiment design. This includes many issues: testing the efficacy of workaday conservation techniques and formulas; the use in experiments of historic materials versus modern testing materials produced under known conditions; the number of samples needed for statistical validity; the applicability of using artificial, short-term, high-temperature accelerated aging to reproduce the effects of long-term, ambient aging (so-called natural aging); and the extent to which an experiment is documented in a refereed publication. These factors and many more make the interpretation of conservation science research literature and the subsequent steering of a course of action an enterprise to be approached with utmost caution.

Consequently (and, to many librarians and archivists, paradoxically), the conservation scientist or conservator who gives an inconclusive response may be imparting far more meaningful or responsibly interpreted information than one who gives a simple answer. With responsibility for decisions affecting the well-being and longevity of their collections, librarians should have a clear understanding of the quantity and quality of research relevant to those decisions. The frequent unevenness of this research accounts, in large part, for the resistance of conservators to immediately embrace new technology and to subject the collections in their care to service as "guinea pigs" in the treatment development process. The history of conservation is filled with examples of materials or treatments originally thought to be safe that resulted in later damage to the artifacts and in the necessity for committing untold resources to undo that damage. Soluble nylon, silking, and lamination (all used to reinforce weak or damaged paper) are examples of conservation treatments that have been discontinued because of unforeseen aging problems.

Philosophical Issues and
Professional Responsibilities

The main professional organization for conservators and conservation scientists in the United States is the American Institute for Conservation of Historic and Artistic Works (AIC). Its purpose is to provide a forum for the exchange of information and promotion of knowledge among all professionals involved in conservation of artifacts. Types of membership range from Associate (any person with an interest in the purposes of the organization) to the categories of Professional Associate and Fellow, which carry certain responsibilities and commitments to professional standards. Members at these levels have agreed to pursue their own continuing education in conservation, to contribute to the field through research, to share their professional knowledge with colleagues and serious students, and to educate the public.

In addition they agree to abide by the Code of Ethics and Guidelines for Practice of the AIC (see the Suggested Readings). An understanding of these will help library staff to understand why conservators act as they do. The code of ethics directs conservation professionals to serve as advocates for the preservation of cultural property. They are required professionally to try to limit damage or deterioration to cultural property; consequently, they will actively intervene if library activities outside the preservation department are damaging to the materials.

Professional Associates and Fellows agree to practice within the limits of their expertise and those of the available facilities. Although circumstances may limit the extent of treatment allocated to an artifact, conservators must not compromise the quality of the treatment. They must recommend the treatment that they deem most suitable to the preservation of the aesthetic, conceptual, and physical characteristics of the piece. If no intervention best serves the interests of the artifact, they are compelled to recommend this, even if it limits their work or income. Whatever treatment is undertaken must be documented and that documentation provided to the owner or custodian.

The conservator has an obligation to ensure that the condition of the object will remain as stable as possible for generations. He or she must consider the consequences of today's treatment on future conservation options for the artifact, and feel fairly certain that materials used and actions undertaken will neither limit future treatment nor involve excessive time or damage to the artifact if they must be subsequently removed. It is not only the specter of needing to remove materials that may prove damaging in the long term. We have seen, too, that the analytic tools available to scholars grow increasingly more sophisticated, and it is necessary to take every precaution to ensure that treatments undertaken today will not hamper future investigation of the artifact.

Treatment Documentation

Once special collections materials have been identified as needing conservation attention, they are reviewed by the conservator and curator in a process known as *treatment specification*. This process ensures that limited conservation resources are applied appropriately and that the treatment chosen is in the best interests of the object and the collection. Conservation treatment should be considered only if an object is threatened by chemical instability or by physical vulnerability to continued use.

Treatment Proposal

The object or collection is inspected by the conservator and a proposal for treatment is drawn up. Preliminary input from the curator can delimit the proposal by providing background information about the piece—for example, its bibliographic or associational value, how it is used and the degree of projected use it will receive, how and where it will be stored, its relationship to other parts of the collection, whether particular parts should be retained, and so on. The treatment proposal contains a verbal description of the item's condition on receipt, encompassing the location and extent of damage, state of chemical deterioration, and any recognizable modifications to the original (including earlier repairs). It will also often contain a description of the original materials and method of fabrication of the artifact. The conservator may need to make tests to determine the physical makeup of the object—for example, what sort of paper fibers and sizing, inks, and adhesives were used—and what the results of the proposed treatment might be to those constituents. The proposal may provide several potential courses of action. It will discuss the benefits of each, the risks and limitations, and the projected treatment time needed.

Once the proposal is drawn up, subsequent discussion between the curator and the conservator provides an opportunity to check assumptions and more fully discuss the treatment options. After a choice is made, the curator signs the proposal to authorize treatment. There is much discussion in the literature concerning who has the ultimate decision-making responsibility, the curator or the conservator. Ideally the decision should be a consensus of the two professionals. Each has the obligation to ensure the object survives for as long as possible and with as little alteration as possible. They approach this responsibility from different vantages and with varying educational backgrounds and experience. Their relationship is an enormously significant one for the health of the collections, and it should be cultivated actively. The greater the communication level, the trust, and the level of knowledge about the other's views on relevant issues of aesthetic, historic, and scholarly value, the more likely these decisions can occur in ways that benefit the collections in their care. If there are a number of curatorial areas and conservators, it is helpful to assign a conservator to a specific curatorial area so that this relationship can develop.

Treatment Report

The second part of documenting the conservation of special collections materials is the treatment report. In addition to being a professional obligation of the code of ethics, documentation serves many purposes: It is helpful to the conservator during the reconstruction portion of the treatment; it serves future scholars and conservators wanting information about the original structure and what was done; and it can function as a learning tool for both conservators and curators, deepening their knowledge about the ways in which historic documents were produced.

The treatment report also details the processes carried out during the course of the treatment, the materials (such as repair papers, adhesives, thread) that were used in the treatment, and a description of parts that were added or removed. Fragments of the original piece that cannot be reused, if valuable enough, can be kept in a separate file or enclosed in the storage box with the piece itself. Such fragments can allow a binding historian to identify the binder by measuring the impressions left by the tooling, or they can provide samples for future scientific analysis. In cases where verbal description is inadequate, photographic documentation is also used; it can provide the conservator with much more detail about characteristics before or during treatment and what, if any, changes have occurred. It also provides documentation of parts that are not retained. Black-and-white photographs should be stored to ensure maximum life expectancy.

The degree of treatment negotiation, research before and during treatment, and documentation are generally linked either to the value or level of interest in the object or to the extent of the treatment. If the conservator learns during the course of treatment that the proposed methods must be altered, he or she will modify the proposal, notify the curator, and get written approval for these changes. Once the treatment is finished, the conservator and the curator sign and date the documentation and it becomes an additional source of information about the object. It is important that the documentation be saved in a manner that ensures its survival and access. Generally it is best to store it with the object itself. If this is not possible, the object should contain a small, tipped-in description of treatment and reference to the location of the complete file.

Treatment Options

Paper artifacts found in library and archival collections include examples of anything ever produced on paper, many of which were never intended to be collected and saved. Each presents its own set of challenges to the conservator: Composition of papers, inks, and adhesives varies widely and results in almost endless and sometimes unpredictable responses to treatment.

Paper artifacts consist of a support and the medium or media. *Support* is a generic term to describe the material (for example, paper, parchment) that physically supports writing or printing. The cellulose fibers of paper are long polymer chains linked by physical proximity and chemical bonds. Deterioration occurs when such elements as acids, present in the paper or introduced by the environment, sever the bonds and shorten the long chains. This shortening of polymer length results in weakening, embrittlement, and discoloration of the paper.

Medium refers to the writing, printing, or imaging substance; in library and archival collections it can include printing and manuscript inks, the dyes and toners of all reproducing technologies, and traditional art on paper materials. Some of these pose a direct conservation problem; many are faded from exposure to light or have damaged the underlying support because of improper formulation in their production. Media can also indirectly present substantial conservation problems to the conservator attempting to treat the support layer because many of the treatments that improve the condition of paper create a high level of risk to the media.

Paper Conservation Treatments

Removing Damaging Mounts   Also called *backing removal*, this treatment is considered when an artifact has been adhered directly to a board or mount that is causing chemical deterioration or physical stress. Damage can be caused by either the board or the adhesive and results in discoloration and possible weakening of the paper. Mounts can also cause damage by setting up stresses in the paper; different rates of expansion between the mount and the artifact when exposed to humidity changes, or shrinkage of the adhesive, can be responsible. The creator's intent in mounting, and issues of the mount's contribution to the provenance of the piece, should be considered before removal. Backing removal can be quite time-consuming so the value of the piece and the degree of threat posed by the mounting are also relevant. The choice of appropriate method depends on the strength of the paper and the sensitivity of the media to moisture, solvents, pressure, and other factors.

Removing Tape   The widespread use of pressure-sensitive tape to mend paper makes this a common problem in libraries and archives, and the damage it causes and the difficulty of removing it accounts for the vehemence with which preservation professionals discourage such mending. As the tape ages, the adhesive softens, often creeping from beneath the carrier tape. Eventually it discolors and hardens, irreversibly staining the paper. To prevent this staining, the tape must be lifted and the adhesive residue removed with solvents.

Tape removal is time-consuming and not always successful. It requires experimentation to discover the solvent or combination of solvents that will soften the adhesive. The solvent also must not disturb the media layer or cause visible alteration to the paper. Work proceeds slowly (up to fifteen minutes per inch) as care must be taken not to work faster than the solvent action (causing removal, or skinning, of the top layer of the paper). The collections may contain more tape-mended documents than there are resources for treatment of them, and priorities need to be set. Conservators can train processing staff to distinguish the most urgent cases.

Removing Stains   Removing unwanted stains is a practice with a long history. References in restoration manuals as early as the sixteenth century mention bleaching with weak acids or sunlight. Chlorine and other forms of chemical bleaches were discovered in the 1780s and used to reduce stains in prints and drawings. Bleaching has been used

to reduce staining that visually interferes with the aesthetic requirements of an object, but increasing knowledge of its drawbacks have led
to an almost total cessation of the practice, at least in library and
archive contexts where aesthetics is not a prime consideration. Damage
can include degradation of the cellulose; bleaching of inks; future staining (so-called color reversion); continued, unwanted bleaching action
because of incomplete removal from the paper; and overall color
change in paper or media.

An old form of bleaching called light bleaching, which had fallen
out of use among paper restorers toward the end of the nineteenth century, is currently experiencing a revival in paper conservation treatment.
It involves the use of sunlight or artificial light of known wavelength,
and it is considered milder, less damaging, and more controllable by
many paper conservators. It can be very time-consuming.

Cleaning   Many stains and forms of discoloration can be removed or
lightened by milder methods than bleaching. Dry cleaning, done
gradually with crumbled vinyl erasers, can remove surface dirt and is
a precursor to washing in water as it prevents settling of the dirt
deeper into the fiber mesh of the paper. Wet cleaning, or washing, is
a highly complex and often (but not exclusively) a beneficial treatment. The extent of water introduced can vary, from total immersion
to more controlled methods, such as mist application of water pulled
through the paper by a vacuum on a suction table, or application of
moistened blotters that wick discoloration from the back of the sheet.
Sometimes solvents, enzymes, or surfactants are added to the water to
increase cleansing. Water used for washing should be purified, with
known beneficial substances (for example, calcium) reintroduced.
Water will remove water-soluble acids in the paper; the addition of
alkaline elements to the water will increase this action. This process
can result in neutralization of the paper, but does not leave a residue
of alkalinity to combat a future rise in acidity. That process is covered
under deacidification.

The decision to wash an artifact is not made lightly. Pretesting of
the media and of the paper (done microscopically) can give the conservator only a sense of the consequences; a medium that does not appear
soluble at the testing stage can soften or dissolve during treatment. In
addition, components of the paper and media can be removed without
immediately visible results, and washing can alter subtle characteristics
of the paper surface, such as burnishing or embossing. Finally, because
the washing process results in the removal of substances, it alters the
evidentiary value of the paper for future analytic investigation. The

potential physical and aesthetic improvements to the object must be balanced against these, and other, possible drawbacks.

Deacidification More precise terminology for deacidification distinguishes neutralization—the application of an alkaline agent that reacts with acids in the paper to form a salt—from alkalization—the deposition of a residue of alkaline material in the paper to buffer against future acidity. The intent of alkalization is to slow the acid hydrolysis of the cellulose, the deterioration process that results in chain breakage and embrittlement. Neither neutralization or alkalization will strengthen the paper or reverse the embrittlement. The present discussion covers those processes delivered on a sheet-by-sheet basis; techniques of "mass deacidification" will not be discussed.

Although the use of alkalization on special collections materials may be called for under certain circumstances, it should never be proposed as a matter of course. It is generally considered when the conservator suspects a high level of chemical instability in the paper.

The most commonly used alkalizing or neutralizing agents are the alkaline earths, calcium and magnesium, which can be delivered in a medium of water or, for water-sensitive situations, mixtures of solvents. Application involves either spraying or immersing the pages; books may have the sewing removed and the sections "taken down." Careful pretesting is done to establish media solubility, effect on observable paper qualities, level of pH, and other factors. Choice of alkalizing agent is affected by paper fiber, size, media, the possibility of metal ions in the paper, and, to some extent, the preference and bias of the conservator.

Side effects can include, among others, color changes in the paper (lignin-containing papers will tend to darken initially, but some test results show this consideration is offset by the comparatively greater darkening of the paper over time if left untreated); sinking of some media (absorption of the media by the paper, which results in increased show-through of the image onto the back of the sheet); a color shift in alkali-sensitive media; decolorizing of some media (such as Prussian blue found in blueprints); or removal of sizing or media binders.

Consolidation This process is used to reattach flaking media or to protect water-soluble media during aqueous treatments. Materials used include natural substances, such as gelatin, parchment size, modified starches, or waxes, and various synthetic resins and emulsions. Considerations include visual alteration of the media (for example, increasing the saturation of colors) and removability and aging characteristics of the consolidant.

Mending Numerous techniques are available to mend tears, fill losses, or give overall support to weakened paper. Mends should be visible but not disturbingly so; should not alter paper qualities, such as transparency or handle; and should not overly strengthen the damaged area because significant differences will cause new damage at the edge of the mended area. Papers used for mending include Western papers thinned along the join to prevent bulking, and Japanese papers, whose long fibers make them very strong in proportion to their thickness. Adhesives can be either starch pastes (with a long tradition of use) or synthetic, nonaqueous resins, like "heat-set." All materials should be of conservation quality.

Tears are usually mended with strips of Japanese paper. Holes can be mended with Japanese paper or with manually or mechanically applied pulp fills. Mechanical "leaf casting" systems are useful in collections with a large amount of damage of this sort—for example, multiple book leaves with insect damage. The system is complex to set up; equipment is needed to measure the amount of pulp to add and to prepare the pulp, as well as the leaf caster or suction table itself.

Overall strengthening of weakened paper can be achieved with adhered linings of paper; the lining is chosen to match the original in its response to humidity, its opacity and color, and other qualities. Ideally, a lining should only minimally alter transparency and reflectance (with thinner objects this may not be avoidable). Sometimes an object cannot tolerate the lining process (the piece may not be able to be placed face down, or to take the expansion and contraction of the process or the pressure of drying). Alternatives include special housings that provide physical support or limit the effects of handling or access.

Book Conservation Treatments

Because the enormous variety of materials and methods of book production vary by period and locale, details of construction can provide bibliographic scholars with information about the date and place of binding. Book conservators play an important role in the development of the young field of bookbinding history. They can avoid unnecessary treatments that may be confusing to bibliographic scholars, and they can record details that are evident only while a book is dismantled.

For a book to be useful for bibliographic research, a scholar must be able to say with certainty what it is or that it is what it claims to be. Alterations, such as mending, complicate this picture; it becomes impossible to say what existed previously and what other (perhaps invisible) alteration has taken place. The book's "bibliographic integrity" has been compromised. For this reason, bibliographers often prefer a damaged book to a repaired one. On the other hand, other scholars may need to use the book, and the damage may be of a sort that worsens with use or time, possibly even threatening loss or irreparable damage to some part of the book. The decision to repair or rebind a book must be made with these issues foremost in mind.

Faced with a book in need of treatment, a book conservator will attempt to design a treatment that can, with the minimum of disruption or intervention, secure the book for safe use and the longest possible continued existence. Depending on the age, condition, and projected use, the treatment may range from a protective box to full conservation treatment. The intention is to stabilize intact but weakened areas or to replace functionally important parts that have broken. It is not the goal of the conservator to return the book to a state resembling its appearance at the time of production, which in any case may not be known with certainty if the book has been previously restored or rebound. As with other forms of conservation, the repairs should be of conservationally sound materials and should be visible, but not distracting.

The issue of conservationally sound materials is still problematic for book conservation. Most particularly, the production of long-lasting leathers is still inadequately understood. The decision to use leather in a conservation treatment should be based on knowledge of current research on preparation of long-lasting leather and of a probable life span of less than a century. If leather is used in covering, the binding should be executed in a manner that isolates the text block from the leather (for example, through the use of paper linings) and minimizes the labor necessary for future rebinding (achieved by release layers of paper linings or the use of nonadhesive structures).

Boxing   A book that will not be receiving heavy use or that possesses artifactual value of a degree that should limit alteration is an ideal candidate for boxing. Customized boxes can be constructed that isolate and protect the volume from abrasion and environmental damage and keep all the attendant parts together.

Minor Repairs   These vary depending on the location of the damage, but are commonly limited to lightweight mending in the area of loss or damage. Although they do not provide the full physical reintegration of more complex treatments (for example, cracks can be visible between previously broken parts), they physically reunite the separated pieces, require little time to perform, and may provide successful treatment for minimally used materials.

Loose pages are typically re-adhered with strips of Japanese paper; unlike "tipping" (gluing) in the pages, "guarding" pages back into the book allows the page to open fully back to the spine and prevents damage to the paper from the breaking edge of a stiff line of adhesive. Text blocks broken in half can be stitched together and lined with a reinforcing layer of cloth or paper. Loose spines can be hinged on with strips of paper or cloth.

Boards that have broken loose can be reattached in a number of ways, resulting in differing levels of strength and "finish." Small holes can be drilled through the shoulder of the spine and the board, with thread used to link them; on small books particularly this provides a surprisingly strong attachment. Although this technique introduces new holes, they are limited in number and discreet, and they allow full visual access to the original structural elements. New attachment can also be provided with paper or cloth strips toned to match the material to be repaired. Depending on the structure of the book and the condition of the materials, these can either be attached to the outer surface of the binding or endpaper or these surfaces can be mechanically lifted and the new material inserted underneath. Larger books may require multiple forms of attachment; very heavy books are usually not appropriate candidates for board reattachment.

Full Treatment   Books whose binding structure has been almost completely destroyed, books that will be subjected to robust use, or books that are severely threatened by their present binding or by chemical deterioration may be good candidates for full conservation treatment. The decision to create a wholly new binding or reuse the original structural components will be based on whether they are contemporaneous with the book, analysis of their condition, whether the original structure is contributing to damage of the text block, and whether the pieces would provide more bibliographic evidence if preserved and stored separately from the text block.

As with unbound material, book leaves that appear chemically unstable, have been severely weakened through fungal or microbial action, or have been distorted by exposure to water, among other criteria, may benefit from washing. In the case of bound materials, there are additional factors to consider. Unlike works of art, where stains and dirt are aesthetically displeasing and distracting to viewing, in library and archival materials they can convey information. Heavily soiled pages can indicate frequently consulted areas of a book, and stains can indicate what pages were originally adjacent.

Books that will be washed must be collated to document their original order of sequence and provide the pattern for their subsequent rebinding. Sheets that do not appear to be a part of the original printing are valuable and should not be discarded. These can include blank pages, advertisements, and illustrations added after publication. The method of drying should not introduce pressure excessive enough to flatten the "punch" (textural distortion caused by the impression of the printing process) nor destroy the textural differences of the wire and felt sides of the paper.

Marginal annotations should not be removed without curatorial direction. Washing alters the size of the sheet slightly, which has consequences for the edges of the text block. Colored or gilded edges will not be smooth following rebinding. Even undecorated edges are affected; the original method of trimming can leave evidence of the tools that were used that may be useful to binding historians. Trimming the edges to restore a smooth edge removes evidence of the original sheet size as well as the original edge treatment, owner's marks, shelf marks, or titling, useful for provenance.

Mending should only restore patently obvious connections and should be done with the knowledge that some tears (for example, those used to signal a "cancel," a printed replacement leaf) have meaning. Endpapers vary in the number of sheets and their method of construction and this information has importance to book scholars. In addition, end papers (and other binding materials, such as boards) should not be reused anywhere but with the book they came from; if a functional component is missing, it is potentially less confusing to bibliographers to supply a new one of modern materials. If fragments of unrelated but important printed matter are found as linings, they should be lifted enough to allow reading but ideally left in place.

Rebacking is a common method of repairing a book reusing its original components, and can apply to both cloth and leather bindings. The old spine is reused if possible, but sometimes embrittlement of the original can render it incapable of the flexing it must be able to bear. On books of bibliographic interest, it might prove useful to save the spine because type or decorative elements can sometimes identify the binder. New cloth or leather is introduced across the spine and underneath the covering on the boards, and the original spine, if reused, is mounted over the new material. Titling may be tooled and some tooling of the newly provided areas done to minimize distraction of the repair, but no attempt should be made, either by coloring or tooling, to disguise the existence of the repair.

If the original parts are not reused, a style for rebinding must be chosen. The previous method of construction may be duplicated, but often changes are made. The conservator may want to alter one or more details of construction used if they have proven damaging. Additionally, the binding in question may not be the original, and the curator or conservator may decide to rebind in a style more in keeping with the book. The rebinding should be nondamaging to the text block, should be suitable for the size and weight of the book, and should function well, opening smoothly and completely without strain to the paper. It should be appropriate to the date and locale of the book in its choice of material and technique. It should be "suggestive" of its historical lineage, not a direct imitation or reproduction of the original binding. Bookplates and other addenda can be either mounted in the new binding or saved with the original parts. These fragments should be housed in close proximity, preferably even in the same rare book box as the volume itself.

Conservation Treatment Programs

Establishing a Program

Advancing beyond the point of providing basic preservation functions (that is, approved storage and handling practices and minor procedures, such as removing staples or constructing customized enclosures) to undertaking full-scale conservation treatment of special collections materials is a significant step and one that should not be taken lightly. The consequences to the collections and the expenditure of money and staff resources can be enormous, and whether the treatment is provided in-house or through contract services, the costs and staffing needs call for a high level of administrative commitment.

Regardless of where the treatment occurs, curatorial expertise will be required for the selection of materials and specification of treatment. To a certain extent, guidelines for these processes can be drawn up, and lower-level staff can provide the initial selection and categorization. But a curator must always review and approve these decisions. Staff are needed for processing the selected materials: charging them out, filling out necessary forms, and providing title and call number information (not a trivial task in many uncataloged special collections). Loan forms, insurance, and packing must be taken care of before materials are sent out for treatment. As items are returned following treatment, they need quality control review, reshelving, and updating of the circulation information.

A staff conservator is invaluable if any degree of treatment activity is planned. He or she will know the collections and how they are used and can specify appropriate treatment, select qualified commercial services, and evaluate quality of the treatment. In addition, the conservator will provide expertise on disaster response, infestation, proper conditions for exhibition, specifications for materials used in the repair and housing of collections, and other technical issues of preservation. In a large institution, these duties can take the majority of a full-time position. A frequent mistake made by institutions beginning to put together a preservation program is to hire a conservator as the first preservation professional. However, a careful assessment of needs may indicate that a preservation administrator is the appropriate position.

Choosing between In-house and Contract Services

Factors in deciding to treat in-house or commercially include an institution's location in relation to contract services, the value of its collections, whether the risks and physical trauma of travel can be considered significant (many collection materials require extreme security, and the hazards of travel include loss, damage, and exposure to widely varying conditions of temperature and humidity), and the ability of the institution to commit the space and money to staff an in-house facility. Beyond the increased safety of the collections, benefits of an in-house facility include increased customization of services, access to materials at all times, the ability to respond quickly to changing institutional priorities or the availability of resources, and close supervision of treatment (including timely negotiation of any alterations necessitated during treatment). Benefits of relying on commercial facilities include an ability to vary the amount of treatment according to the availability of resources and not having to invest in building and maintaining facilities and expertise.

In-house Facility   First and foremost, an in-house facility requires space. Librarians unfamiliar with physical treatment often are astounded at the space requirements; accustomed to the space needs for other technical services in the range of fifty square feet per person, they cannot understand that conservation treatment requires numbers in the range of two hundred to three hundred square feet per person.

Equipment is large; the footprint (including access) for a board shear is over fifty square feet and for a four-by-six-foot table accessible on four sides, it is eighty-four square feet. Efficient work flow means the ability to stack work before, during, and following treatment. Often, work cannot be stacked to dry; it must be spread over plentiful table space. Both collection materials being treated and the supplies needed to treat them require storage equipment. These materials can often be maps, posters, and other oversized items; it all adds up to space.

In addition to space, the facility will require specialized equipment. Wet treatment requires water treatment systems and sinks that do not add unwanted elements to the water. The use of solvents requires a vented fume hood, safe chemical storage equipment, an eyewash stand and chemical shower, and support for disposal of wastes and emergency response. The lab needs to be in a secure area, environmentally controlled (the conditions should at least be no worse than storage areas), and with good illumination.

Designing and equipping a lab require expert advice. Any institution planning a treatment facility should hire the conservator first and allow her or him to design and oversee construction of the facility. Although this means the first year of the conservator's tenure will be largely taken up by the process, it will result in a lab far more useful to the institution and satisfying to the conservator than inheriting a new but inexpertly designed facility.

Contract Services   The availability of contract conservation treatment services has grown in recent years. In addition to private conservators, there are now regional centers sponsored by institutional consortia, as well as privately owned commercial businesses offering treatment for artifactually valuable collections. The American Institute for Conservation has established a referral service; an inquiry to the national office results in a list, by desired specialty, of conservators in the relevant geographical area. (It is important to realize that the referrals are to current AIC members; they do not constitute an endorsement.) Other libraries and archives may also provide referral suggestions. It is important to determine the training, areas of specialty, strengths and weaknesses, length of practice, and membership in professional organizations of potential providers. Once you have compiled a list of suitable providers, obtain references. Inspect samples of their work, obtain additional references, and visit their facility.

It is useful for the conservator or representative of a larger business to visit your institution as well. He or she will need to understand the needs of your institution to develop effective treatment proposals.

Expectations regarding packing, shipping, and insurance should be put in writing. If "mass" treatments are planned, contracts should specify materials and processes to be used. Involvement should of course begin in a limited fashion (both in terms of the quantity and the quality of materials sent), allowing for the growth of the relationship. The processes described earlier in this chapter under Treatment Options are essentially the same; the contracting conservator will need to evaluate the item, provide a treatment proposal (including estimated time and cost), and obtain curatorial approval before treatment.

Evaluating Treatments

Following the guidelines covered in this chapter should ensure that appropriate and responsible treatment is being received, and that materials and techniques are nondamaging. Evaluating the skill of the practitioner is more difficult. Older materials, in addition to bearing the marks of time, were often imperfectly constructed; conservation treatment cannot, and should not, alter these qualities. An excessively neatened appearance might be indicative of restoration (for example, trimmed edges on a book, or an invisible mend to paper). Newly added work should, however, be neatly done. There should be no excessive adhesive present or disruption of the surfaces by burnishing. Paper that has been lined should lie flat; tissue mends should be visible on close inspection. Books should have neatly worked endbands (stitches and beads of even size), evenly formed headcaps, smoothly adhered covering material, and corner turn-ins. If a book has been completely resewn, it should open as easily and as flat as its format allows. Take advantage of collectors and connoisseurs as well as conservators and take every opportunity to discuss with them what they consider excellent workmanship. Look at examples of untreated historical materials to develop an eye for the look of particular periods.

Equally important is a sense of the limitations of conservation treatment. It is often impossible to remove unwanted stains completely. Older materials are variable and unpredictable and often will not respond to treatment as well as the conservator or curator may hope. A conservator will often try several techniques to achieve a particular result and may, occasionally, have to declare defeat. This does not necessarily mean he or she is incompetent; even the most highly skilled and experienced conservators cannot consistently achieve miracles. Depend on the conservator who frankly discusses problems that arose and the techniques used to deal with them, and appreciate that knowing when not to treat or when to limit treatment represents judgment gained through long and often harrowing experience.

Suggested Readings

American Institute for Conservation of Historic and Artistic Works. "Code of Ethics and Guidelines for Practice." <http://sul-server-2.stanford.edu/aic/pubs/ethics.html>.

————. Education and Training Committee. *Conservation Training in the United States.* Washington, D.C.: AIC, 1989.

Clapp, Anne F. *Curatorial Care of Works of Art on Paper.* New York: Nick Lyons Books, 1987.

Clarkson, Christopher. "The Conservation of Early Books in Codex Form: A Personal Approach." *Paper Conservator* 3 (1978): 33–50.

Cullison, Bonnie Jo, and Jean Donaldson. "Conservators and Curators: A Cooperative Approach to Treatment Specifications." *Library Trends* 36 (1987–88): 229–240.

Foot, Mirjam. "Binding History and the Book Conservator." *Paper Conservator* 8 (1984): 77–83.

Frost, Gary. "A Brief History of Western Bookbinding without One Mention of Decoration." *Abbey Newsletter* 2 (1979): 39–42.

Paris, Jan. *Guidelines for Selecting a Conservator.* Washington, D.C.: American Institute for Conservation, 1984.

Pilette, Roberta, and Carolyn Harris. "It Takes Two to Tango: A Conservator's View of Curator/Conservator Relations." *Rare Books & Manuscripts Librarianship* 4 (1989): 103–111.

Ritzenthaler, Mary Lynn. *Preserving Archives and Manuscripts.* Chicago: Society of American Archivists, 1993.

17

Digitization for Preservation and Access

PAULA DE STEFANO

The emergence of digital technology as a way of capturing images of pages for electronic use is a dazzling prospect, especially to professionals who have relied so heavily on a medium as unpopular as microfilm. As a reproduction tool, the strong lure of digital imaging is difficult to resist and has preservation professionals and others scrambling to smooth the high-tech wrinkles out of an unruly set of circumstances. But somehow, the set of preservation problems and the electronic solution to them do not quite line up. The frustration is that, for now, this promising new electronic technology is not yet the panacea needed to completely supersede microfilm as a medium for long-term preservation. As today's preservation specialists contort themselves to become pseudoelectronic wizards in order to embrace this new technology and adopt it for preservation purposes, it seems an appropriate time to reassess the technology's place in preservation activities.

Digital technology and its use as a method of reproducing library materials is, in theory, a welcome innovation. However, reproduction in and of itself is not synonymous with preservation. The mission of the preservation-minded among us has been to rescue the decaying organic materials of value in our libraries and archives and to prolong their content for future scholarly inquiry. By virtue of its reproduction capabilities, and with no established long-term capabilities to recommend it, digital technology is dangerously promoted by some as a preservation technology. The coupling of the terms *digital* and *preservation* is becoming more and more prevalent in the professional literature. This is, perhaps, a consequence of linking the notion of access more and more closely to preservation, as though the two pursuits are inextricably linked. It is true that there is an obvious relationship between them, and they become inextricable when digital technology is involved, but while the use of this technology for access purposes delivers most, if not all, of what it promises, the use of digital technology specifically for preservation purposes is still premature. An analysis of the advantages and disadvantages of this machine-readable technology and its application to the preservation of library materials best begins with an examination of its capabilities in light of the often rigid preservation decision-making process that has guided preservation professionals for many years.

Background

For the sake of simplicity, preservation decision making can be divided into two broadly accepted, time-related categories with two different, equally valid aims (often confused when the term *preservation* is used all-inclusively): long-term preservation and shorter-term preservation. Both employ separate and distinct strategies to achieve separate and distinct results. The logic supporting each differs, as do the types of materials that find their way into these two streams of purpose.

Years of arduous work conducted by preservation and photography professionals resulted in a microfilming strategy that had as its goal the long-term preservation of embrittled scholarly works. Highly acidic, brittle books cannot practically be treated. The only method of salvaging the content of brittle materials is to copy or reformat them to a more stable medium. On the basis of scientific research and testing, nationally accepted standards were developed to ensure the long-term stability of microfilm. These standards assure the preservation of the images captured for several hundred years. Millions of dollars awarded by the National Endowment for the Humanities (NEH) to libraries in eleven years of microfilming grants required adherence to these national standards. Likewise, New York State's Conservation/Preservation Program (CPP) has the same requirement when awarding preservation microfilming grants to repositories in the state. Recommended storage of master negatives under archivally sound environmental conditions in off-site facilities, such as Iron Mountain and National Underground Storage, further ensure the promise of preservation for centuries. Throughout the 1980s and 1990s, microfilm has been the prevailing *long-term* preservation choice for scholarly material meant to be permanently retained.

Shorter-term preservation strategies have been employed to repair and restore fragile and damaged library materials to usable condition and protect them structurally as a way of lengthening their life. For paper-based materials, these methods assume that the paper is treatable and involve conservation treatments performed by trained professionals. Conservation treatments are capable of lasting hundreds of years— we are all aware of the many rare books and manuscripts that have lasted through the centuries. However, because these treatments are applied to materials vulnerable to handling and use, loss, vandalism, theft, and possible disaster as well as the notoriously poor environmental controls in libraries, their life expectancy cannot be scientifically guaranteed. Thus, "shorter-term" refers only in relative comparison to the centuries that microfilm will endure.

When photocopy technology improved and a national permanent paper standard was in place, many libraries proceeded to allocate funds to replace brittle originals with bound preservation photocopies. Among research libraries, this has become a very popular replacement solution for untreatable, paper-based originals. However, in terms of longevity, preservation photocopying must be relegated to the *shorter-term* category of preservation because materials reproduced this way are vulnerable to damage through handling and use, loss, theft, poor environments, and disasters.

In addition to the preservation methods already mentioned, there are other strategies that may be used to continue access to the intellectual content of scholarly materials. Many of our classics have survived in reprint form. Other special materials have been reproduced in facsimile. These methods of reproduction, however, have been primarily employed by commercial publishers for publications with marketable attraction and, therefore, cannot be relied upon by libraries for preservation purposes.

Regardless of the chosen preservation method, nationally accepted standards regarding the stability of the medium, materials, and processes used in preservation and conservation fortify the element of longevity. The long-term preservation achieved by microfilm, for example, is supported by national standards for the chemical stability of the photographic film used in microfilming and duplication projects. The developing and washing of the film, the housing, the storage, the reels, the ties that hold the microfilm in place on the reel, the boxes that house the microfilm, along with the environment in which the film will be stored, are all supported by national standards for long-term stability. Likewise, standards for permanent paper and binding guide the reproduction of deteriorating originals in preservation photocopying projects. The preservation community has relied heavily on standards to make the promise of preservation work.

Digital Media Stability and Obsolescence

Measuring the efficacy of digital reformatting for preservation using the fundamental preservation objectives of longevity and stability is a good starting point for the evaluation of this new technology and its appropriate role in preservation. Based on the physical aspects of digital media—that is, magnetic tape and optical disk—how long will digital media last? As of July 1998, the National Media Lab reports the following:

> With moderate care, most magnetic tapes used for digital data storage will last for 10 years. With special storage and handling, digital magnetic tape formats can reliably store information for 30 years or more. . . . [M]agneto-optical (M-O) and phase change (PD) media have a life expectancy comparable to magnetic tape of 10–30 years.[1]

Although these estimates are trustworthy, the literature is rife with debate over how long digital media will last. Everyone agrees, however, that the obsolescence of electronic hardware and software is far more threatening to the preservation of digital information than the physical longevity of the media on which it is recorded. Electronic information is machine-readable and dependent upon not only the machines used to display recorded texts and images, but the programs that read them and format them for human consumption. Because computer hardware and software are subject to rapid change, the dangers of obsolescence are more insidious than the instability of the media themselves. The solution to this problem is technical rather than physical and therefore presents a distinct departure from the traditional approach taken to resolve preservation problems in the past.

Traditionally, preservation has been accomplished by maintaining library materials in a physical form using proven techniques that would last far into the future. Digital technology eliminates any physicality involved in the problem. Instead, it is the electronic access, use, and ability to manipulate the information that needs to be preserved. Recognizing this departure from traditional values and practice, preservation professionals and others have suggested that a reexamination of the principles guiding preservation is needed in order to embrace this new technology and harness its possibilities for preservation purposes. Many in the library and archive communities agree. As a result, the question of preservation for digitized materials has become more a discussion about continued access to electronic information in the future, rather than a question of how to preserve digital recording media.

Crossing that line has created confusion in the preservation community about how to preserve electronically reformatted materials. Preserving access to digital information has become an urgent objective—urgent because of the short-lived cycles of today's hardware and software. Thus, concerned stakeholders have turned their attention to the issues surrounding continued access to information in the hope of devising an antidote to obsolescence.

Preserving Access to Digital Information

In the face of obsolescence, several preservation solutions to the access problem are currently being explored. *Refreshing* was an early term used to describe the repeated copying of digital information to ensure the persistence of the information. However, refreshing does not account for moving digital information to new systems of hardware or software as systems are upgraded. Rather, *migration* of digital information more accurately describes what technicians believe needs to be done. Repeated migration of electronic information to newer hardware and software systems is seen as one way to avoid obsolescence. Theoretically, if digital information is consistently migrated to new systems before the information becomes inaccessible, the persistence of the information will remain intact.

A number of consortia have wrestled with this idea. In early 1995, the Task Force on Digital Archiving was formed by members of the Research Libraries Group (RLG) and the Commission on Preservation and Access (CPA, now incorporated into the Council on Library and Information Resources). In the words of the task force, its purpose was "to investigate the means of ensuring 'continued access indefinitely into the future of records stored in digital electronic form.'"[2] Their report, published a year later and entitled *Preserving Digital*

Information: Report of the Task Force on Archiving of Digital Information,
proposes a strategy utilizing a distributed network of digital archives to
be responsible for continued access to electronically produced information. It requires repositories to identify themselves as digital
archives and be certified as such to prove their trustworthiness. These
repositories would also be equipped with the legal capacity to launch an
aggressive rescue mission should an organization fail in its commitment to preserve access to its digital files.

At the heart of the RLG/CPA report is the notion of continual
migration of archived digital information as changes in hardware and
software technology threaten to impede access. Unfortunately, the
report concludes with a list of recommendations but no immediate
plans to initiate such a system. Perhaps this is because many very basic
questions have yet to be answered in order to implement a system that
would continually migrate information. For example, no one has determined how a migration system would function, or what the costs might
be. Nor has a system of quality control been developed. Practically
speaking, migrated data would need to be examined for accuracy, but,
as yet, no acceptable method of quality control has been established.
Clearly, quality assurance for content integrity is a crucial aspect of a
migration plan that has preservation as its goal.

Looking ever more closely at the confluence of unresolved issues
surrounding migration today, content integrity may pose the worst
problem of all. In fact, if preservation is a high priority, migration may
be wholly inappropriate. Technical experts warn that transferring data
to accommodate new software systems almost always requires some
kind of technical conversion of the data to satisfy the needs of the
newer system. That means that repeated conversions when migrating
to new systems are liable over time to corrupt the integrity of the original data. Some progress has been made toward creating a format for
which conversion and data integrity will be minimized. The Universal
Preservation Format (UPF) is currently under development and seeks
to create a "neutral container" to envelop a digital file without altering
its integrity during conversion or migration. Still, a rigorous and
dependable system of quality control would be needed before migration endeavors are viable for preservation purposes. With such doubts
and unanswered questions still lingering, it is difficult to predict
whether any migration system will ever be safe enough to use as an
antidote to obsolescence.

Jeff Rothenberg says the ideal solution would be to always view
digital information using the original software; however, the ware-
housing of obsolete software and hardware would eventually prove

futile because of the cost of repairing and replacing worn-out components, or even retaining the expertise to do so. An alternative would be to build computer systems that would emulate the behavior of outdated hardware and software. This approach would obviate the need to continually convert the data and would allow originals to remain unchanged. However, experts tell us this is not yet technically feasible.[3]

At present, archiving digital information with the hope of preserving access through migration or emulation seems far off. Without some viable plan for a method of long-term storage that resolves the access problems associated with obsolete software and hardware, long-term preservation of digitized materials is not yet possible. In the meantime, some repositories plan to rely on the backward compatibility built into today's software. Most software these days is backward compatible, at least for a few generations. However, unless software and hardware manufacturers are sympathetic to the long-term needs of the digital repositories, it is unlikely that backward compatibility will be any more than an interim solution to the problem of obsolescence.

Lack of Standards

Another practical deterrent to the use of digital technology for preservation is the lack of standards and guidelines. Standards based on scientific testing have become a staple in the field of preservation, the basis from which preservation solutions proceed. They assure the longevity of paper, binding, photography, moving image, and sound transfer. The creation of standards was a critical step in the development of preservation policy and cooperation among institutions. Standards endow preservation efforts with reliability and credibility; they enable technical negotiations between clients and vendors; and they assure institutions and funding agencies that scarce resources will be well spent.

For preservation purposes, no standards exist to support the manufacture of digital media for long-term stability; nor are there standards to support archiving and migration protocols, emulation techniques, or backward compatibility requirements for hardware and software. Nor has there been any scientific testing toward these goals for preservation purposes. The absence of standards has stymied the use of digital technology for preservation reformatting and there has been little movement forward beyond demonstration projects except by an intrepid few.

The impediments to using digital technology to preserve original materials are clear. However, though the long-term preservation of digital information looks bleak and despite the lack of standards and problems of continued, long-term access, there are several reliable and appropriate ways of incorporating digital imaging in preservation initiatives. For now, the desired goal must be to exploit the access capabilities of digital technology and combine them with the longevity of proven preservation methods. Very simply, this means preserving original material through conservation treatment or one of the accepted preservation reformatting methods (microfilm or photocopy), and producing a scanned version for access purposes as well.

Digital Scanning and Microfilm

Several demonstration projects have successfully pioneered the concept of combining digital scanning with preservation microfilm initiatives. Most notable among them were the projects at Cornell and Yale Universities. Early interest in digital technology focused on what the technology could do in terms of image capture. An initiative led by Anne Kenney at Cornell investigated the possibility of reformatting brittle books using a digital imaging system that included a flat-bed scanner at the front end of the process, with digitally produced microfilm, also known as computer output microfilm (COM), at the final end. Moving from digital scan to microfilm, Kenney focused on the quality of the image during the initial capture process.

Theoretically, the project determined to emulate the strong, measurable image quality capabilities relied upon in micrographics. Kenney sought to translate the Quality Index (QI) measurements used in microphotography to digital scanning using mathematically reliable formulas. She proved it to be a trustworthy and reliable method to determine digital image quality. In this way, scanning resolutions for high-quality images could be estimated and assured. Formulas were developed to estimate not only image quality, but also file size (an important consequence of image quality), transmission time, and display resolutions. A loose-leaf workbook entitled *Digital Imaging for Libraries and Archives*, published by Cornell's Department of Preservation and Conservation, describes the methodology and includes instructions for how to use the formulas (see Suggested Readings).

Earlier attempts at digitizing, without demonstrated methods of ensuring quality in the scanning process, forced institutions to rely only on anecdotal evidence when converting library materials to digital formats. The groundbreaking Cornell digital project was a giant step toward solving the problem of definable image quality. In the field of preservation, a history of trust has been built upon the high image quality demanded and produced photographically in microfilm. The Cornell benchmarking methodology permits the same trust when producing high-quality digital images.

More to the point, when combining digital imaging with microfilm technology for long-term preservation purposes, the digital image quality will determine the image quality of the COM produced. Kenney proved that COM produced from high-quality digital images could satisfy and pass the high standards required for preservation microfilm. The combination of the long-term preservation capabilities of the microfilm and the enhanced access of the digital images proved ideal.

Donald Waters and Paul Conway at Yale University reversed the approach taken at Cornell to investigate the possibility of scanning existing microfilm in a demonstration project entitled Project Open Book. Here, too, the strategy was to link the desirable access capabilities of electronic imaging with a reliable preservation method. This film-to-digital approach proved more difficult because of technicalities of the original filming. Nevertheless, it was a successful demonstration project and provided the preservation community with a method of digitizing preserved images for which originals no longer exist.

With respect to the two different approaches, there is some debate over the digital-to-film approach established at Cornell and the film-to-digital approach developed at Yale. At issue is the level of quality when re-scanning is necessary. Theoretically, if the digital file is lost, the microfilm copy could be re-scanned. There has been some conjecture that digital images produced from COM film may be inferior to the digital image resulting from photographically produced microfilm and, therefore, filming should always be done first, from the original, to ensure the high quality of the microfilm. However, this question has not been rigorously tested and remains to be resolved.

Clearly, the attraction of the Cornell and Yale methodologies to the preservation community rests with the assurance of the long-term preservation capabilities that reside in the film. Without this, neither approach would satisfy preservation needs. The life of the digital file becomes less critical because the microfilm can be re-scanned if necessary. At the same time, the enhanced access capabilities of the electronic file are far more palatable to researchers than a positive use copy of the microfilm.

Digital Scanning and Photocopying

The reformatting of embrittled, out-of-print books using xerographic technology is a popular choice, especially for materials that are not suitable for microfilming. Improvements in the quality of photocopies and the emergence of a national standard for permanent paper provided preservation specialists with the ability to produce pristine, high-quality copies of deteriorated materials on alkaline, permanent paper that could be bound. In most cases, the deteriorated original is discarded.

The only drawback to this activity has been that once produced, if the bound photocopy disappeared, there was no way to rescue or preserve the content. (In addition, photocopying does not contribute to the national preservation effort by sharing the cost of first capture.) Preservation photocopying produces one copy to replace the original. If that copy is lost or stolen, nothing has been preserved. Digital technology used in place of photocopying can diminish that concern, first, because it can be used to produce a printed replacement copy on permanent paper and second, because it exists as a reproducible file should the printed copy be lost or stolen. In other words, books can be scanned, output to alkaline paper, and bound, leaving a digital file behind as a backup.

The use of digital scanning to reformat brittle materials, instead of preservation photocopying, is an attractive choice for research libraries that want to retain paper copies of their brittle books. The digital-instead-of-photocopy approach is not foolproof, however. For the short term, the digital files can back up the digitally output paper copy and vice versa, but, should the digital file become inaccessible and the paper copy become unavailable, the content would be virtually lost. Harking back to the original decision to reproduce the item, one assumes that if long-term preservation had been a concern, a combination of microfilm and digital conversion would have made more sense than the shorter-term solution: digital conversion and paper copy. Nevertheless, insofar as digital copies provide a replacement solution that is superior to the preservation photocopy replacement solution, it is worth considering.

Digital Scanning for Surrogate Use

Another appropriate use of digital technology for preservation purposes exists when a digital image is used to provide a surrogate copy of an original. In this way, the digital image acts as an agent for preservation because it allows information to be used and handled without damage to the original. High-quality photocopies and microfilm have been used in the past to relieve originals from the wear and tear of repeated use. Digital technology brings an added value to this effort because surrogates can be used over and over again without loss of quality, unlike microfilm or photocopies. When creating surrogates, high-quality image capture becomes essential; otherwise, the researcher may not be satisfied with the surrogate copy.

Practical Advice for Digital Projects

When digital projects are called for as part of a preservation initiative, policy decisions will need to be made for image quality as well as preservation and treatment of originals during and after scanning. A high-quality imaging system is warranted where preservation is concerned for several reasons. Materials that find their way into the preservation stream are in poor condition and cannot undergo the stress of repeated scanning. Therefore, it is best to scan once for the best possible image, making sure that resolution, tonal range, and color are adequately captured. In addition, as stated earlier, if converted images will be used as surrogates, researchers will not be appeased unless the quality is high enough to satisfy their needs; and, when COM is involved, high-quality image capture is needed to produce microfilm that will pass the rigorous standards required for preservation.

Determining optimum image quality before scanning will avoid the need to repeat the task later. Image quality is usually equated with the ability to reproduce a specific level of detail in the original. In order to determine that, collection specialists should be consulted regarding who is likely to use the digitized material and how it will be used in the future. For example, if text is involved, a high image quality may be needed to facilitate optical character recognition (OCR) conversions in the future, in which case, a high level of detail will need to be captured.

Decision making for image quality involves certain technical specifications for image capture, such as the type of scan (binary, gray scale, color), the dots per inch (dpi) to be used in the capture process, and what file types and compression schemes will be used for storage purposes. Although there are no established guidelines within the preservation community for obtaining quality images, generally speaking, the higher the resolution (dpi), the higher the image quality. Higher resolutions, however, result in large files that require more storage space. Because storage space represents a cost, high levels of image quality need to be justified. The Kenney/Cornell system of benchmarking using the smallest important detail within the image, or text, and the desirable QI is a reliable method to predetermine image capture resolutions. Ideally, the decision making for image quality should be shared between technicians, who understand equipment and image capture specifications, and curators, who are familiar with the use of the materials and able to anticipate future user needs.

In addition to issues surrounding image capture and preserving access to them, preserving the integrity of digital files is a concern and challenge. In the digital environment, files can be altered and manipulated, sometimes deliberately, sometimes inadvertently, sometimes maliciously.[4] Precautions should be taken to protect the intellectual content and integrity of a digital document or image. Usually this means providing some fixity to the data through time-stamping, or hashing. Although there are no established standards or guidelines for doing so, here again, a preservation application that includes microfilm will diminish the concern for document integrity because the intellectual content will be protected by the existence of a preserved microfilm copy.

Before adding digital imaging to the list of options available for preservation reformatting, file maintenance schedules and procedures should be established. Maintenance for digital files may or may not be an activity for the preservation department. In fact, it is quite likely maintenance will need to be the responsibility of an institution's computing technology office, or an equivalent office with technical expertise. Even so, the preservation department will need to plan for storage space, determine accessibility needs for the materials (online, off-line, near-line) and predetermine a schedule for maintaining the files. Commitment to the latter activity is essential for continued access even for short lengths of time.

In-house versus Outside Contracting

In the Cornell and Yale projects, most of the scanning process was conducted on-site in the preservation department using very expensive state-of-the-art equipment. Both endeavors were funded as demonstration projects and involved the technical expertise of specialists both inside and outside of these institutions. Since then, however, the trend is to use outside contractors for image scanning, with good reason. Given the expense of scanning equipment and the rapid changes in technology, it is far more economical to contract with a knowledgeable, experienced commercial vendor for scanning services than attempt it in-house, especially for large projects. The amount of technical knowledge and expertise needed to purchase, configure, use, and maintain hardware and software can be daunting. An important by-product of the Cornell and Yale projects was practical recommendations for preparation, processing, and work flow of materials to be converted. When contracting for vendor services, institutions can specify required image capture resolutions more accurately and verify the result when scanned images are returned. Of course, even when contracting to an outside vendor, some equipment is needed. A scanning workstation, including a flat-bed scanner, a high-quality monitor, a processor, and storage, is necessary in order to conduct tests and perform quality control.

Conclusion: Preservation or Access?

The digital landscape looks bleak for preservation purposes. The technology that Margaret Child referred to in the 1987 documentary *Slow Fires* as being "on the horizon" is still on the horizon for preservation purposes; however, it has crested the wave for access purposes.[5] How to include digitization for preservation and access purposes continues to be a question and a frustration among preservation professionals. It is interesting that much of the confusion stems from the relationship between preservation and access.

Preservation and access share a correlative relationship: One directly implies the other. They also share a causal relationship: The need for access to an item triggers the need to preserve it, just as the preservation of an item provides continued access. Logically, it's obvious that the two are reciprocal: What purpose is there to preserve information that won't be accessible to a researcher? The impulse to preserve did not emerge in libraries with the intent to make preserved materials inaccessible. In practical terms, what library would engage in or fund such an activity? Despite their reciprocal relationship, preservation and access have traditionally involved very different sets of activities. Organizationally, especially in larger institutions, preservation and access have been the responsibility of two separate departments and administered by two sets of trained professionals. Preservation and conservation professionals have worked collaboratively with those expert in "access" (that is, cataloging professionals) to update records to show changes in the status, format, or location of preserved materials.

Very little in the literature closely connected preservation and access, beyond their obvious, reciprocal relationship, until the emergence of federal funding for preservation microfilming grants. Soon after the early Research Libraries Group cooperative microfilming projects began, the Commission on Preservation and Access was established in 1986. Following that, the NEH joined two once-separate offices to create the Division of Preservation and Access. With the promise of funding, what was previously a tacit, but obvious, relationship became a largely politicized combination of two separate activities.

Today, with the emergence of electronic information, access has become even more consequential. Without electronic access to machine-readable information, for all practical purposes, the information might as well not exist. It is at this point that the relationship between preservation and access becomes more than reciprocal—it becomes almost synonymous. In the digital world, access supersedes preservation.

In today's world of electronic information, the oneness of access and preservation is causing confusion, distortion, and conflict within the field of preservation as practitioners grapple with highly technical electronic environments. Some preservation professionals argue that now more than ever, the link between preservation and access is inextricable and, in one sense, it is. However, the opposing argument is that despite their reciprocal relationship, preservation and access need to be distinguished from each other, pulled apart again, into two related but separate activities. The advantage of this perspective is that it puts the access issue more appropriately into the hands of technical experts, which will undoubtedly allow the problem of continued access to digital information to move forward more rapidly toward a resolution. In the future, the digital conversion of texts may become the responsibility of computer technicians, and preservation may revert to traditional treatment activities.[6] Preservation of electronic information clearly requires technical expertise, and the electronic expertise that today's trained preservation professionals possess is limited at best. Preservation professionals must be present in this effort to advocate long-term preservation of electronic information, but the technical aspects of that goal more practically rest with individuals expert in electronic technology.

The consequences related to software and hardware obsolescence stand squarely in the way of employing digital technology in the preservation process (beyond a hybrid approach as described earlier). For now, an examination of the facts reveals that Don Willis's hybrid approach is still the most solid application of digital technology in preservation endeavors.[7] Six years later, a new report by Paul Conway, Anne Kenney, and Stephen Chapman, entitled *Digital Imaging and Preservation Microfilm: The Future of the Hybrid Approach for the Brittle Books Program*, reaffirms Willis's hybrid approach.[8] Not until digital preservation can satisfy national standards for quality and permanence will it replace microfilm.

Notes

1. From the National Media Laboratory's web page entitled "Media Stability," under the section "Information on Storage Media Longevity," July 17, 1998 <http://www.nml.org/MediaStability>.

2. Commission on Preservation and Access and the Research Libraries Group, *Preserving Digital Information: Report of the Task Force on Archiving of Digital Information* (Washington, D.C.: CPA, 1996), iii.

3. Jeff Rothenberg, "Ensuring the Longevity of Digital Documents," *Scientific American* 252 (January 1995): 45, 47. Also see Rothenberg's report, *Avoiding Technological Quicksand: Finding a Viable Technical Foundation for Digital Preservation*, available early 1999 from the Council on Library and Information Resources.

4. Peter S. Graham, *Intellectual Preservation: Electronic Preservation of the Third Kind* (Washington, D.C.: Commission on Preservation and Access, 1994).

5. The Council on Library Resources, the Library of Congress, and the National Endowment for the Humanities, *Slow Fires: On the Preservation of the Human Record*, a Terry Sanders film presented by the American Film Foundation, 1987.

6. Dan Hazen, "Preservation as Vanishing Act (and Art?): Print Era Organizations in the Electronic Age," in *Advances in Preservation and Access*, edited by Barbra Buckner Higginbotham, vol. 2 (Medford, N.J.: Learned Information, 1995), 16.

7. Don Willis, *A Hybrid Systems Approach to Preservation of Printed Materials*. (Washington, D.C.: Commission on Preservation and Access, 1992).

8. Paul Conway, Anne Kenney, and Stephen Chapman, *Digital Imaging and Preservation Microfilm: The Future of the Hybrid Approach for the Brittle Books program*, working paper, Council on Library and Information Resources, Washington, D.C. <http://www.clir.org/pubs/archives/hybridintro. html>

Suggested Readings

Bellinger, Meg. "The Transformation from Microfilm to Digital Storage and Access." *Journal of Library Administration* 25, no. 4 (1998): 177–185.

Cloonan, Michèle Valerie. "The Preservation of Knowledge." *Library Trends* 41 (spring 1993): 594–605.

Conway, Paul. *Conversion of Microfilm to Digital Imagery: A Demonstration Project. Performance Report on the Production Conversion Phase of Project Open Book.* New Haven: Yale University Library, August 1996.

———. "Preservation in the Digital World." *Microform & Imaging Review* 24, no. 4 (fall 1996): 156–171.

Hedstrom, Margaret. "Digital Preservation: A Time Bomb for Digital Libraries." *Computers and the Humanities* 31 (1998): 189–202.

Kenney, Anne R. *Digital to Microfilm Conversion: A Demonstration Project 1994–1996.* Final Report to the National Endowment for the Humanities, PS-20781-94. Ithaca, N.Y.: Cornell University Libraries, Department of Preservation and Conservation, 1997. <http://www.library.cornell.edu/preservation/pub.htm>

Kenney, Anne R., and Stephen Chapman. *Digital Imaging for Libraries and Archives.* Ithaca, N.Y.: Department of Preservation and Conservation, Cornell University Libraries, 1996.

Lynch, Clifford. "The Integrity of Digital Information: Mechanics and Definitional Issues." *Journal of the American Society of Information Science* (December 1994): 737–744.

Mohlhenrich, Janice, ed. *Preservation of Electronic Formats: Electronic Formats for Preservation.* Fort Atkinson, Wis.: Highsmith, 1993.

Trant, Jennifer. "Framing the Picture: Standards for Imaging." Paper prepared for the International Conference on Hypermedia and Interactivity in Museums/Museum Computer Network Joint Conference, San Diego, Calif., October 1995.

Van Bogart, John W. "Electronic Technology as a Preservation Strategy." In *Association of Research Libraries Proceedings of the 125th Meeting,* October 19–21, 1994, 55–78. Washington, D.C.: ARL.

Weber, Hartmut, and Marianne Dörr. *Digitization as a Method of Preservation? Final Report of a Working Group of the Deutsche Forschungsgemeinschaft (German Research Association).* Washington, D.C.: Commission on Preservation and Access, October 1997.

18

Preservation of Information in Nonpaper Formats

ELEANORE STEWART
and PAUL N. BANKS

The range of newer media in libraries and archives is broad and growing rapidly: still and motion pictures, audio and video recordings, computer media. Within each of these broad categories is a seemingly endless range of ramifications. For example, just in the forty or so years of video recording, there have been about one hundred formats—mostly incompatible with each other—and one or two new video formats appear each year.

Libraries and archives have been able to assume a life expectancy for their books and records of fifty or one hundred years or more, longer than the career span of any individual librarian or archivist. But the information in most newer media remains retrievable for only ten or twenty years.

Most newer media are much less robust than printed books and paper documents because:

They are less stable chemically than even poor-quality paper, so they deteriorate more rapidly even when stored unused in reasonably good environments.

They are machine dependent; that is, they must move in machines to provide their information. In most cases, this motion incurs wear.

They are totally system dependent for retrieval of their information. When the system is no longer sustainable, the information will be lost unless it has been migrated to a newer system.

Information technologies rely on ever greater data packing densities, making the information ever more vulnerable to large losses from small incidents.

Failure for many newer media is often unpredictable and sudden, and may result in total loss of the information.

The rapid move toward digitization adds another layer of complexity to the preservation picture. In addition to textual and numerical information, still and moving images and sound are increasingly being produced, processed, and distributed in digital form. The undoubted advantages of digital form for information of all kinds are accompanied by at least as large a set of perils for its long-term survival for future research:

Accessibility to digital information depends entirely on intricate edifices of hardware, operating systems, applications software, and storage media.

Most such systems are heavily proprietary, which leaves those concerned with long-term preservation at the mercy of the marketplace.

Changes in technology are almost wholly driven by business and consumer forces; libraries and archives have virtually zero influence on these developments.

Although there are many—and crucial—standards, both formal and de facto, in the digital domain, developments in technology often move faster than the standards process.

The imperative of frequent active intervention that these factors entail places managerial and economic demands on libraries and archives that are quite without precedent, and whose dimensions are only beginning to be realized. Furthermore, for many newer media there is little experience with their maintenance and preservation, and new media—for example, various digital video recording formats and media, the Advanced Photographic System films, or thermal dye transfer prints—are introduced so frequently that reliable information upon which to base permanence estimates or treatment options is rarely publicly available.

The useful life of newer media can be extended significantly by providing the best possible environment and by strictly controlling how they are used. For many modern media for which it is desired to retain indefinitely the original object in usable condition—for example, color photographs—providing an optimum environment is essential. For some media, however, especially those used in digital systems, the obsolescence of the systems upon which access depends may outpace deterioration of the recording medium, making obsolescence the limiting factor. When the information in those media must be preserved indefinitely, programs of periodic migration become inescapable.

Environment

There is no doubt that the initial and operating costs of maintaining an optimum preservation environment for nonpaper media are high, although they can be to some degree contained by thoughtful facilities design. The cost-effectiveness of improving or optimizing environment for long-term preservation for newer media is thrown into stark relief by examining some examples of the cost of preservation alternatives:

Restoring a feature-length motion picture costs hundreds of thousands of dollars.

Removing the image pellicle from a single shrunken cellulose acetate negative costs $50 or more.

Copying one hour of videotape to a new preservation master costs $150–$300.

The effects of temperature and RH on deterioration of all organic materials are, practically speaking, the same: Higher temperature and higher relative humidity accelerate chemical deterioration. However, a broad range of newer media is particularly sensitive to environmentally accelerated deterioration.

For example, research at the Rochester Institute of Technology's Image Permanence Institute has shown that for acetate film stored at 70°F, lowering the relative humidity from 60% to 20% can increase the life expectancy by a factor of four; at 50% RH, lowering temperature from 70°F to 40°F increases life expectancy by a factor of nearly ten. Similarly dramatic increases in the stability of dyes in color photographs can be attained by improving the environment.

Environmental cost-benefit studies for newer media can be useful in establishing priorities for action and in making the best resource allocations. The isoperm and time-weighted preservation index concepts discussed in chapter 7 are a basis for such estimates.

With few exceptions, standards for long-term preservation of newer media are remarkably consistent: maximum temperature 65 or 70°F, and relative humidity of about 30%, with allowable fluctuations of ±2° and ±5%. The exceptions are for color photographic materials and materials on cellulose acetate or nitrate base, for which colder conditions are specified.

The stringent environmental requirements for most nonpaper media normally dictate that they be segregated from people activities and, to contain costs, from less sensitive collections. Prefabricated cool or cold storage vaults are increasingly being used for this purpose where separate storerooms with their own environmental conditions are not feasible. Although there are some risks and logistical problems involved, commercial vaults having suitable conditions may be the only practical alternative for many institutions for storage of sensitive and valuable media.

Light exposure is an issue for photographic and many computer output media if they are to be exhibited. Exhibition conditions are discussed in chapter 11, Exhibition Policy and Preparation.

Handling and Use

All handling and use cause deterioration of objects, however imperceptible the wear and tear from each use may be. Even use in the form of exhibition inherently accelerates deterioration of any light-sensitive media. When transported through a machine, as use for most of the media covered in this chapter requires, the likelihood of serious wear or damage is increased. The common threads through discussion of preservation of all machine-dependent media are suitable equipment, meticulous maintenance, and adequate training for everyone who handles the media.

Most machine-dependent information media, and especially newer ones, operate with extremely close tolerances, sometimes, as with computer hard drives, on the order of a monomolecular layer of air. Many will have seen a diagram of the size of a speck of dust, a human hair, and a blob of tobacco smoke in relation to the size of the gap between a videotape and the read-write head. In general, wear from use can be reduced by handling media in an essentially dust-free environment with clean cotton gloves when the actual media must be handled, or by supplying users only with surrogates. Professional media copying and restoration facilities generally maintain nearly clean-room conditions.

For machine-dependent media, remote access or provision of service copies is essential for long-term preservation. Audio and video archives typically provide only remote access, with original media handled only by staff. For most libraries and archives for which remote listening or viewing setups are not feasible, professionally made service copies should be provided. Service copies have the obvious additional preservation advantage of reducing even staff handling of originals.

Media should always be promptly returned to their appropriate containers after use.

Copying, Migration, and Refreshment

At one time or another, copying of most of the media discussed in this chapter is essential for preservation. Some media must be copied to survive either media deterioration or system obsolescence; service copies or visual indexes may be necessary to protect originals; or copies may be needed for user purchase.

The purpose or purposes of making copies should be carefully thought out before programs are begun. Although it is hubristic to believe that any copying is once-and-for-all, the costs of copying are such that it is unfortunate to dissipate scarce resources on ill-conceived projects. Copying is always expensive; even making a simple photocopy takes staff labor (often professional staff), a real cost that may not be fully recognized. Major distinctions might be made among copies made for indexing purposes, which can be of low quality; service copies, which usually need to be of generally high quality; and preservation masters, which need to capture all the original information with all the fidelity that is technically and economically feasible.

The question of fidelity is not necessarily simple. Most copying technologies permit at least some degree of "improvement"—correcting color, reducing noise, and so on—but this always entails interpretation by the operator or loss of some original information. Especially when preservation masters are being made, a widely used practice is to make a "straight" copy that captures as much as possible of the information in the original; there can be no ethical or research issues about then applying "improvements" to subsequent generations as long as the unaltered master survives.

Similarly, the copying of photographs requires both skill and judgment, in part because modern materials generally do match the tonal range of historic ones. For example, nominally black-and-white albumen prints have strong color tones that are not captured in a modern black-and-white copy; color copies may be required (with, however, obvious cost and preservation implications).

The most critical issue in copying machine-dependent media *for preservation purposes* is that professional-quality equipment and adequately trained personnel must be used. For making preservation masters from deteriorating or obsolescent audiotapes or videotapes, for example, it is obvious that it is important to capture as much information as possible before the original becomes unplayable. Even for making service copies or copies for sale where the original is to be retained, running a film or tape through a machine places it at great risk of damage or, in extreme cases, even destruction.

When preservation master copies of deteriorating audiotapes and videotapes need to be made, a great dilemma is whether to copy to a digital or an analog format.

There is strong impetus now to copy to a digital format, not least because once digitized, the information is readily available for transmission over networks, including the Internet, or incorporation into multimedia presentations. In addition, digital information, unlike analog, can be recopied bit for bit indefinitely, with little or no generational loss. And it is generally easier to process digital information—to eliminate noise, correct color shifts, and so on.

There are at least as compelling reasons to copy to an analog format. By far the most compelling is the rapid obsolescence of digital systems. Although analog systems become obsolete also (and indeed as a class are generally losing ground to digital systems), they are on the whole much simpler systems that would be possible to replicate in the future in a way that digital systems would not.

Moreover, digitizing is by definition sampling the original information, not replicating it entirely. Sampling rates—resolution—are increasing, relatively rapidly in some cases, but if the copy is a replacement for a deteriorating original, some portion of the original information will be lost in the digitization process. In addition, many digital systems (for example, most digital video) entail "lossy" compression, in which some original information is simply discarded in order to manage storage and transmission requirements.

Management

The short useful lifetimes of most newer media require substantially more aggressive preservation management than libraries and archives are accustomed to for traditional media. Preservation entails surveying to establish priorities, optimization of storage, use and handling policies, and copying and migration programs. Underlying all these, needless to say, are adequate budgets.

Unlike specific-media archives, such as the UCLA film and television archives and the Rodgers and Hammerstein Archive of Recorded Sound at the New York Public Library, general research libraries, archives, and special collections departments may not be able to support the infrastructure—specialized equipment, personnel, and storage facilities—necessary for long-term preservation of newer media.

Even within the overall, generally short useful lives of the newer media, there are differences in life expectancy, but resources for preservation copying or other appropriate options to deal with the entire category or collection are rarely available. A crucial first step, then, is to establish priorities.

Rational priorities should be based on a combination of the importance of the content to the collection and the estimated endpoint of the medium. For example, "acetate" direct recording disks have limited life expectancy, failure is irrecoverable when the coating bearing the image begins to flake, and the information on them is often unique. Computer and instrument data of permanent value must be migrated while the system needed for reading it is still operable. Cellulose acetate film or tape that is reaching the critical point of vinegar syndrome may need to be copied urgently, especially if cool or cold storage is not available.

Because specialized knowledge is required to assess the remaining useful life of media and systems, it may be appropriate to have the collections surveyed by one or more specialists as a first step in establishing priorities for action.

A fundamental consideration in the preservation of computer data is the locus of responsibility. Archives and research libraries know the significance of such information that they are responsible for, understand the implications of preservation for posterity, and are aware of any applicable access restrictions. In most cases, however, they lack both the specialized personnel and the equipment to manage digital data. A central computing facility will almost certainly have such requisites as well as established error tracking, refreshment, and migration routines.

A somewhat parallel situation exists for audio and moving image information. Libraries and archives generally do not have the requisites for preservation copying, or even for safely making reference copies from valuable or unique originals. It must be emphasized that general audiovisual or multimedia laboratories also may not have staff or equipment appropriate for making *preservation* masters or for safe copying of valuable originals.

Preservation copies of newer media, then, must usually be made by outside vendors. Many vendors work primarily for commercial customers whose requirements are not as critical or stringent as those for preservation copying. It may be wise to seek recommendations about a suitable supplier specializing in preservation work from a major library or sound, video, or motion picture archives, and close quality control should be maintained. Bid documents and contracts need provisions for handling and safety of originals as well as for the quality of the duplicates. Visits to the facility and trial batches are essential for this kind of work.

Magnetic Media in General

Because magnetic media will be found in audio, video, motion picture, and computer data collections, we will discuss their common characteristics here.

The fundamental components of magnetic tape (and floppy disks as well) are a support and a magnetizable layer. The support of nearly all flexible magnetic media is polyester film, although early audiotape was on paper or cellulose acetate base. Fortunately, polyester is a highly permanent and durable material.

The magnetizable layer has most often consisted of gamma ferric oxide (rust, in effect) particles dispersed in a polyester-urethane resin of widely varying composition. The traditional iron oxide particles are quite permanent, but the need for other characteristics, especially higher data densities, has led to the use of iron metal particles and evaporated metal coatings, both of which are far more vulnerable to oxidation than ferric oxide.

The urethane binder is the most vulnerable component of most magnetic media. It interacts with humidity in the air by a process called hydrolysis to soften and become gummy. In this state, the surface of the magnetic layer transfers to recording and playback heads and tape transports, interfering, sometimes fatally, with playing the tape. Consistent maintenance of moderately low relative humidity is crucial to tape preservation.

Satisfactory performance of all magnetic tape is subject to mechanical distortions, and careful maintenance of the tape pack is also crucial.

The two interacting factors are linear and lateral distortions. Linear factors are stretch from too high tension, and slippage from tension that is too low. Both are caused by improper rewinding tension before storage or fluctuating temperature and relative humidity. Lateral tape problems arise from physical or mechanical edge damage, mainly from storing tapes after stop-and-start playing—that is, without their having been evenly rewound first. Tape that is loose from the linear problems just mentioned is then also subject to these lateral problems. Inappropriate reels can also cause edge damage.

An additional problem affecting some analog tapes is print-through, in which a "ghost" of the image on one layer of tape transfers over time to an adjacent layer.

To minimize these problems, it is important that tapes are always run end to end at appropriate tension before storage, and that optimum temperature and relative humidity are maintained. In addition, it is also generally recommended that tapes be "exercised"—run from end to end at controlled tension—every two or three years, although it is not clear how many facilities actually carry out this time-consuming operation.

ANSI/PIMA IT9.23-1998, *Imaging Materials—Polyester Base Magnetic Tape—Storage*, is a useful guide for preservation of tape.

Specific Media

Still Photographs

Photographic collections in libraries and archives contain examples of a wide variety of historic processes dating from 1839—from early ones, such as daguerreotypes and albumen prints, through black-and-white films on cellulose nitrate or cellulose acetate, to modern color slides and prints and digitally processed thermal transfer prints.

Photographs are composites made of an imaging medium, a support layer, and, generally, a third component, a binder, which suspends the imaging particles and ties them to the support. The image medium consists, most frequently, of finely divided particles of silver or platinum, which produces a black-and-white image, or of organic dyes found in color processes. The binder layer has included, through the course of photographic history, such film-forming materials as albumen, collodion (a form of cellulose nitrate), or gelatin. The support layer may be metal, glass, paper, or plastic film.

Silver image-forming particles are vulnerable to high humidity and pollutants and respond by fading, discoloring, or producing an iridescent metallic surface sheen known as "mirroring." The dyes in color transparencies and prints are particularly sensitive to light, heat, and, to a lesser degree, humidity, and most will fade or shift color through the preferential fading of one component of the dye mix, even in the dark.

Support layers deteriorate from differing causes: Metals rust, paper and cardboard become brittle, glass can corrode or break. The most widespread support layer problem is found in cellulose nitrate and acetate films, which deteriorate as chemicals released by the breakdown of the film in turn attack the film to cause further breakdown until the film base is completely destroyed. Some resin-coated (RC) print papers, especially early ones, are subject to yellowing and even cracking of the emulsion-bearing polyethylene layer.

The role that environment plays in photographic deterioration has been outlined earlier; it should come as no surprise, then, that the most effective means of preserving a collection lies in controlling environmental factors.

Current ANSI standards (ANSI/NAPM IT9.20-1996) recommend a maximum temperature of 65°F and humidity ranging from 30% to 50% for black-and-white prints, and 36°F and 30% to 40% for color prints. ANSI/NAPM IT9.11-1993 specifies 70°F maximum and 20% to 30% RH for black-and-white films, and 36°F and 20% to 30% RH for color negatives and transparencies (with somewhat higher RH permissible with lower temperatures). The *IPI Storage Guide for Acetate Film* (see Suggested Readings), although not setting specific conditions, delineates the increased life expectancies for that material (and by inference for nitrate film) from reducing temperature or humidity or both.

A great variety of enclosure materials and designs are available, each with varying benefits and drawbacks. Many—or possibly even most—storage envelopes, folders, and boxes used in the past are damaging and need to be replaced. Compatibility of the enclosure material to the photographic process and knowledge of access and handling patterns, environmental conditions, and type of shelving or storage unit are important criteria in selecting new enclosures. For example, in many cases, paper housings may be preferable to even plastics known to be unreactive, because paper does not trap gaseous deterioration products to the degree that plastics do. There are also mechanical factors, such as the shiny surface and hard, sharp edges of polyethylene terephthalate (PET, polyester, Mylar), that should be considered.

ANSI Standard ANSI/PIMA IT9.2-1998 specifies the characteristics necessary for storage materials (both paper and plastic) in direct contact with photographs. In addition, ANSI Standard ANSI/NAPM IT9.16-1993 describes the Photographic Activity Test (PAT), which describes the evaluation both of new enclosures and of housing materials already in the collection.

Some photographs require forms of protection more substantial than sleeves or folders. Fragile photographs, like glass plate negatives, should be stored in containers that protect them from breakage. Daguerreotypes must have a cover glass to retard tarnishing. If the binding structure can tolerate the added bulk, photos mounted in scrapbooks or albums can benefit from inserted sheets of thin, nonreactive paper to protect them from being damaged by adjacent materials, such as platinum prints, album pages of unrefined paper or board, or gilded decorative elements.

Policies for access, housekeeping, handling, loan, and exhibition should be developed and implemented to reduce the effects of use on photographs. These policies should include such things as requiring users to wear cotton gloves when handling photographs, prohibiting the use of pens in the reading room, establishing guidelines for processing newly acquired collections (removing damaging enclosures and paper clips; segregating different types of photographs; and providing suitable protective enclosures), and restricting exhibition length of exposure and quality of illumination to reduce fading.

A fundamentally important way of reducing damage to photographs from handling is to provide either reference copies or visual indexes. Service copies are especially important when the collection holds only a negative. When only a print is in the collection, making a copy preservation negative and a service print is an important, if expensive, insurance measure against loss, damage, or deterioration of the original.

Visual indexes, although expensive to produce, can dramatically reduce the need to handle originals, are a great convenience for users, and can reduce staff labor by permitting users to browse at will without having to retrieve the original photographs until the ones actually needed are identified. In the past, microforms and analog videodiscs have sometimes been used for visual indexes; the advent of computer-based imaging technologies, including relatively inexpensive scanning and various optical storage media (including the Kodak PhotoCD), makes visual indexes more feasible.

Collections should be screened to locate vulnerable materials like nitrate- and acetate-based film. These materials are deteriorating rapidly, and the risk of losing the information they hold is high. Deterioration of acetate film is signaled by a vinegar smell (acetic acid), brittleness, bubbling or buckling of the emulsion layer, or crystals on the film surface.

Although cool, dry storage retards further deterioration of these types of film, ultimately their images must be preserved by copying them onto polyester-based film and processing and storing them according to archival standards. Unfortunately, there is no way of determining the life expectancy of any given piece of film, and often, by the time the damage is discovered, it can be too late; buckling and curling can prevent good-quality reproduction without delicate and expensive restoration treatment.

Photographs that are important enough to retain in their original format and that require conservation treatment should also be identified. The sorts of problems that should receive priority treatment by a photographic conservator are daguerreotypes with deteriorating glass covers; photographs on glass or metal that has broken or corroded; photographs with mold or with visible flaking or lifting emulsion; photographs adhered with pressure-sensitive tape or rubber cement; or photographs that are stuck to their framing.

Motion Pictures

There have been many motion picture formats since the introduction of movies in the 1890s, although only a relatively small number are likely to be found outside of specialist archives. Since the beginning of the medium, 35-mm stock has been the standard for theatrical films; most educational films are on 16 mm; and amateur films have most often been on 16-mm, 8-mm, or super-8-mm formats. The field is complicated, however, by different sound systems (optical, magnetic, stereo, surround-sound); formats used abroad (9 mm, 28 mm); and wide-screen formats (70 mm, VistaVision, Cinemascope, and so on). An additional complexity is that film production elements (negatives, answer prints, "full-coat" magnetic film, and so on) may find their way into archival collections.

Major preservation issues with motion pictures are deterioration of cellulose nitrate and acetate bases, color fading, and their extreme vulnerability to damage during projection. An equally great issue is the very high cost of restoration and copying.

As acetate or nitrate film base shrinks with age and deterioration, the pitch of the sprocket holes no longer matches the sprockets of the projector, often causing either damaged holes or broken film. Even undeteriorated films are subject to serious damage in projection from poorly maintained equipment or careless handling. Shrinkage also means that satisfactory copies (whether onto film or videotape) can be made only on specialized equipment.

Motion pictures on cellulose nitrate base (not made in the United States since 1951) are extremely hazardous and should never be kept in libraries and archives other than in vaults that meet National Fire Protection Association and local codes. When nitrate film reaches an advanced stage of deterioration, it can ignite spontaneously at a relatively low temperature. Burning nitrate film cannot be extinguished, so it will seriously increase the severity of a fire even if it is not itself the cause. (Still negatives on nitrate base, while still hazardous, are not as severe a hazard because less autocatalysis occurs than with the dense mass of motion pictures.)

The fundamental strategies for motion picture preservation are cool (or, for color, cold) and dry storage, as for still photographs, and avoidance of projection.

As with other machine-dependent media covered in this chapter, motion pictures for which long-term preservation is desired should be projected only by technicians who understand how to handle them, and on meticulously maintained equipment. In some cases, it may be acceptable to allow a user, wearing clean cotton gloves, to view a film on a Moviola viewer or an editing table (such as a Steenbeck) that does not use sprocket wheels. Unfortunately, such equipment is rarely available in libraries and archives.

The obvious answer is to provide service copies to users—obvious except, of course, for the very high cost of copies. In addition, even high-quality videotape copies, which are far cheaper than film copies, entail loss of quality as well as a different viewing experience.

Motion pictures are customarily housed in relatively tightly sealed metal or plastic cans. As experience in dealing with the vinegar syndrome grows, however, it now appears that it is preferable to house acetate film in containers of suitable plastic (not metal) that allow acetic acid vapor to dissipate so that it does not accelerate the autocatalytic generation of more acid. In addition, deteriorating acetate and nitrate films need to be segregated, also to reduce autocatalytic deterioration.

Motion picture archives are now almost always equipped with cool or cold vaults. For institutions having a few films that need long-term preservation and for which a climate-controlled vault is not feasible, there appears to be no real alternative to having service copies made (probably on videotape) and storing the originals in a commercial film vault or the vault of a cooperative institution.

The Society of Motion Picture and Television Engineers (SMPTE) has issued a useful document titled "Recommended Practice: Storage of Motion-Picture Films" (see Suggested Readings).

Sound Recordings

The experimental recording of sound began in the second half of the nineteenth century. Thomas A. Edison's phonograph combined a diaphragm and stylus that engraved primitive undulating marks on a sheet of tinfoil wrapped around a cylinder. Subsequent developments saw the production of more permanent recordings in a variety of formats: cylinders, discs, wire, and tape.

Cylinder recordings, "shellacs" (roughly corresponding to 78-rpm recordings), and vinyl LPs (including 45-rpm recordings, usually actually polystyrene) all have reasonable life expectancy if properly stored and handled. Shellacs, however, are especially vulnerable to mishandling as they become more brittle with age. Celluloid cylinder recordings are subject to fungal attack if stored in humid conditions. Vinyl LPs sometimes distort spontaneously from relaxation of stresses molded in at the time of manufacture, and they are subject to cold flow as, for example, from leaning on the shelf or imprinting by irregular surfaces, such as wrinkled album liners.

"Acetate" direct recordings and magnetic tape, on the other hand, have limited life expectancies even when carefully stored and handled, and the information on them is often unique. For these reasons these two types of recordings should have high priority for preservation assessment and attention. "Acetate" disks consist of a core of aluminum, glass, or cardboard with a coating of (usually) plasticized cellulose nitrate, which shrinks and peels on aging. Unlike other disc types, which are "pressed" (molded) in multiple copies, acetates, sometimes also called instantaneous recordings, are engraved directly. Frequent recognition points are the composition of the core (which can be seen at the edge of the center hole), two or three holes, and a handwritten or typed (rather than printed) label.

Although sound recordings are somewhat less sensitive to chemical contamination from housings than are photographs, their surfaces need to be protected from dust, dirt, and handling, and they need suitable support. Suitable housings for most types of sound recordings are available from conservation suppliers. The size and weight of disks require special shelving, and the shelving system should permit them to be stored exactly vertically.

As dynamic media that must be run on machines for use, all sound recordings, with the exception of compact disks, are worn by playback. The provisions discussed earlier under "Handling and Use" should be followed for audio recordings, and, as with other dynamic media, service copies or remote access are essential for the preservation of important recordings.

Cleaning of sound recordings must be approached with great caution and performed only by knowledgeable staff. The ability to recognize the material composition of the recording is critical; cleaning methods that are safe for one may seriously damage another.

When sound recordings must be copied for preservation, analog recording onto quarter-inch, polyester-based, standard-play tape with a ferric oxide coating is generally recommended. Ideally, two copies should be produced—an unfiltered preservation master and a service copy that can be "cleaned up" as desired. Service copies may be made on a more convenient access format, such as audiocassette or CD.

When original recordings remain playable, it is highly desirable to retain the originals. Only part of the evidential value of recordings is preserved in copying—for example, the format, the label, and the housing can often be used to date or identify discrete recordings. In addition, the quality of re-recording technology is constantly improving; access to the originals allows these benefits to be realized.

Video Recordings

Of the hundred or so extant video recording formats, only a relatively small number are likely to be of long-term preservation concern in nonspecialized libraries and archives. The most widespread open-reel formats are 2-inch quad, 1-inch type C, and 1/2-inch EIAJ. The common cassette formats are 1/2-inch beta, 1/2-inch VHS, and 3/4-inch U-matic.

With the exception of laser discs and now digital versatile disks (DVDs), all video recording is based on magnetic tape, and the guidelines in the section on "Magnetic Media in General" are applicable. As with most media discussed in this chapter, providing optimum environment is the first line of defense for video media.

The major preservation issues with videotape, as with magnetic media in general, are wear from playback, system obsolescence, binder hydrolysis, contamination, and tape pack deformations.

Because of the enormous amount of information that must be contained in video signals, some information is omitted in most video recording formats, and compression schemes are used in digital video recording. As a consequence, video recordings are especially vulnerable to quality loss in copying, and the choice of a format for preservation masters of deteriorating or obsolete video recordings is also crucial. These are additional reasons that it is so important to choose a facility with appropriate personnel and equipment for preservation copying. Currently, Betacam SP and Digital Beta are the formats often being recommended for preservation masters.

SMPTE's Recommended Practice RP103-1995, *Care, Storage, Operation, Handling and Shipping of Magnetic Recording Tape for Television*, will be useful to institutions holding videotapes of long-term value (see Suggested Readings).

Computer Data Media

Although the life expectancy of most computer data media, especially those based on magnetic systems, may be relatively short, the limiting factor for accessibility of digital information is almost always obsolescence of one or more components of the system necessary to retrieve information: hardware, operating system, application software, or storage media. This places an ongoing burden on those responsible for the perpetuation of the information, and it presents a particular challenge to archives that may not receive information for decades after it was created.

Systems in the mainframe world seem to change less rapidly than those of desktop computers, but data are more likely to be in custom formats that may not be easily migrated. Centralized computer facilities using mainframes (and now, increasingly, workstations) are operated by specialist staff and are more likely than personal computers to be subject to systematic backup, refreshment, and migration routines. Networked desktop computers perhaps fall in the middle, at least to the extent that information for which preservation is a concern resides on servers rather than on individual machines.

Although issues of preserving mainframe or networked data should not be minimized or underestimated, long-term preservation of data from individual desktop computers appears to present nearly overwhelming challenges. Operating systems, application software, and even physical storage media evolve with stunning rapidity, and with only limited backward compatibility. The increasing size of computer files and the persistence in desktop computers of the 3¹/₂-inch floppy disk with its limited capacity has led to a wide range of almost wholly proprietary and noninterchangeable high-capacity and exchange media, including various tape, floppy disk, optical, and magneto-optical systems. An example of the preservation issues is high-capacity Syquest disks; these had a relatively broad installed base (especially among graphic artists), inspiring some confidence in their longevity, but Syquest appears to have gone out of business, leaving a moderately widely used system orphaned.

The principal preservation activities for computer data are refreshment and migration. Refreshment refers to simply copying data from a medium that is deteriorating or obsolescent to newer media. Much more complex is migration, which involves moving data into current operating system environments or software applications. Although refreshment can generally be carried out without loss of data as it is done on a bit-by-bit basis, there is always risk of losing data or functionality in migration. Although the actual migration of information will probably be carried out by technical personnel, it is important for librarians or archivists, whose responsibility is the long view, to be involved in the process.

To the degree that there is a twenty- or thirty-year time lag between the creation of records and the time they are accessioned into archives, and the accessibility of most desktop media is five to ten years, archives will only be able to hope to preserve digital information by taking an active role in its maintenance early in its life cycle.

Computer Output Media

Both textual and pictorial material are increasingly being produced by a range of computer printers and plotters as well as the technically similar digital photocopiers. The advance of printing technology is remarkable; small desktop printers costing under $300 can produce color prints of nearly photographic quality, and billboards are produced on ink-jet printers sixteen feet wide. Computer-mediated devices are widely used not only for desktop printing, but for architectural and engineering drawings, posters, pseudo- and actual photographs, and even fine art prints. Their growing pervasiveness raises yet another set of preservation concerns for libraries and archives. There are few published studies on the life expectancy of these media, but in many cases the omens are not encouraging.

Some prints—for example, those from Iris ink-jet printers, which are sometimes sold as fine art prints—are extremely sensitive to water, so that a sneeze or a damp finger can damage them. Many digital prints are based on dyes with limited lightfastness, but permanence is as much dependent on the substrate as on the inks. Thermal dye ("dye sublimation") prints are increasingly replacing conventional photographic color prints, as in the printers found in photo stores. One type of thermal color print will retain acceptable quality only for months at temperatures above 75°F, according to the manufacturer's care guidelines.[1]

There are somewhat fewer concerns about the longevity of electrostatic copies from photocopiers and laser printers. ("On-demand" publishing and digital printing will surely dramatically increase the number of electrostatically printed books in research libraries, incidentally.) The carbon and iron pigments used in black toners are highly permanent, and color toners are most often based on pigments rather than the dyes typical of most true photographic and ink-jet printing processes, and thus are likely to be more stable.

The long-term permanence of electrostatic copies depends largely on adhesion of toner to paper. Recent copiers and laser printers seem to have overcome the poor bonding that sometimes occurred earlier, although there is some concern about color prints because of the multiple layers of toner that make up the image. Many resins have been used in toner formulations since the inception of electrostatic copying in 1960, and little has been published about their long-term integrity. It is known that some are softened by contact with plasticized polyvinyl chloride plastics, and it seems probable that prolonged exposure to ultraviolet radiation would cause some breakdown. In practice, however, there appears to have been little problem with toner breakdown thus far.

Newer media have revolutionized human existence since early in the nineteenth century, and there is no indication that their growth and mutation will slow their impact on civilization. Their almost unimaginable benefits have been accompanied by far higher risk of rapid loss of the information that they contain. These greater risks place an almost wholly new kind and level of responsibility on librarians, archivists, and curators who are given the task of preserving the human record. This responsibility entails levels of fiscal, managerial, and technical resources for which archives, research libraries, and historical societies may not be fully prepared.

Note

1. <http://www.kodak.com/global/en/service/faqs/faq1527.shtml>, accessed 29 November 1999.

Suggested Readings

Commission on Preservation and Access and the Research Libraries Group. Task Force on Archiving of Digital Information. *Preserving Digital Information*. Washington, D.C.: CPA, 1996.

Davidson, Steven, and Gregory Lukow, eds. *The Administration of Television Newsfilm and Videotape Collections: A Curatorial Manual*. Los Angeles: American Film Institute; Miami: Louis Wolfson II Media History Center, 1997.

Geller, Sidney B. *Care and Handling of Computer Magnetic Storage Media*. NBS Special Publication 500–101. Washington, D.C.: National Bureau of Standards, 1983.

Henderson, Kathryn L., and William T. Henderson. *Conserving and Preserving Materials in Non-book Formats*. Papers presented at Allerton Park Institute, Urbana-Champaign, Ill.: Board of Trustees of the University of Illinois, 1991.

Norris, Debbie Hess. "Preservation Planning for Diverse Photographic Holdings." In *Photographic Preservation and the Research Library*, edited by Jennifer Porro, 19–27. Mountain View, Calif.: Research Libraries Group, 1991.

Puglia, Steven. "Cost-benefit Analysis for B/W Acetate: Cool/Cold Storage vs. Duplication." *Abbey Newsletter* 19 (1995): 71–72.

Reilly, James M. *Care and Identification of 19th-Century Photographic Prints*. Rochester, N.Y.: Eastman Kodak, 1986.

———. *IPI Storage Guide for Acetate Film*. Rochester, N.Y.: Image Permanence Institute, 1993. Includes calculating wheel.

———. "Preserving Photographic Collections in Research Libraries: A Perspective." In *Photographic Preservation and the Research Library*, edited by Jennifer Porro, 7–17. Mountain View, Calif.: Research Libraries Group, 1991.

———. *Storage Guide for Color Photographic Materials*. Albany: New York State Education Department, 1998. Includes calculating wheel.

Ward, Alan. *A Manual of Sound Archive Administration*. Aldershot, England: Gower, 1990.

Wilhelm, Henry, with contributing author Carol Brower. *The Permanence and Care of Color Photographs: Traditional and Digital Color Prints, Color Negatives, Slides, and Motion Pictures.* Grinnell, Iowa: Preservation Publishing Company, 1993.

Formal Standards and Recommended Practice Documents

American National Standards Institute. *American National Standard for Imaging Media—Reflection Prints—Storage Practices.* ANSI/NAPM IT9.20-1996. New York: ANSI, 1996.

———. *Imaging Materials—Photographic Processed Films, Plates, and Papers— Filing Enclosures and Storage Containers.* ANSI/PIMA IT9.2-1998. New York: ANSI, 1998.

———. *Imaging Materials—Polyester Base Magnetic Tape—Storage.* ANSI/PIMA IT9.23-1998. New York: ANSI, 1998.

———. *Imaging Materials—Processed Photographic Plate—Storage Practices.* ANSI/NAPM IT9.18-1996. New York: ANSI, 1996.

———. *Imaging Media—Photographic Activity Test.* ANSI/NAPM IT9.16-1993. New York: ANSI, 1993.

———. *Imaging Media—Processed Safety Photographic Films—Storage.* ANSI/PIMA IT9.11-1998. New York: ANSI, 1998.

Society of Motion Picture and Television Engineers. *Care and Preservation of Audio Magnetic Recordings.* SMPTE Recommended Practice RP190-1996. White Plains, N.Y.: SMPTE, 1996.

———. *Care, Storage, Operation, Handling and Shipping of Magnetic Recording Tape for Television.* SMPTE Recommended Practice RP103-1995. White Plains, N.Y.: SMPTE, 1995.

———. "Proposed SMPTE Recommended Practice: Storage of Motion-Picture Films." *SMPTE Journal* 103 (1994): 201–205. Also available as SMPTE, *Storage of Motion-Picture Films.* RP131-1994.

INDEX